Becoming the Boss

BECOMING THE BOSS

New Rules for the Next Generation of Leaders

LINDSEY POLLAK

HARPER
BUSINESS

An Imprint of HarperCollins*Publishers*

HarperCollins books may be purchased for educational, business, or sales promotional use. For information, please e-mail the Special Markets Department at SPsales@harpercollins.com.

FIRST EDITION

Designed by Fritz Metsch

Library of Congress Cataloging-in-Publication Data has been applied for.

ISBN 978-0-06-232331-6

14 15 16 17 18   OV/RRD   10 9 8 7 6 5 4 3 2 1

To Chloe
and new leaders everywhere

ACKNOWLEDGMENTS

Thank you first and foremost to the enthusiastic team at Harper-Collins who made this book possible: Colleen Lawrie, Hollis Heimbouch, Leigh Raynor, and Renata Marchione. Thank you to my literary agent, Michelle Wolfson, for many years of encouragement and advice. (We knew we'd work together someday!)

Many thanks to each of the new leaders, established leaders, and leadership experts who shared your personal experiences and insights for this book: I am so appreciative of your honesty and generosity. For assistance with research, writing, and editing, thank you to the talented Paige Arnof-Fenn, Kevin Grubb, Michelle Hainer Calcaterra, and Amy Orlov.

Thank you to everyone at my corporate partner The Hartford for a wonderful and productive relationship, especially Liam McGee, Lori High, Laura Marzi, Wendy Wojdyl, Michelle Loxton, and Kelly Carter. And thank you to the hardworking and gracious women of Emanate: Kiersten Zweibaum, Alexis Odesser, Ginny Webb, Jenna Hoops, and Kristen Massaro.

It's not easy to build a business and work mostly alone, so I'm forever grateful to the professional networks that have provided community, resources, support, friendship, and cocktails at so many important moments over the last fifteen years and counting. Thank you to the leaders and members of Rotary International, TARA, The Li.st, The YEC, and the Freelancers Union.

A million thank yous to my amazing network of friends, mentors, clients, and colleagues who have supported me personally and professionally over so many years. Thank you to Amy Abrams, Laura Baird, Susan Phillips Bari, Gillian Baudo, Derek Billings, Lynn Carnegie, Jason Criss, Diane Danielson, Cher Duffield, Carol Frohlinger, Jodi Glickman, Joanne Gordon, Christine Hassler, John Hill, Natasha Hoehn, Cassandra Krause, Donna Kalajian Lagani, Mignon Lawless, Alexandra Levit, Danielle Martin, Nicole Mills, Solana Nolfo, Shreya Oswal, Mary Ellen Slayter, Cari Sommer, Trudy Steinfeld, Manisha Thakor, and Tammy Tibbetts.

Thank you to Mom, Dad, Rob, Anne, and Laura for a lifetime of love and encouragement to be true to myself. Thank you to Meredith Bernstein, the Rahos, the Goodman/Ramsays, and Vivian, Georges, and Valerie Gotlib, for your support and love. And to Etel Lima, thank you for being the most wonderful caretaker imaginable and a true member of our family.

Finally, thank you to my amazing husband, Evan, and our daughter, Chloe. There is nothing I am more grateful for than you.

CONTENTS

Part III: **Last**

Becoming the Boss

Introduction

Early in my career, I worked at a start-up called WorkingWoman .com. (Never heard of it? You'll see why in a moment.) After about a year, I received my first-ever promotion and was told to hire a junior person to handle some of my workload. I chose a friendly, eager, recent college grad named Alex. It was my first experience managing someone and I was excited to become a mentor to my brand-new protégé. I managed to read about ten seconds of *The One Minute Manager* before my employer went bankrupt, as many dot-coms did in the spring of 2001. I had been a manager for three whole weeks.

I thought my leadership career had stopped in its tracks, but I couldn't have been more wrong. During my "exit meeting," along with the manila envelope containing my severance package, the head of the company handed me back the company laptop I'd just relinquished and said, "Keep it. Use it to go start your own business." Without any other prospects on the horizon, I took his advice.

But let's back up for a moment. How did I land at WorkingWoman .com in the first place and know what kind of business to start when I left that job? Where did my career journey *really* begin? Although the similarities pretty much end here, my leadership origin story begins in the very same place as Facebook founder Mark Zuckerberg's: a college dorm room.

My Story

I discovered my passion as a senior in college while serving as an RA (aka resident advisor, which we called freshman counselors at my university). I loved everything about the role: advising college students on their academics, extracurriculars, career paths, and life choices, and serving as a resource for administrators, parents, and other "grown-ups" who wanted to understand the students I was advising. It was truly one of the best years of my life.

After college I received a Rotary Ambassadorial Scholarship, which sent me to grad school in Melbourne, Australia (and saved me from the huge potential mistake of applying to law school). I chose to study women's entrepreneurship based on some classes I'd enjoyed in college, not realizing then that I was studying my own future. After two and a half years I received a master's degree in women's studies and returned to the United States, ready to begin an awesome career, even though I wasn't entirely sure what that career would be.

During my first job interview back home, for an HR-related position at a Fortune 500 company, the interviewer looked at my résumé and said, "A master's degree in women's studies? That'll get you nowhere."

That experience led to three months of staying under the covers in my childhood bedroom, eating frozen yogurt directly from the carton (as I described in full, rainbow-sprinkled detail in my previous book, *Getting from College to Career*), and wondering if my glory days were behind me. Eventually I started meeting with people and sending out résumés. One day I met with a career coach who asked me to describe the best job I'd ever had. I immediately started telling her how much I loved being an RA and wished I could do that forever.

"So do that forever," she said.

"Um, there are no RA jobs in the real world," I replied.

"So start your own business," she advised.

As with much good advice, I completely ignored it and eventually landed the job at WorkingWoman.com.

(You already know how that turned out.)

So it wasn't until the *second* time someone told me to start my own business that I actually listened. After leaving WorkingWoman.com I started freelance writing on career issues and giving speeches on the only topic I knew anything about: how to be a young person figuring out what to do with your life.

Slowly but surely since then, I've built a speaking and consulting business, providing professional development training to college students and young professionals and advising organizations on managing, and marketing to, young people. Just as I did as an RA, I spend my days guiding young people to their careers and helping the "grown-ups" understand the next generation. I've delivered more than a thousand speeches and consulting engagements across several countries; blogged about workplace issues for such outlets as the *Huffington Post*, ABC News, and FastCompany.com; and served as an official spokesperson for companies such as LinkedIn, Levi's, and The Hartford—a leading insurance company whose research and leaders will appear throughout this book.

I've worked very hard and I'm proud of my list of professional accomplishments and affiliations. But running my own business hasn't been easy. Some leadership qualities like vision, confidence, and self-discipline came relatively naturally to me (I should mention I am a perfectionist, type-A, Virgo, firstborn child). But I'm the first to admit that being a good people manager did not come naturally to me at all (maybe because I'm a perfectionist, type-A, Virgo, firstborn child).

Over the years I've managed dozens of part-time employees, interns, consultants, and virtual assistants, and I've often found that people management is the hardest part of my job. I've struggled with giving clear instructions, delegating authority, and providing feedback, among countless other leadership and management mistakes I'm sure I've made. And that's why I wanted to write this book: so you can learn from my experience and not have to suffer through the same challenges on your leadership journey. As I did with the job search process in *Getting from College to Career,* in this book I will share everything I've learned about becoming the boss. That includes everything I'm still learning and everything that young professionals like you—through conversations, e-mails, social media posts, and responses to an online leadership survey I fielded while writing this book—have told me you want to know about leadership, whether you are an entrepreneur like me or you work for someone else.

Of course you'll find much more than my individual experience and advice in these pages. In my day-to-day consulting and public speaking, I work with leaders across a wide variety of job functions, industries, and regions, and they've generously shared their advice and opinions throughout the upcoming chapters. I've also interviewed hundreds of additional leaders of diverse generations and industries—from students to CEOs, from finance to food service—to offer as many perspectives on leadership as possible. My goal is to provide you with the most comprehensive information out there about how to be the best leader you can be, with a particular focus on your first months and years as the boss.

WAIT, HOW ARE WE DEFINING *LEADER*?

We'll explore this question in greater detail throughout the book (spoiler alert: it's really a question each person has to answer individually), but for now I'd like to define the word *leader* quite broadly, as someone who has influence over others, with or without formal authority. Even if you don't yet have anyone reporting to you, or you work alone, or you're a student, or you're a stay-at-home parent, you have every right to call yourself a leader and this book is absolutely for you. More than anything else, I believe leadership begins on the inside with the way you approach the world and your desire to make a difference.

Is Leadership Different Today?

The subtitle of this book is "New Rules for the Next Generation of Leaders," because I believe that today's leaders require some different training from leaders of the past. However, before we get too far, let us hereby acknowledge that:

Some classic rules of leadership and success will never change.

Qualities such as confidence, intelligence, ethics, and drive have always been important and will always be important for leaders. Charisma and presence will never go out of style. Treating people as you want to be treated is good. Screaming at people is bad. And as "flat" as organizations are becoming, with fewer levels of management between the entry level and the CEO, we will always need people to step up and take on responsibility. So in no way will I suggest in this book that we need to toss out all of the management and leadership theories of the past. In fact, the entire next section of the book is dedicated to ensuring that you know your history.

The problem, however, is that too many leadership and management books are written by, yes, incredibly successful people, but those who are often at the ends of their careers. While that perspective is important and valuable, I believe you need more up-to-the-minute advice, too. As you'll see below, enormous demographic, economic, and technological shifts are taking place right now—in business, government, law, the media, health care, the nonprofit sector, and almost any other realm you want to work in. These shifts are both exciting and daunting, and they are fundamentally changing the world in which you'll lead today and into the future. The leadership advice of the past is simply not enough to prepare you for today's complex realities.

You Will Lead Through a Demographic Revolution

First, we are in the early years of a fundamental demographic shift in the United States and around the world. Here at home, a tidal wave of baby boomers—those born approximately from 1946 to 1964, so most of your parents—will be leaving the paid workforce over the next two decades. According to PwC, 63.3 percent of American executives will be eligible to retire in the next five years. An even larger tidal wave of your generation, the millennials—defined as those born approximately from 1982 to 2000, also known as Generation Y—are flooding in. By 2020, millennials (comprised of more than 80 million Americans, compared to roughly 76 million baby boomers) are projected to make up a full 50 percent of the entire U.S. workforce. This means that the baby boomer attitudes, leadership styles, and management practices that have dominated American business and culture for the past several decades will give way to millennial preferences. This demographic revolution is even more pronounced in places like China, where millennials already comprise 50 percent of that country's workforce, and India, which is on track to become the world's youngest country by 2020.

Becoming the boss in a time of demographic change means that you will need to build your skills in communicating with, and managing, people of multiple generations who have different expectations and different styles of working.

You Will Lead Through an Economic Revolution

Speaking of China and India, you will also likely preside over the United States' loss of global economic dominance. The United States has been the world's largest national economy since at least the 1920s (and Western nations overall have dominated for two centuries), but China is now on track to become the world's largest economy by 2030, with India taking third place behind the United States. Only five European nations will be in the top twenty then, compared to being in the top eight today.

As this economic change is happening globally, millennial leaders will reckon with new economic realities at home, such as the fact that living a middle-class American life will be more expensive than for any previous generation. College tuition fees in the United States have surged 1,120 percent (more than triple the inflation rate) since records began in 1978, medical expenses have climbed 601 percent, and the price of food has increased 244 percent over the same period. And due to those huge tuition costs and the higher cost of living overall, today's young people will confront more debt than ever before: two-thirds of 2011 college graduates carried an average student loan debt of $27,500. Contrast that with 1993, when less than half of students graduated with debt, and those who did averaged $9,350. (In today's dollars, that's about $15,000.) Overall, there is $1 trillion in total outstanding student loan debt in our country today.

Perhaps the greatest economic shift is in the American job market. You are becoming the boss in what some economists call a "post-employment" economy, in which companies can function and thrive without hiring as many workers or paying them as highly as in the past. According to U.S. Census Bureau data, from 1950 to 2000, the average household income of American families rose steadily. From 2000 to 2010, when many millennials entered the workforce, median household incomes fell for the first time since World War II. For the next several years at least, you'll likely need to learn how to lead within the confines of a limited budget and a limited number of employees, both of which may become the new norm.

You Will Lead Through a Technological Revolution

The final major shift millennial leaders will face is the extraordinary pace of technological advancement. It's no secret that today's young people have grown up with unprecedented technological change, but the facts are truly staggering. Smartphone usage has outpaced nearly any comparable technology in history: It took landline telephones about forty-five years to rise from 5 percent to 50 percent penetration among U.S. households. Mobile phones took just seven years to reach similar levels. From 2000 to 2012, there has been a 566 percent growth in Internet usage worldwide, and if Facebook were a country, it would be the third largest nation in the world. New technological advancements such as 3-D printing, virtual reality, and nanotechnology are sure to catapult us into even faster and more dramatic transformations. Perhaps the most shocking tech-related statistic of all is that experts predict a whopping 45 percent of American jobs are at high risk of being replaced by computers within the next two decades.

As a boss in high-tech times, you'll need to become an expert at managing through technology, including overseeing virtual employees, handling the etiquette of new communication tools, and keeping current with important new apps, networks, and devices.

All of these demographic, economic, and technological shifts add up to the fact that we are living in a make-or-break moment in modern history. It is a moment that will require a new generation of leaders who are as dynamic and revolutionary as the times we are experiencing. I firmly, deeply believe that today's young people—that you—are up to the challenge. And I promise by the end of this book you will be more than ready to seize your moment.

BY THE NUMBERS:
THE FUTURE IS IN YOUR HANDS

61 percent of millennials are worried about the state of the world and feel personally responsible for making a difference.

(Cone Millennial Cause Study, 2012)

Generation What?

If you're confused by the terms *millennial* or *baby boomer*, you're not alone. You probably just think of yourself as you, not part of some monolithic demographic group. But thinking of yourself as a member of a generation is valuable because it can help you understand why your motivations and preferences seem different from those of your older or younger colleagues (or family members, for that matter), and why certain issues or goals are more important to you. It's similar to the way you might feel intrinsically different from someone raised in another country or someone of a different gender or ethnic background. In fact, human resources leaders now consider generational differences to be a workplace diversity issue that requires monitoring and training. I've personally seen a tenfold increase in requests from my corporate clients for speeches and workshops on the topic of generational differences.

The primary reason everyone is talking about generational differences today is because for the first time in American history, four distinct generations are sharing the workplace at the same time. (That's right; it's not just the baby boomers and millennials playing in the sandbox.) Below is a quick primer on each of those four generations, members of which you are guaranteed to encounter in your new leadership role, no matter what industry, region, or organization you work in. Note that these are primarily American categories until we arrive at the millennials, who are widely considered to be our first truly global generation.

Traditionalists (born approximately from 1922 to 1945)

Traditionalists in the U.S. population: 50 million
Defining characteristics: loyal, cautious, formal, proud

Tom Brokaw wrote a bestselling book naming the traditionalists the "greatest generation." They are also known as the GI or World

War II generation, because fully half of men in this age range served in the U.S. military. The majority (but not all) of traditionalists are retired at this point, but their influence is still heavily felt in the militaristic structure of many organizations. Think: top-down hierarchy, clear reporting structures, and the "uniform" of a suit and tie. Women of this generation primarily worked in the home as mothers and homemakers.

As survivors of the Great Depression, traditionalist men and women are also characterized by their frugality, risk-aversion, and loyalty to large institutions. When you think of diligently climbing the career ladder at one organization and retiring forty years later with a gold watch, think traditionalist. When you wonder where so many seemingly arcane, formal, conservative organizational practices came from, remember the mind-set of the cautious, rule-following traditionalists.

Baby boomers (born approximately from 1946 to 1964)

Baby boomers in the U.S. population: 76 million
Defining characteristics: optimistic, self-focused, competitive, forever young

The children of traditionalist parents, the baby boomers seemed to run full-force in the opposite direction. Raised in the postwar boom times of the 1950s and 1960s, the boomers were, for most of their lives, the largest cohort in American history. To stereotype: they grew up with suburban homes, convertible cars, rock 'n' roll music, American dominance on the global scene, and, significantly, television. The boomers were the first group to experience mass culture and mass marketing, and thus became mass consumers: they wore jeans, drank Coca-Cola, and bought Hula-Hoops. They invented the concept of being a carefree, fun-loving teenager. Socially minded and rebellious against traditionalist values and authority, they fostered the civil rights and women's rights movements, which expanded opportunity but also created more competition in the workplace as women and minorities began to take on jobs previously held in the traditionalist era only by white men.

Because of their vast numbers, for most of their lives boomers have completely dominated American society: think presidents (Bill Clinton, George W. Bush, and Barack Obama), pop culture (from the Rolling Stones to Steven Spielberg to Oprah Winfrey), and corporate leaders (Bill Gates, Carly Fiorina, and the late Steve Jobs, to name just a few). By the end of 2014, all baby boomers will be over the age of fifty, but they are still heavily involved in the U.S. work-force, thanks to their "forever young" natures and the global reces-sion that began in 2008 and forced many boomers to postpone their retirement plans. When you think of corporate all-hands meetings ("just like Woodstock!"), casual Fridays (boomers love their jeans), and "don't retire; rewire!" think boomer. When you wonder why it's so hard for organizations to pivot their HR or marketing strate-gies to the different style of the millennials, remember that they've been focusing on the massive baby boomer generation for the past thirty or forty years.

Generation X (born approximately from 1965 to 1981)

Generation Xers in the U.S. population: 46 million
Defining characteristics: independent, skeptical, tech pioneers

The children of the older baby boomers, born approximately from 1965 to 1981, Gen Xers represent the smallest generation in the workplace today. I'm a member of this clan and we were known in our day as the "baby bust." (Not very motivating, huh?) The rebel-lious and reinventing boomers had created a massive surge in the U.S. divorce rate in the 1960s and 1970s, and many Gen Xers were the children of those divorces. Combined with a difficult economy and increasing opportunities for women to build careers, these social and familial changes led to the phenomenon of latchkey kids—children who, their parents either divorced or both working, would come home from school in the afternoon, unlock their front doors with keys tied around their necks, and take care of themselves until a parent came home several hours later. Thanks to the new technologies of the time, Xer kids also had new "babysitters"—microwave ovens, personal computers, and video games—to take care of them.

At the same time, the world outside the typical Gen Xer's home became a lot scarier. When the U.S. economy soured in the 1970s, the "sex, drugs, and rock 'n' roll" fun of the baby boomer era gave way to dangers like AIDS, crack cocaine, and urban blight. Take it from a Gen Xer like me, the seventies and early eighties were kind of a bummer and pretty scary, too. No one paid a lot of attention to the effects that growing up in this era would have on us kids, a small generation totally overshadowed by our boomer predecessors, so we grew up independent, self-reliant, and supportive of technology that helped us take care of ourselves. Now just imagine what happened when we entered a workplace dominated by all of those rah-rah-rah baby boomers: we felt alienated and unimportant, knowing that we would never be a big enough group to have a huge impact at work.

So in the 1990s, as the economy improved and we joined the workforce in the biggest numbers our little generation could muster, aspiring Gen X leaders followed our independent instincts and moved to Silicon Valley. The Google guys Larry Page and Sergey Brin, along with many other high-tech start-up founders, are quintessential Xers. Of course there are many Gen Xers in more traditional roles and industries, but if you have trouble understanding an Xer on your team, it helps to think of them as Googlers, wanting to be independent, self-sufficient, and out of the mainstream. Plus, we Xers are often a little bitter that we got stuck between two mega-generations—the boomers and the millennials—and never really had a chance to make our own mark on society. In fact, I predict that very few Gen Xers will take on the largest leadership roles in American society. While many Gen Xers are and will be financially successful and happy, I don't believe we'll ever see a Gen X president of the United States.

Millennials (born approximately from 1982 to 2000)

Millennials in the U.S. population: 80 million

Defining characteristics: self-expressive, group oriented, global, tech dependent

The millennials, also known as Generation Y, are the children of the younger baby boomers. Thanks to increased birthrates due to economic improvement and a spike in immigration, particularly among the Hispanic population, the millennials are an even larger group than the massive boomers. American millennials are also known for the way they were parented: Many of the competitive, youth-focused boomers raised their kids as best friends (dubbed peer-enting), staying heavily involved in their kids' lives from birth to work. These helicopter parents hovered over their kids and swooped in when those kids needed support. (Really intense helicopter parents are known as black hawks.) Even if you were a millennial with strict parents who didn't hover, the U.S. education system shifted around this time toward the building of self-esteem and creativity rather than the rote learning of facts.

Other generations often criticize millennials for acting entitled, wanting constant feedback, and thinking they deserve a trophy just for showing up. I believe that these criticisms—I call it millennial shaming—can be traced back to the way many Gen Ys were parented and taught. (It's not your fault if you were praised a lot as a child! And, for the most part, having a healthy self-esteem is a good thing, especially for a leader.) But you need to be aware of the negative perceptions of your generation because you will likely face some bias in the workplace. Unfortunately, based on my work with dozens of companies struggling with issues of generational difference, I'm sorry to say that the biggest complaints about millennials tend to come from my own group, Gen Xers. Remember that bitterness I mentioned? Think of us as older siblings, resenting the fact that our younger siblings seem to have things so much easier and get so much more attention than we ever did.

Another significant trait of millennials is that you were born into technology. Sometimes referred to as digital natives, many of today's young professionals clicked a mouse before reading a book, and that has a major impact on how you see the world and interact with others. For many Gen Ys, face-to-face interactions don't come as naturally as texting and instant messaging. You often don't mind (or, actually, prefer) to talk to a computer customer service rep or GPS navigator than a human being. And thanks to the Internet, you have the expectation that every piece of data in the universe is available at your fingertips (because it actually is). Having an innate comfort with technology and an expectation of total access to information gives you a confidence that can make other generations a bit uncomfortable (and a bit envious).

BY THE NUMBERS: OUCH!

Millennial shaming is quite rampant in corporate America. While you are a unique individual, prepare to face some bias because of the traits commonly associated with your generation. A 2013 study by Beyond.com found some painful disconnects between the way millennials view themselves and the way older professionals perceive them:

• 82 percent of millennials rated themselves as loyal to employers, versus only 1 percent of HR professionals who think their youngest employees will stick around.

- 86 percent of millennials rated themselves as hard workers. Only 11 percent of HR professionals agreed.
- 40 percent of millennials think they have what it takes to lead. Just 9 percent of HR professionals think so, too.

Thanks to the Internet and all of the access to information and people it provides, along with more accessible and affordable international transportation, the millennial generation is also our first truly global generation in history. Terms like *baby boomer* and *Gen X* don't really translate to other countries' populations, but *millennial* does. I've read articles from all corners of the world talking about millennials and their shared characteristics. And because you've been able to read about and connect with your global counterparts for your whole lives, you and your peers tend to be more accepting of each other's diverse lifestyles and perspectives. Most millennials are actually uncomfortable when they work in nondiverse environments or teams.

So, to recap: the traditionalists and Gen Xers are small and cautious generations; the boomers and millennials are large and bold. Boomers have been in charge for decades, but even that "forever young" generation eventually will become too old to work and will pass on. Gen X is too small (and not entirely interested) to fill all of the leadership roles that boomers will vacate. This adds up to the fact that if you're a member of the millennial generation and you're not already a leader, odds are you'll have the opportunity very soon. The numbers confirm this: a 2013 international study by Deloitte found that 50 percent of working millennials are already in leadership positions. And a study I conducted in partnership with The Hartford found that 78 percent of millennials consider themselves to be leaders in some area of their lives, professional or personal.

BY THE NUMBERS:

DO YOU CONSIDER YOURSELF TO BE A LEADER?

The Hartford's 2013 Millennial Leadership Survey asked millennials to identify the areas of their lives in which they consider themselves to be leaders.

Base: Millennials who consider themselves a leader in some aspect	Total (680)
Family/Friends	64%
Personal interests/hobbies	50%
School/education	36%
Business/workplace	35%
Sports/athletics	24%
Volunteer/community/non-profit	22%
Arts/entertainment	19%
Social media/web presence	19%
Religious organizations	10%
Politics/government	8%

Yes, the millennial generation is large and well on its way to being in charge. But—and this is extremely important—remember that today and for a couple more decades at least, other generations (Gen Xers in particular) are still alive and kicking. You must always keep in mind that a large part of your success will depend not only on your ability to create the coming millennial-led world, but also on your ability to understand and get along with other generations while the transition process is taking place.

Quiz: Wait, Do I Act Like a Millennial?

If you're still not sure what characterizes a millennial, here are some common attributes. Yes, there is some stereotyping here, but if you check off more than five of the points below, your colleagues would definitely characterize you as a millennial and you'll have to manage expectations accordingly:

❏ I don't have a landline telephone; I use only a cell phone.
❏ I send or receive more than thirty texts a day (the average for a millennial is sixty).
❏ I have multiple social networking profiles and check them daily.
❏ I first used e-mail as a student and not as a professional.
❏ I have my own Web site or blog.
❏ I frequently have several IM conversations going at one time.
❏ I consider one or both of my parents to be my best friend.
❏ I call most of my parents' friends and my friends' parents by their first names.
❏ I don't personally know all of my Facebook friends.
❏ I had a double or triple major in college.
❏ I've received a trophy or certificate for participation at some point in my life.

Want to learn more about common characteristics associated with your generation? Check out this quick and spot-on quiz from the Pew Research Center, "How Millennial Are You?": pewresearch.org/quiz/how-millennial-are-you. (For the record, I clock in at 85 percent.)

If, like me, you can't get enough of this generational differences stuff, then I encourage you to read more about it. Neil Howe and the late William Strauss are the authorities on generational study and, in fact, invented the term *millennial*. I owe them a great debt as their research and insights heavily inform the work that I do and the generation-related information that I share. You can check out Strauss and Howe's books, articles, and research at LifeCourse.com.

The Key Trends Affecting Your Career

Finally, let's take a look at some additional conditions in which you'll be launching your leadership career. You'll find each of these topics discussed in more detail in the Trend Watch boxes throughout the chapters to come, which are based on my ongoing series of "Tomorrow @Work" trends forecasts, written in my role as spokesperson for The Hartford's "My Tomorrow" campaign.

CEO of You

First and foremost, know that your career path is in your hands. Years of corporate restructuring initiatives and the recent global recession have virtually ended the assumption that anyone will work for one company for an entire career and retire with a gold watch and an ice cream cake party. This means that instead of seeing your career as a ladder to climb, you now need to think of your career as a business and brand to manage, and as an asset to protect: you are the CEO of You, Inc.

This may involve actually starting your own business—according to the Ewing Marion Kauffman Foundation, 54 percent of millennials want to start a business or have already started one—or you may just want to think entrepreneurially even if someone else employs you. Ninety percent of millennials say that being an entrepreneur is a mind-set rather than the specific role of being a business owner (which, by the way, I completely agree with). If you haven't already, now is the time to begin thinking like the CEO of You and build and maintain your own personal brand, both online and offline. We'll dive into this topic in chapter 2, "Be," and chapter 3, "Be.com."

A VIEW FROM THE TOP

I think millennials are going to be great leaders. The adaptability of that generation, their ability to multitask, their ability to see things in many different avenues and think about the possibilities, that is what is going to be the hallmark of their generation.

—Lori High, chief sales and marketing officer,
Group Benefits, The Hartford

Tech Talk

One of the biggest workplace changes I've noticed over the course of my own career is how much quieter offices are these days. When I had my first internship in the mid-1990s, most people used just a landline and a nonnetworked computer to conduct business. When you walked through an office, you heard the constant sound of ringing telephones and overlapping conversations. Today, you mostly hear just the discreet tap-tap-tapping of keyboards and mobile device screens. However, that doesn't mean that face-to-face or voice-to-voice interaction is out of style. In fact, it may be more important than ever to be skilled at high-touch in a high-tech world. We'll talk about the right mix of technology and old school communication methods, and how to do them both well, in chapter 4, "Listen."

Multiple Mash-ups

Today's workforce is more diverse than ever before, encompassing people of different generations, genders, ethnicities, abilities, countries of origin, personality types, and work styles. You never know what mix of traits will make up your colleagues, clients, and customers, so you have to be prepared to relate to them all. Some people will expect you to be formal, some will expect you to be friends. Some will expect you to make decisions behind closed doors, some will expect you to be transparent about everything, including disclosing your own salary. How do you deal with difficult personalities, mediate awkward situations, and generally be a good boss? That's the topic of chapter 5, "Manage."

Work-Life 3.0

The issues of work-life balance and "having it all" have always been hot topics, but never more so than now. Thanks to Wi-Fi, mobile technology, virtual networks, and teleconferencing, work can take place literally anywhere, and employees want to take advantage of that. For millennials in particular, balance and flexibility are no longer considered luxuries to earn, but necessities to expect. How will this affect your career and personal life and your ability to manage employees seeking their own visions of work-life integration? And how can you maintain your sanity in an always-on world? See chapter 6, "Prioritize."

Retro Rolodexing

"It's not what you know, it's who you know" is more true today than ever. The busier and more tech-enabled the world becomes, the more important authentic, trusted relationships will be. I profoundly believe that your relationships are the core of your success no matter what you ultimately aspire to do. And the people who are peers early in your career will likely turn into some of your most important colleagues in the future—whether those relationships are formed and maintained face-to-face or entirely online. Learn more in chapter 7, "Connect."

Customization Nation

This final trend is one that may not even feel like a trend because it's become so commonplace. It's the idea that pretty much everything can and should be customized to your personal preferences, ranging from toys (Build-A-Bear Workshop) to clothing (design your own fit of jeans) to credit cards (choose your payment due date and reward perks). In my opinion, the desire to customize everything is one of the most significant traits of the millennial generation and it's rubbed off on the rest of us, too. So I'll end the book on this topic, how you can continually customize your career as your life expands and changes, in chapter 8, "Grow."

Sprinkled throughout the book in boxes, you'll find additional categories of advice as well.

- How to Say It: guides for challenging communications.
- There's an App for That: recommendations of apps, Web sites, and other tech-based management, productivity, and professionalism tools.
- A View from the Top: wisdom from successful leaders.
- By the Numbers: factoids, statistics, and charts related to the topic at hand.
- More, Please: more in-depth advice on various topics that might not apply to all readers.

If at any point while reading this book you have a question, a comment, or an aha! insight, please share it with me and the Becoming the Boss community on Facebook at Facebook.com/lindseypollak or on Twitter @lindseypollak.

This Book Is for You

As I hope you have already gleaned, this book is not for seasoned executives, jaded entrepreneurs, or other leadership veterans. This book is for you as you take your very first steps as a leader. My mission is to provide absolutely every bit of information and guidance I can, combining the best of yesterday's advice with up-to-the-minute tips from today's trenches, and lots of predictions on what you'll need to do to continue to thrive in the future. In addition to extensive leadership advice, I'll offer my best overall career management strategies as well.

When I wrote *Getting from College to Career* I included all of the advice, tips, tricks, and inspiration I could—ninety topics in all—about finding your first job out of college. My hunch was that young professionals weren't finding that information elsewhere, and I turned out to be right: the response was overwhelming, and the many readers who used the book to land their dream jobs started posting, tweeting, and e-mailing me almost immediately to ask, "Okay, I've got the job and it's going great. What's next?"

What's next is becoming the boss. So whether you are in a leadership position now or plan to be soon, let's get started.

PART I

Learn

Catch Up

Winning Friends, Moving Cheese, and Breaking All the Rules

Remember that feeling of walking into a classroom to take an exam when you knew you'd studied as hard as you could and were as prepared as you could possibly be? In your new role as a leader, one of the ways to achieve that calm confidence is to know your history. Yes, you are building your career in a completely different world from leaders five hundred, fifty, and even five years ago, but some things will never change. No matter how modern or high-tech the world becomes, you'll still hear frequent references to various leadership and success theories, practices, people, and platitudes from the past.

Even if your aim is to disrupt your industry or be the polar opposite of every leader you've ever had, in today's multigenerational workplace you still have to speak the same language and have many of the same reference points as the people you will encounter. (This is why many companies put their executives through intense cultural training before they take on an international assignment.) I can't tell you how impressed baby boomers and Gen Xers are when a younger colleague references a classic book like *The 7 Habits of Highly Effective People* or *Good to Great*. It's an instant credibility builder. As Harry Truman once said, "Not all readers are leaders, but all leaders are readers."

While I absolutely encourage you to become a well-read expert on the history of business, management, career success, and leadership, I know that you may not have the time for that right now. In fact, you may have downloaded this book at midnight because you're starting a new job tomorrow morning. So I'm going to attempt to distill about two thousand years of theory into the fifteen-minute *CliffsNotes* version.

Here is my ridiculously oversimplified but factual overview (vetted by several respected—and slightly horrified—MBAs in my network) of the top leadership, success, and management books you need to know about. There is a strong bias toward books published over the last five to ten years because those are the titles you are most likely to come across today and the ones you will want to be most familiar with.

Please note that the mention of a book or author here doesn't necessarily mean that I agree with his or her advice or opinions; it just means that I think they are important to be aware of.

The Art of War by Sun Tzu (second century B.C.)

The Art of War, written more than two thousand years ago, is generally defined as the earliest known book on military and political strategy. Modern military leaders read it. Many salespeople, politicians, and CEOs have it visibly displayed on their office shelves. Here are some highlights of Sun Tzu's aggressive advice:

- Warfare (and business) are about deception.
- Attack when they (your competitors) are unprepared.
- Do not make a move unless it is advantageous.

The Prince by Niccolò Machiavelli (1532)

Machiavelli's ideas and his book *The Prince* have influenced kings, America's Founding Fathers, and modern leaders for centuries. Have you ever heard someone describe another person or their actions as "Machiavellian"? You guessed it, that reference traces back to Niccolò. (It refers to situations when a clever trick is used to get something.) Here are a few more bits of the book's philosophies:

- A prince (or leader) might be a good person, but it's only essential for a prince to *seem* good to others.
- Don't be too generous, as it will only cause more greed.
- It is better to be feared than loved.

How to Win Friends and Influence People by Dale Carnegie (1936)

It might be fair to say that *How to Win Friends and Influence People* is the polar opposite of *The Prince*. It was one of the very first self-help books and it's still amazingly relevant. Here are some of the book's tips for making people like you. (FYI, the original edition also included tips for wives like "Don't nag your husband," but those were, thankfully, removed later.)

- Be genuinely interested in other people.
- Smile. (I know it sounds ridiculously obvious, but I swear that recruiters tell me the characteristic they most remember from candidates they meet at job fairs is whether or not a candidate smiled.)
- Be a good listener. Encourage others to talk about themselves. A person's favorite word is his or her own name.

Atlas Shrugged by Ayn Rand (1957)

Rand's novel *Atlas Shrugged* (the only fiction book on this list) explores a dystopian America where some of society's most successful citizens protest against government taxation by deciding to disappear, demonstrating that the destruction of the profit motive destroys society. Rand is also the creator of objectivism, a deep belief in individual rights and the pursuing of one's own happiness above all else (known in economics circles as rational self-interest). Before *Atlas Shrugged*, many business leaders felt somewhat apologetic for their success and wealth. This book made them (and many of their contemporary counterparts) feel like heroes. Here are two representative quotations:

- "Do not let the hero in your soul perish, in lonely frustration for the life you deserved, but have never been able to reach . . . The world you desired can be won, it exists, it is real, it is possible, it's yours."
- "He was guilty of nothing, except that he earned his own fortune and never forgot that it was his."

Confessions of an Advertising Man by David Ogilvy (1963)

Ogilvy has often been called the father of advertising, so his name is mentioned frequently. If you are a fan of *Mad Men*, as I am, then you've heard some of Ogilvy's wisdom doled out by various characters on the show. Probably his most famous quotation is "The consumer isn't a moron; she is your wife," but I don't see much modern application for that one. Here's a better one: "It is useless to be a creative, original thinker unless you can also sell what you create."

The Effective Executive (1967) and *The Essential Drucker* (2008) by Peter F. Drucker

If Ogilvy is the father of advertising, Peter Drucker is the father of management. I chose *The Effective Executive* for this list because Drucker's influence was particularly strong in the late 1960s (and rumor has it that Amazon CEO Jeff Bezos requests that all of his top executives read it). But Drucker wrote dozens of important books on management, leadership, success, and business, which is why I also recommend *The Essential Drucker*, a greatest-hits collection of his sixty-plus (!) years of writings. I guarantee you will hear someone quoting Peter Drucker in a meeting or presentation sometime soon (whether that person knows he or she is quoting Drucker or not), so you must know his name. Here are two of his most well-known pieces of wisdom:

- "What's measured improves."
- "Management is doing things right; leadership is doing the right things."

Servant Leadership by Robert K. Greenleaf (1977)

While it is a timeless concept, perhaps traceable to the *Tao Te Ching*, Robert K. Greenleaf coined the term *servant leadership* in a 1970 essay called "The Servant as Leader," which was published in book format in 1977. According to Greenleaf, traditional leadership generally involves the accumulation and employment of power by the person at the "top of the pyramid." In contrast, the servant leader shares power, puts other people's needs first, and helps people develop and perform to the best of their abilities. Servant leaders judge themselves by the satisfaction of their employees and their service to the greater good in society. Here is the theory in Greenleaf's words:

- "The servant-leader *is* servant first . . . The best test, and difficult to administer, is: Do those served grow as persons? Do they, *while being served*, become healthier, wiser, freer, more autonomous, more likely themselves to become servants?"
- "This is my thesis: caring for persons, the more able and the less able serving each other, is the rock upon which a good society is built."

The One Minute Manager by Kenneth Blanchard and Spencer Johnson (1982)

When I reached out to dozens of colleagues to ask what their favorite business book was, *The One Minute Manager* received the most mentions. Consider this super-short book a "management for dummies" that's really very smart. It basically boils down to this:

- Set one-minute goals that you can write in 250 words or fewer. (If Twitter had been around in 1982, Blanchard and Johnson probably would have recommended 140-character goals.)
- Give one-minute praise and one-minute reprimands for behavior to keep people on track toward their one-minute goals.

We'll come back to the *One Minute Manager* in chapter 5 because Blanchard and Johnson's advice is still so relevant and easy to apply today.

In Search of Excellence by Thomas J. Peters and Robert H. Waterman Jr. (1982)

In Search of Excellence is one of the best-selling and most widely read business advice books of all time, and Tom Peters is still considered one of the world's top management gurus (more on Peters in chapter 2). When you think of the go-go-go 1980s, think of this book. The authors studied forty-three top American companies of the time period and came up with eight principles of management these companies had in common. Here are a few of them:

- Make decisions and solve problems as quickly as possible. In other words, get on with it.
- "Stick to the knitting," i.e., stay with the business that you know. (I honestly did not know why people said "stick to the knitting" in business meetings until I saw it in this book.)
- Keep your staff lean and have minimal staff in your headquarters. (Note: the 1980s saw the first massive layoffs of middle management staff. Corporate America hasn't looked back since.)

The E-Myth (1986) and The E-Myth Revisited (1995) by Michael E. Gerber

As an entrepreneur, I have often been recommended *The E-Myth* over the years. Most important, and most applicable to your career whether you want to be an entrepreneur or not, is Gerber's insistence on the importance of working *on* your business and not just *in* it, meaning that you as the leader need to pay more attention to the structure, processes, and operations of your organization or team than to your product or service. Here is the key concept of the book, underlined *and* highlighted in my own copy:

- "The technical work of a business and a business that does that technical work *are two totally different things!*"

  In other words, as Gerber points out, a great barber does not necessarily make a great barber shop owner and a great musician does not necessarily make a great music store owner. Similarly, as you'll read in chapter 5, being great at doing your job does not make you a great manager of other people doing that job.

The 7 Habits of Highly Effective People by Stephen R. Covey (1989)

I was a freshman in high school in 1989 and I remember how insanely popular *The 7 Habits of Highly Effective People* was when it launched, even though most of my attention at the time was focused on boys. It's probably the book I've seen on successful businesspeople's book-shelves more than any other and the book I recommend most to oth-ers. Here are my three personal favorites of the seven habits:

- Habit 2: "Begin with the end in mind." Covey advises creating a mission statement for your life and making daily choices based on that statement. In other words, whenever you want to do anything, weigh the decision against your long-term goals.
- Habit 3: "Put first things first." Prioritize, plan, and execute your to-do list based on your life priorities (along with, when at work, your organization's priorities), not just what seems urgent in the moment.
- Habit 7: "Sharpen the saw." Covey's final habit is to spend time daily "preserving and enhancing" your physical, spiritual, mental, and social/emotional self. Exercise, read books, spend time with people you care about—take care of yourself. As Covey writes, this is "the habit that makes all the others possible."

Emotional Intelligence by Daniel Goleman (1995)

When you hear people talk about EQ, this is what they are talking about. Emotional intelligence relates to your skills in dealing with and reading emotions. Goleman argues that EQ can be even more important than the cognitive skills (your IQ) that are usually cited as the reason for someone's success or career advancement. Here's how he has described the main concept of the book: "If your emotional abilities aren't in hand, if you don't have self-awareness, if you are not able to manage your distressing emotions, if you can't have empathy and have effective relationships, then no matter how smart you are, you are not going to get very far." Many aspects of EQ are also referred to as soft skills, which is a term you'll hear a lot in today's workplace. Many recruiters and human resources executives agree that soft skills, such as communication and relationship building, are often more important to your leadership success than the technical skills you possess.

Who Moved My Cheese? by Spencer Johnson (1998)

Who Moved My Cheese?, by the coauthor of *The One Minute Manager*, is the best-selling business book ever. It was an insane phenomenon. It's also really, really short. *Who Moved My Cheese?* is written in the style of a fable about, yep, mice looking for cheese. On a higher level, it's about the need to adapt to change. Here are two of the book's simple but profound lessons:

- The quicker you let go of old cheese (translation: an idea, product, job, or career path that isn't working), the sooner you find new cheese.
- In business or in any aspect of life, what you are afraid of is never as bad as what you imagine. The fear that builds up in your mind is worse than the situation that actually exists. Johnson was the first to ask, "What would you do if you weren't afraid?"

First, Break All the Rules by Marcus Buckingham and Curt Coffman (1999)

This was Buckingham's first big best seller, but he is equally well known for the follow-up book with Donald O. Clifton, *Now, Discover Your Strengths*. Buckingham's books are based on his work at the

Gallup Organization, which conducted huge surveys of managers (eighty-thousand-plus participants) to determine what makes them succeed. Some of Buckingham's most important takeaways are:

- "Focus on strengths" rather than trying to improve your weaknesses, which the authors believe is a waste of time.
- "Find the right fit" for yourself and employees by carefully matching people with positions in which they will have the greatest chance of success. In other words, play to employees' strengths and don't try to shove a square peg into a round hole.

The Tipping Point by Malcolm Gladwell (2000)

The Tipping Point was another total phenomenon. If you haven't heard someone reference a "tipping point"—for a fad, a popular song, an idea, anything—you will soon. Essentially, *The Tipping Point* describes the point at which a fad becomes a fad and the people, known as "connectors," who can speed up that process. Here are two quotations that sum up the book:

- "The tipping point is that magic moment when an idea, trend, or social behavior crosses a threshold, tips, and spreads like wildfire."
- "There are exceptional people out there who are capable of starting epidemics. All you have to do is find them."

In addition to *The Tipping Point*, Gladwell has created an industry out of exploring interesting social phenomena. In *Blink* (2005), he addressed how and why people make instant decisions; in *Outliers* (2008), he analyzed the factors—such as studying or practicing for more than ten thousand hours—that lead someone to become extraordinarily successful; and in *David and Goliath* (2013), he explored the relationship between underdogs and favorites.

Good to Great by Jim Collins (2001)

Think of *Good to Great* as a kind of reboot of *In Search of Excellence*. Written twenty years later, Collins's book explored the characteristics of another set of successful companies, identifying what made them not just good companies, but great ones. It was a mega–best seller and must read for many years. Here are some of the most often cited theories from the book, notable as well for Collins's memorable turns of phrase:

- Good is the enemy of great. Lots of organizations feel that it's acceptable to be good enough, so they don't try harder to achieve true greatness. The same is true of people who settle for being good when they could be great.
- The best leaders are called level 5 leaders, who focus not just on the current success of their organizations, but on "enduring greatness."
- Set big hairy audacious goals (BHAGs). This concept actually originated in Collins's earlier book, *Built to Last*. It means to set really huge, visionary, ten- to thirty-year goals, such as reducing lung cancer by 50 percent or putting a composter into every home. (You can set BHAGs in your career, too.)
- The flywheel effect (a cycle that builds momentum through persistence) will win out over the doom loop (a reaction without understanding with little or no buildup). In other words, be consistent and accumulate strength and energy rather than trying to create sudden momentum by making a radical choice. (Collins advises this strategy with your career as well.)

Getting Things Done by David Allen (2002)

Allen is a productivity guru whose tips for organization and time management are legendary. His book *Getting Things Done* is so popular, especially among entrepreneurs, that it has a cult following of people who simply refer to it as GTD (and there are many blogs dedicated to Allen's philosophies). Here are three popular GTD strategies that I try to live myself:

- When a thought pops into your head while you are engaged with something else, write it down on a big list (real or virtual). When a paper crosses your desk while you are busy, put it in a central in-box. Then review all of these notes and papers once a day. This way, you can stay focused on the task at hand while never forgetting anything.
- Follow the two-minute rule: if you determine an action can be done in two minutes, just do it right then because it will take longer to put it aside, think about it later, and then do it, than to actually finish the task the first time you notice it.
- Break down amorphous blobs of undoability, (e.g., write a book) into manageable, measurable steps (e.g., write the first sentence). This is probably my favorite productivity tip of all time, and how this book was written!

Never Eat Alone by Keith Ferrazzi with Tahl Raz (2005)

Never Eat Alone is a modern-day *How to Win Friends and Influence People*. As you might guess from the title, it's about why you need to spend more time networking. If your brain immediately associated networking with schmoozy wheeling and dealing, Ferrazzi would want you to stop that right now. His book is about genuine relationship building and the mutual benefit that you and another person can provide each other. As he says:

- "Success in any field, but especially in business, is about working *with* people, not against them."
- "Don't keep score."

The overall takeaway from *Never Eat Alone* is that truly powerful and successful people support each other so that everyone wins.

A Whole New Mind by Daniel H. Pink (2005)

Besides being one of my all-time personal favorites, *A Whole New Mind* helped mark a key turning point that we're still experiencing in business today: the notion that creative, innovative thinking is the most valuable asset in an organization. In a time when technology might do it faster, outsourcing might do it cheaper, and we have more choice than ever before, Pink makes the case that creativity is necessary to survive in business. His six "senses" (you can consider them "essentials") for today's business include:

- Story: what's the narrative of your product?
- Symphony: have the big picture in focus and be able to link seemingly unconnected elements.
- Meaning: understand that defining your life's purpose is critical to people and thus critical to business.

Pink has written additional leadership favorites, including *Free Agent Nation* (2001), in which he posits that a growing number of us will be working for ourselves in the future, and *Drive: The Surprising Truth about What Motivates Us* (2009), which asserts that purpose and the desire to direct one's own life are people's true motivators, not external rewards like money or promotions.

The 4-Hour Workweek by Timothy Ferriss (2009)

While a four-hour workweek is a pretty over-the-top promise for a book title, Ferriss claims to live this reality—mostly through outsourcing as much of his work as he can. His key philosophy is that happiness is defined by having control of your time. *The 4-Hour Workweek* received (and still receives) major buzz and led a lot of people to embrace the concept of using technology and virtual assistants to handle time-consuming tasks such as answering common e-mail requests, booking travel, or dealing with the cable company. Here is the book's money quote, so to speak: "$1 million in the bank isn't the fantasy. The fantasy is the lifestyle of complete freedom it supposedly allows."

The Innovator's Dilemma by Clayton M. Christensen (2011)

Clayton Christensen, a Harvard professor, tackles the idea of innovation with research that explains how even efficient, customer-centric businesses are not immune to failure. The crux of his advice is that businesses that focus only on what their customers need now may be blind to what their customers will seek in the future. *Forbes* said, "This book ought to chill any executive who feels bulletproof—and inspire entrepreneurs aiming their guns." And if you're among an Ivy League crowd at work or expect to be, a Harvard Business School alum friend once told me, "If you want to impress a boss who went to Harvard, mention Clay Christensen."

Quiet by Susan Cain (2012)

While not yet a full-blown classic, Susan Cain received so much press for *Quiet: The Power of Introverts in a World That Can't Stop Talking* that a lot of business schools are now talking in leadership and communication classes about introversion. According to Cain, who calls herself an "introvert spokesperson," there are far more introverts in the world than you might think. You may be one yourself and, no matter what field you work in, you will certainly have introverts in your network and as colleagues in your job. *Quiet* teaches you what makes introverts tick and how to communicate better across personality types in general. Here are two of my favorite quotations from the book:

- "There's zero correlation between the gift of gab and good ideas."
- "Don't think of introversion as something that needs to be cured."

Lean In by Sheryl Sandberg (2013)

It's probably too soon to know if Sheryl Sandberg's *Lean In* will have lasting impact, but there is no question that this book, written while she was the chief operating officer of Facebook, was the hottest topic of discussion inside corporations, governments, small businesses, and kitchens when it first arrived on the scene. Perhaps because of the lack of women business gurus throughout history, Sandberg became *the* contemporary voice for ambitious women who want both a big career and a happy home life. Although some people criticized the book (for its lack of attention to the diversity of women's economic situations, for instance), several of Sandberg's key themes really struck a chord:

- To men: For women to reach fifty-fifty equality at work, then men need to reach fifty-fifty equality at home. If men took more responsibility for childcare, housework, and other domestic tasks, women would be able to achieve more in their careers.
- To women: "Don't leave before you leave." I was in the audience when Sandberg first gave this advice publicly at the TEDWomen conference in Washington, D.C., in December 2010. At the time I was seven weeks pregnant with my daughter, and Sandberg's advice not to "take the foot off of the gas" of one's career before even having a child was incredibly relevant to me. I believe this

advice extends more broadly as well—don't count yourself out for an opportunity because you think it might be too hard to handle.

MORE, PLEASE: THE BEST, CONTINUED . . .

There is, of course, no way this list could possibly be 100 percent complete or satisfy everybody, so here are some other lists of best or most important business and leadership books:

- *The 100 Best Business Books of All Time*: a whole book about business books! (100bestbiz.com)
- *Business Insider*'s "27 Books Every Entrepreneur Should Read": good ideas for business launchers and employees alike (Businessinsider.com/best-business-books-for-entrepreneurs-2013-5)
- *The Personal MBA*'s "99 Recommended Business Books": a categorized list of books on every conceivable business topic (Personalmba.com/best-business-books)

And here are some additional authors to check out on particular topics:

- Entrepreneurship: Guy Kawasaki.
- Sales: Jeffrey Gitomer; Zig Ziglar.
- Marketing: Seth Godin; Jay Conrad Levinson; David Meerman Scott.
- Negotiation: Roger Fisher; Carol Frohlinger; Deborah Kolb; William Ury.
- Women and Business: Gail Evans; Lois Frankel.

From Sun Tzu to Sandberg, you should now have a pretty good foundation of knowledge of major business book concepts, authors, and themes that you may hear referenced as you build your career. Moving forward, I hope you'll become an ongoing student of success literature. You don't have to read every sparkling new self-help business book or blog, but do pay regular attention to the nonfiction best-seller list and note what titles, authors, or experts your fellow leaders are talking about.

CHAPTER 1

Prep

Feeling the Fear, Filling the Tanks, and Perfecting the Pots

When you're launching a new product, restaurant, campaign, or leadership career, you need to prepare first: "Get ready for your close-up," as they say. In this chapter, we're going to put the pieces in place that will ground you as a leader and give you the foundation you can rely on when the going gets tough (or when it gets complicated, reorganized, downsized, disrupted, hacked, or anything else that comes your way).

How well you are capable of leading other people begins, first and foremost, with how well you lead yourself. You may be surprised at how far you'll read in this book until I start talking about managing other people. This is because you will be a far, far better leader of others if you spend time building your knowledge, your mind-set, and your attitude first. When those elements are in place, so much else will follow. Herewith are five key ways to become a leader on the inside so you're ready to be a leader on the outside.

Don't Fear the Fear

Career fear is totally natural. I suffer from it all the time. So do all the young professionals I meet. Here are just a few of the professional fears that I've felt myself and have been shared with me over the years: fear of failure, fear of success, fear of being too ambitious, fear of not being ambitious enough, fear of being disliked, fear of being inexperienced, fear of being overqualified, fear of tweeting, fear of not tweeting, fear of a nasty boss, fear of a backstabbing coworker, fear of a challenging client, fear of asking for a promotion, fear of leaving a job without another one, fear of launching a side business, fear of getting fired.

I'm not going to tell you to let go of any fears you might have. In my experience, that's next to impossible. What I am going to tell you is that it's completely normal to have fears about your work and career. After all, we are talking about your livelihood, your future, your ability to put food on the table and buy stuff on iTunes. The trick is to keep moving forward despite the fear.

What can you do when you feel fear surrounding your career or any leadership action you want to take? Whenever I feel profession- ally scared, I try to remember one of my favorite quotations. Bill Cosby once said:

Decide that you want it more than you are afraid of it. ◄

And then I think of all the times I've made the decision to over- come fear. Did I want to go to Yale more than I feared being rejected? I did. Once I got there, did I want to sing in one of Yale's prestigious a cappella singing groups more than I feared not making it when all of my friends did? Yes. Later, did I want to launch my own business more than I feared running out of money and moving back in with my parents? Yes. (I totally failed at the a cappella one, by the way. Twice I auditioned and was rejected. It was painful and embarrassing and I cringe even mentioning it, but I don't regret trying for it. And maybe the rejection helped nudge me away from singing on stages and toward speaking on them.)

Deciding that you want it—a leadership position, a promotion, a bylined column, a Kickstarter-backed start-up, an elected office—more than you are afraid of it is not just about moving past fear; it's also about committing 100 percent to what you want. In the business world and many other "grown-up" realms, few things will be handed to you (no matter what the millennial shamers say about today's young people being entitled). You'll have to reach for what you want with conviction. When it comes to leadership, in particular, fear is okay but wishy-washiness is not.

Fill the Tanks

After writing all of those book summaries in the previous chapter, I was in desperate need of some procrastination. I opened up my Pocket app (see box on page 46) and started reading an article about how writer-director-producer-cult-hero Joss Whedon is so unbelievably productive. Among many great tips he shared in the article, this piece of advice jumped out to me, mostly because I happened to be following it at that precise moment:

> Fill the tanks, fill the tanks, fill the tanks. Constantly watch things and things you don't [normally watch]. Step outside your viewing zone, your reading zone. It's all fodder.

Whedon's advice is to be a sponge, and not just in your own field. You can be a really good engineer if you read and learn a lot about engineering. But you can be a superstar engineer if you know a lot about engineering and you also listen to opera, tour a lavender farm on vacation, and watch the Sunday morning political shows. Because what happens when you fill the tanks with ideas from other realms is that you start to make random connections and come up with really creative ideas. You start to connect dots that other people aren't connecting and stand out from the crowd with your vision and innovation.

For example, I once walked into the wrong breakout session at a conference and sat through a presentation on postrecession housing trends. (The room was so empty that I felt too guilty to get up and leave once I'd realized my mistake.) I not only learned a ton, but also had a big aha! that the way millennials want career advice is similar to the way today's young professionals want real estate brokers to provide them with guidance. Six months later, I was also able to use the information I had gained when I received an out-of-the-blue request to speak for a professional association in the lumber and building materials industry. This might have been a complete coincidence, but I was glad to have some small knowledge of the housing industry when that opportunity came along.

What can you do to fill your tanks? Try a few of these actions:

- Subscribe to a blog, magazine, or industry e-newsletter that has absolutely nothing to do with your job, your personal interests, or even your region of the world. You don't need to read every article; just scan through the headlines and top stories to expose yourself to the main ideas.
- Talk to your friends about their jobs. And I don't mean just saying, "Hey, how was work?" Ask them to describe what they do all day, what issues are important to their companies, what news they are following closely at the moment. If you're comfortable with your nonindustry friend and the information isn't proprietary, you can even talk through some of your current challenges and ask for advice from that person's external perspective. This is why corporate and nonprofit boards of directors are composed of people from a wide variety of industries and areas of expertise.
- Whatever your favorite news outlet or app, subscribe to the "editor's picks" feed of stories from across a range of categories. (This is how I recently acquired a tiny bit of knowledge about avalanches, Scientology, and Maine lobster bakes.) If you're going

to read about topics that are not your first choice, you may as well read the best content available.

- Go to a movie theater or flip to a TV movie channel and watch the next film that is playing, no matter what it is.

Do any or all of the above with no agenda other than to fill your tanks. I don't know when or how or where your newfound, random chunks of knowledge will help you grow as a leader, but I'm positive they will. Fill the tanks, fill the tanks, fill the tanks . . .

THERE'S AN APP FOR THAT: POCKET

I know this is a bold statement, but Pocket (Getpocket.com) may be my favorite app of all time. Here's what it does: let's say you come across an article or video while sitting at your desk, but you don't have time to read or watch it at that very moment. Save it to Pocket and the article or video will be waiting for you whenever you have time. I subscribe to tons of e-newsletters, so I have developed the habit of quickly scanning them in the morning and adding anything interesting to Pocket. Then, over time, I read the saved content while I'm in a cab, waiting in a long line, or reading before bed. You don't even need an Internet connection to view your saved items.

Three Steps to Fill the Gaps

One reason Joss Whedon can focus on filling his tanks with content from other fields is that he spends most of his time excelling at his main work, which is making films, comic books, and television shows. He is tremendously skilled and experienced at his craft.

Are you?

It's a blunt question, but a crucial one. Before moving on to talk about the various elements of leadership and long-term career success, you have to "qualify" first. In other words, I can't help you become your hospital's youngest-ever chief of surgery if you haven't graduated from medical school yet.

Now, of course, anyone can declare herself a CEO and launch a business with no credibility or strong management skills, and many less-than-exceptional people have risen up the ranks of their organizations or industries. But are those the people you admire and want to emulate as leaders? I don't think so. We all have room for improvement; true leaders are regularly assessing what their gaps are and making plans to improve their knowledge and skill set.

Representative Aaron Schock of Illinois is the first U.S. congressperson born in the 1980s and for the first few years of his tenure was the youngest member of Congress at the time. I asked him how he was able to build credibility with his (much) older congressional colleagues and his answer was simple and profound: "Know your stuff. Do your homework, learn about the work you do, and be able to demonstrate that knowledge. It might not be flashy or attention grabbing, but hard work and knowledge go a long way in any field. Outperform your competition and people will take notice and give you opportunities for advancement."

Here is a three-step plan to do the same in your world:

Step 1: Assess Your Current Skill Set

The first step is to assess yourself honestly. Here are some questions to help:

- Do you possess the same educational degree or comparable experience/learning as the majority of people who are leaders in your field?
- Do you receive mostly positive feedback about your current job or the work you are now doing?

- In what areas have other people encouraged you to improve, and have you done so?
- Are there any technical skills that you know you need to attain now or in the next few years in order to become a leader in your field (e.g., understanding a profit and loss statement, mastering Salesforce)?
- In what soft skills areas do you personally feel you need to improve to be as successful as possible (e.g., negotiation, public speaking, making small talk)?

If you want to test your assumptions, try these strategies:

- Check out the LinkedIn profiles of people whose careers you admire in your field and compare them to your own qualifications. Look specifically at these sections:
  –Education: What educational degrees do those successful people have?
  –Skills and Endorsements: What words or phrases have they listed on their profiles, and which of these have received the most endorsements from people in their networks? See if you notice a pattern of skills that most of your role models possess and are celebrated for. Do you have these skills? Can you attain them?
  –Experience: What roles have these people held and what specific accomplishments have they achieved in those roles? Do you notice any commonalities? What experience do they have that you might need to achieve to move up in your career?
- View job postings for the leadership positions that you aspire to. (If you want to be a successful entrepreneur, look for job postings for leadership positions in businesses similar to the one you want to launch.) While you don't have to possess every single qualification or skill that a job is seeking, do you possess most of them? What are you missing?

- Go back to your university career center and set up a session with a career coach. (This is usually free or low-cost for alumni.) Career counselors are generally familiar with a wide variety of industries and organizations, so they can compare your skills and experience to the thousands of people they've already worked with.

Again, there are many examples of people who have succeeded as leaders without traditional education, skills, or experience (Steve Jobs, Mark Zuckerberg, and Rachael Ray, to name a few), but those people are not the norm. When possible, it's best to have the strongest foundation possible. Which leads to step 2 . . .

Step 2: Take Immediate Action to Fill the Gaps You Identify

In the last section you identified the skills you need to acquire or improve. Great. Don't wait another minute to start getting what you need. Don't worry about becoming a master; just stop being a beginner. Put aside this book (but don't forget to come back!) so you can take one or all of the following actions:

- Take whatever skills you want to acquire (leading meetings, speaking Arabic, creating a marketing plan) and go find the very best book on the subject. Commit to finishing the book in one to two weeks by adding reading time to your calendar. (If I come over to your place and see the book sitting unread on your nightstand, you're in big trouble!)
- Subscribe to multiple blogs and/or e-newsletters on the topic(s) you want to learn or improve. Google "best blog on . . ." or "best e-newsletter on . . ." and subscribe immediately. Then read the blog posts or articles during your scheduled reading time.
- Download the iTunes U app (Apple.com/apps/itunes-u) and register for a free class on the topic you want to improve. As

long as you're committed to watching the lectures and doing the homework, you can learn from some of the best professors in the world. Even if you listen to just one talk, you'll know more than you did before.

• If you don't want to take an entire class on a particular subject, you can watch free educational videos on thousands of topics at KhanAcademy.org or university-level lectures at AcademicEarth.org.

• Take a low-cost class. Who cares if it's not the Ivy League? Community colleges, public libraries, the Learning Annex, the YMCA, and other local institutions offer catalogs full of great classes at reasonable prices and reasonable hours for working professionals. As a bonus, many of these classes are taught by local professionals and community leaders, who may become good networking contacts for your career moving forward.

MORE, PLEASE:
SHOULD YOU GO TO GRAD SCHOOL?

When is it worth it to commit to a year or more of graduate school to truly master a skill or subject area? This is one of the most common questions I receive from aspiring leaders. Educational decisions are personal and depend on a variety of career, academic, economic, and industry-specific factors, so I can't give you a definitive yes or no here. (Sorry!) What I can do is provide you with the right questions to ask to help you make the best decision for you:

Question 1: Why Do You Want to Go to Grad School?
Education is a wonderful, valuable endeavor and a worthy goal in itself, but when it comes to graduate school, you should always have an end result in mind. Grad school is way too expensive to be used as a journey, a place to ride out the bad econ-

omy, or "a way to figure out what I want to do with my life."

Asking this question can also help you decide where to apply. It might even guide you to a less expensive, possibly online, option. For instance, if you want to go to business school to help you make a career change from one industry to another, your top priority should be finding an institution that is known for guiding people into careers in the new field you want to join. Or, you might look at other ways, besides an advanced degree, to make a career change, such as taking on volunteer work related to your new industry.

If your reason for wanting to go to grad school is to increase your technical knowledge of, say, accounting and financial management (for instance, to gain a higher position or salary bracket in your current organization), then the school name may not be as important as simply gaining the knowledge you need. On the other hand, if your number one goal is high-level networking in an industry such as management consulting where an MBA is crucial, then a "brand name," top-ten business school might be the choice for you.

Question 2: What Do Your Future Colleagues Advise?

In addition to thinking about your own reasons for wanting an advanced degree, it's important that you survey people in your specific field (or the field you want to enter after grad school) about how much the degree matters. Obviously, in some fields, such as medicine, law, or psychology, the degree is 100 percent required. But what about journalism? Computer science? Nonprofit management? Seek out people in the jobs you might want in the future (your university alumni network is a great place to find them) and ask what they would recommend based on their personal experiences. When in doubt, get more information from people who've been in your shoes.

> **Question 3: How Will You Pay for It?**
>
> Remember that statistic in the introduction that the average millennial already has $27,500 in student loan debt? I don't want you to add a penny to that number without giving it a lot of serious thought and looking into potential grants or scholarships to mitigate the expense. Unless you're independently wealthy or someone else is footing the bill, money must factor into your decision. Put together a realistic budget for how you'll live during your graduate school years—including whether or not you can work in addition to studying—and understand what your monthly loan payment would be afterward. And determine what a realistic starting salary might be after you graduate. Can you afford the debt you would be taking on?

Step 3: Practice Daily

Practice is a key component of success in any field. Just as a professional musician or athlete continues to practice every day, so must you practice skills like negotiation, public speaking, fund-raising, writing effective e-mails, giving feedback, and more. Keep getting better. Once you feel that you have mastered a skill, that's a sign that you're in danger of becoming complacent. The best leaders (and musicians and athletes) continually assess their skill sets and continually improve.

The fact is, you will become smarter and better at anything just by committing to doing it a lot. Let go of perfection and focus on practice. There is a parable (that I learned about from a Tumblr reblog, of all places) that makes this point beautifully:

A ceramics teacher announced on the first day of class that he was dividing the students into two groups. All those on the left side of the studio, he said, would be graded solely on the quantity of work they produced; all those on the right side would be graded solely on quality. His procedure was simple: on the final day of class he would bring in a bathroom scale and weigh the work of the quantity group: fifty pounds of pots rated an A, forty pounds a B, and so on. Those being graded on quality, however, needed to produce only one pot—albeit a perfect one—to receive an A.

Well, when grading time came around, a curious fact emerged: the works of highest quality were all produced by the group being graded for quantity. Apparently, while the quantity group was busily churning out piles of work—and learning from their mistakes—the quality group had sat theorizing about perfection, and in the end had little more to show for their efforts than grandiose theories and a pile of dead clay.

HOW TO SAY IT:
WHAT IS YOUR GREATEST WEAKNESS?

Here's a bonus to all of this work and learning and practice: you know that pesky question that recruiters love to ask during job interviews (even for CEO positions), What is your greatest weakness? You now have the ideal answer if you are interviewing for a new leadership position. This is what recruiters have told me is the very best type of response to that question:

> Well, I try to regularly assess my skills, and I recently identified grant writing as an area where I needed some improvement. I read a great book on the subject and took an excellent six-week class at the nonprofit resource center. I was able to improve my skills quickly, practice them often, and now feel much more confident as a grant writer.

With this answer, you are showing that you can honestly identify your flaws and that you are the kind of person who takes action to improve yourself when necessary. That is the type of employee—and, more important, leader—that any organization would love to have.

The Confidence Factor

Filling your gaps is important for another reason: I call it the confidence factor. There may be times when you first become a boss and throughout your leadership when you will feel unsure of yourself or perhaps like an impostor who might be unmasked at any moment. Many prominent leaders have admitted to experiencing "impostor syndrome" but, in my observation, it's usually the ones who are most qualified and experienced—and therefore most likely to be hard on themselves. While impostor syndrome is usually a temporary emotion, a great way to combat it is to remind yourself of your training. For instance, if you're on stage at a conference about to speak on a panel with a group of dauntingly impressive people, remind yourself that you worked hard to get there; you know vastly more about your business, company, or product than most people in the audience; and you were invited to be part of that panel for a reason. If you've been steadily filling your gaps and practicing your skills daily, you'll be able to brush aside your insecurities and focus on wowing the crowd with all the knowledge and brilliance you've worked so hard to obtain.

Make New Friends

Sometimes you seek and receive stellar career advice; sometimes you stumble into it. The latter is how I learned this tip. It was the summer of 2001, just after my three glorious weeks of being a first-time manager. I was enjoying a month of severance pay and trying to drum up clients for my new business (while, I admit, simultaneously look-ing at job postings in case entrepreneurship didn't work out). Most of my friends were employed full-time, so they were at work all day. This meant that I started to hang out with the handful of entrepre-neurs and freelancers I knew. Through these people, I met more. And more. And more. And it was one of the best things I ever did for my career as a business owner.

I hate to say it and it's not always the case, but sometimes your oldest and dearest friends (and even family members) won't get what you want to achieve. I'm certainly not suggesting that you drop all of your friends and hang out only with leaders. What I am suggesting is to make sure you create a support network of people—it can be just a few—who understand your leadership goals and what it will take to achieve them. Find a community where it's okay to talk about being successful, achieving big things, changing the world, making a fortune, or whatever your biggest dreams are. If you aren't naturally coming across other young leaders, check out chapter 7 (which is all about networking) and the resources guide at the end of this book for suggested organizations. You can also research and join local groups in your area, such as:

- Nonprofit organizations, especially committees and advisory boards.
- Local sports leagues (I swear that my friend Diane has met better business contacts on the soccer field that I have met through years of networking in professional associations).
- LinkedIn groups.
- Meetup groups.
- Your university alumni association or club.
- YoPros (young professionals) groups, often associated with your company or local chamber of commerce.
- Professional industry associations.

- Political clubs.
- Religious organizations.
- Toastmasters public speaking clubs.
- Rotary or Kiwanis clubs.

By the way, I know that some of the above suggestions may seem a bit old-fashioned, like Rotary clubs. But take it from someone who received a Rotary Ambassadorial Scholarship that (1) paid for me to earn my master's degree in Melbourne, Australia, (2) allowed me to spend two and a half years living in that amazing city, and (3) helped build my skills as a professional speaker through the extensive experience I gained speaking to Rotarians in Australia and back home in the United States: sometimes the most traditional organizations can be the ones that are most interested in cultivating young leaders and the most valuable for you to join. They've lasted this long for good reason and they are eager to continue into the future.

Develop Global Competence

Globalization could probably win a prize as the most overused buzzword of the twenty-first century so far, but that doesn't mean the concept is any less important for today's leaders to embrace. As Thomas Stewart, chief marketing and knowledge officer of Booz & Company, has said, "For boomers, an expat assignment was a good way to ruin a promising career; that's how hard it was to get back on track. Now it's impossible to imagine a CEO candidacy that doesn't include a gig abroad."

Dan Schawbel, CEO of Millennial Branding and author of *Promote Yourself*, agrees: "Global experience is crucial for millennials because it's a global economy, all countries are connected now more than ever before, and because you can apply for jobs and advance around the world if you choose." It becomes more important every day of the twenty-first century to be mindful of how business is done differently in other cultures than one's own. Alexandra Levit, author of six business books and a millennial leadership expert, has termed this skill "global competence."

Here are a few ways to ensure your leadership toolkit includes global competence, even if you have not yet lived or even traveled abroad:

- Talk to people from other countries. The millennial generation is the most diverse in American history, so it's likely you know many people who were born outside the United States, have family in other countries, or have spent significant time abroad. Actively seek out their points of view as you build your career. Most people are thrilled to share their global perspective with an interested listener.

- Read *The Economist*. It wasn't until I lived in Australia that I realized how astonishingly America-focused America really is and how little global news is available through most American media outlets. The antidote is *The Economist*, a UK-based publication that is widely read by international CEOs, elected officials, entrepreneurs, and other leaders. If you want to amp up your global IQ, add it to your e-reader.

- Travel abroad. This is the most obvious and effective way to gain a global perspective. I know that international travel can be expensive, time consuming, and uncomfortable, especially if you're a novice. Do it anyway. Get a passport if you don't already have one, sign up for discount travel e-mails to alert you to cheap fares, pack your suitcase, and go. When you get to wherever you are going, learn as much as you can, particularly about the industry in which you work. If your career is in government, talk to people about their political system and their view of ours (cabdrivers are an especially bountiful source of political opinions). If you run a marketing agency, take photos of advertising billboards and study the ads in local magazines. If you work in finance, read the business section of the local newspaper and ask about the local stock market. Browse the supermarkets, shop in the stores, eat at the restaurants, listen to the music, and watch the most popular TV shows. (P.S.: Spending a college semester abroad and hanging out only with Americans and visiting a country's major tourist attractions doesn't count as global experience!)

- Volunteer for an internationally focused nonprofit organization. I have learned more about international relations from my volunteer work than from any other source. In my role as chair of the board for She's the First, a nonprofit that sponsors girls' education and develops young leaders worldwide, I've been exposed to Facebook conversations, blog posts, Google+ Hangouts, and speakers that have educated me about girls' education in countries ranging from India to Tanzania to Guatemala. Find an organization that works on international issues you care about—access to water, education, the environment, children's health, etc.—and learn while you volunteer.

- Take a trip on YouTube. According to Tammy Tibbetts, founder and president of She's the First, online video is another great way to build your global competence. "Let people tell you about their lives and countries in their words," she says. "Watch movies. Look at the amazing documentaries out there. In my world of girls' education there are amazing documentaries like *Girl Rising* and *Half the Sky*, or She's the First's own documentary, *Magho*. Thanks to these films, the average person can be in tune with what it's like to be a girl who lives in Uganda or the Middle East or Peru. Take the initiative to educate yourself."

"Take the initiative to educate yourself" is ideal advice when it comes to every element of preparing for and thriving in a leadership position. Leaders don't wait for someone to guide them to where they need to be; they take a deep breath, roll up their sleeves, and pursue the necessary action.

We are now at the end of your official prep period, but the topics in this chapter will continue to recur throughout this book and over the many years of your leadership journey. As a leader, your education is never complete.

CHAPTER 2

Be

Building Your Brand, Polishing Your Presence,
and Dealing with Being Booped

What does it mean to you to be a leader? Or, to put it another way, what kind of leader do you want to be?

Whether you've fallen into a leadership position or you've been dreaming your entire life of being an entrepreneur, a CEO, or PO-TUS (that's president of the United States, if you weren't as big of a *West Wing* fan as I was), it's important to think about not only what you want to *do* as a leader, but also what you want to *be* as a leader. This is where the concept of personal branding comes into play. I know some people dislike the term *personal branding,* so whatever you prefer call it, we are talking about defining and managing your professional reputation.

Welcome to You, Inc.

Let's start with the personal branding guru himself, Tom Peters. In 1997, Peters, who was already an established management guru, wrote an article for *Fast Company* magazine called "The Brand Called You." In this article, he introduced what was a pretty radical idea at the time: that we all need to be the CEOs of our own reputations and careers instead of relying on an employer to manage our paths for us. People immediately embraced this concept and it hasn't lost steam since. Here is Peters's key insight:

> We are CEOs of our own companies: Me Inc. To be in business today, our most important job is to be head marketer for the brand called You.

What I love about the concept of personal branding is that it places your reputation and career management almost entirely in your control. That is so empowering and so different from the days when you had to wait and hope that a high-level person would notice you, realize you had some potential, and decide to groom you for a leadership position. And I've found that the concept of personal branding resonates particularly strongly with today's young professionals. When you've had some kind of online identity since age six, you're pretty much a natural at self-marketing.

TREND WATCH: CEO OF YOU

While no one works for the same company for an entire career anymore, keep in mind that future generations—the ones you'll be leading—may never even know the concept of having a single full-time employer. As benefits such as health insurance and retirement savings plans are increasingly separate from one's job, we may even move toward a "permalance" economy, where everyone is essentially a free agent and companies employ almost all talent on a temporary basis. This may sound like a scary concept to older generations that committed to one employer for life and that employer committed to them, but it may sound completely obvious to generations of the future.

As a leader today, it's important that you acknowledge the

different ways that each generation perceives their career trajectories so you can manage their expectations accordingly. Millennials tend to think of their careers as "lattices" (in the words of *Mass Career Customization* authors Cathleen Benko and Anne Weisberg) or "jungle gyms" (à la Sheryl Sandberg), whereas traditionalists and baby boomers, along with many Gen Xers, see their careers as one-way-only ladders. Part of your job as a manager in the twenty-first century will be to help all employees see themselves as CEOs of their own careers and personal brands, whichever career paths they choose to follow.

The Four Essential Elements of Your Personal Brand

As you begin to think about your personal brand and how you'd like to be perceived as a leader, here are four overarching areas to focus on.

1. Visibility

Do people in your organization or community know who you are? Is your presence felt by the people you lead or the people you want to lead? Are you findable where your desired networking contacts are looking? Do you appear in the media, at industry events, in the company cafeteria? Leaders need visibility.

2. Differentiation

What are you known for? What can you offer that other people can't? If someone walked into a meeting of you and your team, could that person tell that you are the boss? While leaders today need many skills, it can be helpful to have a few areas where you really excel. This is what gets you noticed and what gets you continually promoted.

3. Consistency

Can people depend on you to behave in a similar way across a variety of circumstances? Do you treat people equally? Is your image consistent across all social media and your in-person persona? This quality is particularly important: consistency regularly ranks as one of the most desired qualities of a strong boss or leader. Nobody likes surprises, especially in their leaders.

The consistency of your style is important for another reason as well: it sets the tone for your team to be consistent. It's like the physics principle of entrainment: a roomful of pendulums will eventually all begin to swing at the same pace. If you are consistently optimistic and reliable, your team will (under most circumstances) be consistently optimistic and reliable. If you are moody and unpredictable, your team will become moody and unpredictable, too.

4. Authenticity

Are you genuine in your image and your outreach to people? Are you comfortable in your leadership skin? In no way should you interpret personal branding as the need to put on a persona or be fake in any way. While you certainly want to own your authority and power, you can do so in a way that feels natural and comfortable to you. Maintain your personal integrity always.

A VIEW FROM THE TOP

A leader can't have a bad day. Your team depends on you and looks to you for inspiration, motivation, and rational thinking. No tantrums. Have an open door. Be honest. Be clear. You want people to be able to deliver the tough news without fearing that you'll bite their head off. 　　—Erin Moran McCormick, CEO, Year of Action

What Are You Known For?

Keeping in mind the need for a leader to have visibility, differentiation, consistency, and authenticity, let's start to home in on your unique personal brand as a leader. The truth is that you have a personal brand. We all do. Especially if you are established in a particular organization, and definitely if you hold a leadership position, it's simply a fact that people have opinions about you. You want to know what your current reputation is so you can continue to reinforce what you are doing well and build your reputation in new areas you want to be known for.

For example, if you have been a very successful advertising salesperson for the past few years, you may have built up a reputation for having excellent client relationships and great skill at closing deals. That is fantastic and important. But let's say you've just been promoted to sales manager and you're now responsible for a team of salespeople. You want to maintain your reputation for being a great salesperson, but also add new skills to your brand, such as being a terrific motivator and a supportive boss. In addition to building these skills, you'll need to make sure that people in your organization know that you now have these skills. That's what personal branding is all about.

Here are a few ways to glean what your current professional reputation is:

- Ask people you trust. I know it might feel a bit weird, but ask a handful of friends, mentors, colleagues, or family members to provide a few words to describe your professional skills and reputation. Ask people to be as specific as possible, and write down and compare their answers.
- Revisit recent reference letters, performance reviews, or other official documents in which someone has described you

professionally. What words and phrases do they use? What words and phrases *don't* they use that you wish they had?

- Look at the Skills and Endorsements section of your LinkedIn profile and see what skills people in your network have endorsed. Some people don't love this feature of LinkedIn because it feels too "gamey" or they've been endorsed for skills they don't possess or don't want to be known for (an audience member at one of my speeches told me that a friend had jokingly endorsed him for breathing). While it may be true that some of your endorsements might not be very helpful or valuable, I have found that the cream rises to the top. On most people's profiles, a few skills receive many more endorsements than all of the others. It's these most-endorsed skills that you should pay close attention to. Do you like your top three to five most endorsed skills on LinkedIn? Are they what you want to be known for? If not, you have some work to do. (See chapter 3 for more about creating a strong LinkedIn presence.)

What Do You Want to Be Known For?

Now let's work on reinforcing the elements of your existing brand that you want to keep and incorporating the elements you hope to add. Here's a simple exercise to help: if you overheard the people you lead talking about you, what words would you hope they would use to describe you? Remember, of course, that authenticity is key: to really be known for something, it has to be true.

❑ Appreciative

❑ Assertive

❑ Authentic

❑ Bold/courageous

❑ Calm

❑ Cautious/careful

❑ Charismatic

❑ Client-focused

- ❏ Commanding
- ❏ Committed
- ❏ Communicative
- ❏ Compassionate
- ❏ Confident
- ❏ Conscientious
- ❏ Consistent
- ❏ Creative
- ❏ Decisive
- ❏ Dependable
- ❏ Discerning
- ❏ Easygoing/flexible
- ❏ Encouraging
- ❏ Enthusiastic
- ❏ Ethical
- ❏ Fair
- ❏ Funny/witty
- ❏ Generous
- ❏ Hardworking
- ❏ Honest
- ❏ Humble
- ❏ Intelligent
- ❏ Intuitive
- ❏ Kind
- ❏ Logical
- ❏ Loyal
- ❏ Motivational
- ❏ Open-minded
- ❏ Optimistic
- ❏ Organized
- ❏ Patient
- ❏ Persuasive
- ❏ Positive
- ❏ Rational
- ❏ Realistic
- ❏ Resourceful
- ❏ Respected
- ❏ Responsible
- ❏ Risk-taking
- ❏ Serious
- ❏ Skillful
- ❏ Straightforward
- ❏ Strict
- ❏ Strong
- ❏ Successful
- ❏ Tactful
- ❏ Talented
- ❏ Thoughtful
- ❏ Tough
- ❏ Trusting
- ❏ Trustworthy
- ❏ Vulnerable
- ❏ _____
- ❏ _____
- ❏ _____

BY THE NUMBERS: WHAT MAKES A LEADER?

How do your leadership attributes compare with what your peers are looking for in their leaders? The Hartford's 2013 Millennial Leadership Survey asked millennials what they believe to be the most important characteristics of a leader. Here are the top answers:

		Total (871)
	Intelligent	69%
	Ethical/moral	61%
	Passionate	49%
	Charismatic	28%
	Empathetic	24%
	Financially astute/responsible	23%
	Healthy (mind & body)	19%
	Persuasive	16%
	Competitive	10%

It's always satisfying to place a checkmark in a box, but what can you actually do with these words once you identify them as qualities you want to be known for? Here are some suggestions for translating what you hope people say about you into what they actually say about you:

- Start to sprinkle these words into your conversations with the people you lead. For instance, if *realistic* is part of your personal brand, when one of your staff members comes to you with a challenge, you might say something like, "Let's come up with a few realistic solutions to this issue." As long as you are being authentic, the way you talk about yourself will ultimately become the way other people begin to talk about you.

- Use these words in written representations of yourself, including your résumé, professional bio, performance reviews, and LinkedIn profile. Of course you don't want to write, "Owen is the witty, consistent, resourceful, and trustworthy manager of fund-raising for Small Nonprofits, Inc." That would be pretty off-putting to most readers. The trick is to use the words to describe your work, not yourself. For example, a bullet point on your résumé or LinkedIn profile might read: "Raised more than $5,000 for a local playground renovation by implementing consistent and witty Twitter campaigns." Or, "Working with limited resources, developed relationships of trust with local foundations by attending weekly chamber of commerce events."

- Finally, use your personal brand traits to check in with yourself when making decisions big and small. For example, if you chose the words *ethical*, *positive*, and *risk-taking*, then make sure you are hewing close to these traits when selecting a course of action. In other words, live your values on a daily basis.

HOW TO SAY IT: REQUESTING A REFERENCE

When you ask people for references, you can politely suggest that they use some of your key brand attributes in their endorsement of you if they agree you possess these qualities. Here is an example of an e-mail request for a written recommendation:

Hi, Anne,

It's been such a pleasure to have you as a client and I really appreciate your ongoing support of me. As you know, I am in the process of applying for a promotion to vice president of client services, and I was wondering if you would be willing to provide a brief reference letter for me? In particular, I'd love to talk about the results we accomplished on the Jeep campaign and the Big Brothers Big Sisters toy drive. I'm hoping to point out that I am hardworking, trustworthy, and organized, if you agree I possess those qualities. Thank you for considering my request. And of course please let me know anything I can do to support you at any point.

Best regards,

Owen

MORE, PLEASE: "WHAT IF MY PERSONAL BRAND TURNS OUT TO BE 'ANNOYING JERK?'"

In some instances, you may discover that you are known for a few negative qualities or qualities that other people might perceive in a negative way. Even if it surprises you or hurts your feelings, this can be a gift to learn early in your career because you can take action sooner rather than later.

Let's say, for example, you learn that you have a reputation for arrogance. What can you do?

• Don't panic. One negative characteristic (or even a few) isn't going to sink your career and clearly it hasn't already. Try to view this feedback as constructive and valuable information that will help you become a better leader.

- Decide if you can live with it. For some leaders, particularly in certain realms such as politics, finance, fashion, or Hollywood, being perceived as arrogant (or aggressive or nitpicky or egotistical) may not be so bad. We can all name quite a few successful leaders who possess these qualities, and there is nothing wrong with having some aspects of them. I'll admit I've heard that I am sometimes known as self-promotional, which some people perceive as a put-down. But as an entrepreneur whose business is, well, me, I've decided I can live with the critique even if I don't love it. I believe I have to be somewhat self-promotional to be successful. That said, if I learned that I was known for being rude or unethical, I'd want to do something about it.

- Tone it down. If you decide your reputation contains some negative elements you want to change, you don't need to overhaul your entire personality. Instead, just turn down the volume a bit. For instance, if you're known for being hotheaded, then challenge yourself to stop sending angry e-mails or making angry phone calls and commit to waiting at least thirty minutes before responding to bad news. If you can commit to small changes in specific areas, you can slowly turn your reputation around.

What Would a Leader Do (WWLD)? How to Be a Leader if You're Not Yet in a Leadership Position

I'm aware that you may be reading this book before you are actually in a leadership position. Maybe you're in your first job and still learning the ropes. Maybe you have vague visions of hosting your own talk show someday. Maybe you have an idea for a business you want to start but haven't pursued it yet. Whatever stage you're in, here are three ways to build your leadership brand before you've got the title or responsibilities to go with it.

Take Initiative

In *Getting from College to Career*, I wrote about the importance of gaining leadership experience in college to landing a great job afterward. I interviewed Alice Korngold, a nonprofit leadership expert, and I loved what she said about why employers care so much about leadership experience. "Leaders are what make things happen. Period," she told me. "Every organization, from business to nonprofit to politics to coffee shops, needs people who will say, 'This is where we need to go' and will make sure you get there." What stands out to me about this quotation is that you don't actually need a designated leadership role to do what Alice is describing. All you need to do is get things done.

So no matter what you are doing now, in any situation, you can ask yourself: what would a leader do? Where in your current role—be it a full-time job, part-time job, volunteer position, or otherwise—can you make something happen? Where can you say, "This is where we need to go" and take action to get there? If you work in a coffee shop, can you suggest a more organized system for expediting food orders? If you're an analyst at an investment bank and you notice that no one can ever find the various industry reports on the company network, can you volunteer to organize it all into a shared folder?

BY THE NUMBERS:

A GENERATION OF VOLUNTEERS

If you're a millennial, it's likely you are already committed to volunteer work, which is a significant form of leadership in itself. In 2009, the National Conference on Citizenship reported that millennials "lead the way" in volunteering with a 43 percent service rate, compared to only 35 percent for baby boomers. Among college students, the volunteerism rate is 53 percent, of which 41 percent say they serve a few times a month at least.

Even if you aren't yet ready to take on a project of your own, you can choose to go above and beyond on any assignments you receive from a higher-up. For example, if your manager asks you to put together a list of potential locations for a client dinner, you can choose to include a few Yelp reviews for each restaurant to help her decision making. If you are taking messages for your boss while he is in an all-day meeting, you can ask each caller the best time to reach him or her the following day to save your boss from playing phone tag. I know these may sound like small actions, but, in the words of Keith Ferrazzi, author of *Never Eat Alone*, "little choices make big impressions." You never know who is watching when you go the extra mile, and you never know how that experience might teach you a good lesson for your future leadership roles. If you really want to be a leader, the first step is to stop being a bystander.

Show Commitment

If you are now part of an organization in which you want to rise up the ranks (be it a corporation, a political party, a university alumni community, or any other group of people), it's important to demonstrate your allegiance to that institution. Initiate and take part in conversations about long-term plans for the organization. Volunteer for formal and informal committees and task forces. Attend nonrequired events, such as picnics, parties, information sessions, and community service projects. Join and become an active participant in the organization's LinkedIn group. Follow the organization on Twitter, Facebook, and elsewhere, and share some updates with your networks. Offer to help the organization with recruiting efforts and refer good candidates for job openings. Members of the millennial generation are often criticized for a lack of loyalty, particularly when it comes to job-hopping from employer to employer, so your commitment will stand out even more.

Act Like a Leader

I've never loved the saying "fake it till you make it" because I don't think there is anything fake about acting in a way that is consistent with a role you want to hold in the near future. But I do agree with the sentiment behind the phrase: a great way to become a leader (or any other position you aspire to) is to start acting—appropriately— like you already have the job. The classic wardrobe advice to "dress for the job you want, not the job you have" is a cliché, but there's a reason it has stuck around for so long. Take that advice to heart and apply it to other aspects of your job: compose e-mail for the job you want, speak in meetings for the job you want, use social media for the job you want (much more on this in the next chapter), and build work relationships for the job you want. In general, when taking any professional action, ask yourself: WWLD?

How to Handle "You're Young Enough to Be My Daughter/Son/Grandchild" (aka the "Boop")

No matter how expertly you manage your personal leadership brand online and offline, occasionally you will not be perceived the way you want. Well into my thirties and established as a business owner, I was invited to appear as an expert at a client's trade show booth during a financial services industry conference. I was wearing a conservative navy blue suit, tasteful jewelry and makeup, and professionally styled hair. During some downtime, a man working in the next booth came over to introduce himself and chat. He asked about my business, I asked about his, we exchanged cards. Then as the conference attendees began returning to the trade show area, I said I had to get back to work. "Of course," he said, "It was nice to meet you." And then, before turning to go, he reached out, touched a fingertip to the end of my nose and said, "Boop!"

Yes, this actually happened to me!

What do you do if you find yourself in a similar situation, being treated like a child when you're at work? After recovering from the initial shock, I believe you have three options:

Ignore It

This is the option I chose following the boop and here's why: the booper was significantly older (in his sixties or seventies), the action was inappropriate but not aggressive, no one else was around to witness it, and I would likely never see the guy again.

Deflect It

Deflection is usually your best option when someone treats you like a child in front of other people. Your goal with deflection is to appear polite but firm, and not to let the comment or action undermine your authority. For example, several years ago I attended an exclusive dinner at the Four Seasons restaurant in New York with fellow contributors to a magazine, who were all amazing writers and businesspeople I couldn't wait to meet. An owner of the magazine moderated a discussion among the guests. One by one, he asked each person about his or her work, upcoming book topics, opinions on current events, and so forth. When he got to me, he said:

> Well, Lindsey, you just look so young! I suppose my only question to you is, just how young are you?

I have no doubt I turned bright red and that everyone in the room felt a knot in their stomachs wondering how I would handle the question. Thankfully, I'd had some media training that taught me how politicians use deflection when they don't want to answer an interviewer's question. So I smiled politely (but not too politely) and said,

"That's a question I didn't expect! I'd actually love to tell you about a new book project I'm now researching . . ." Then I launched into the topic I wanted to discuss.

Deflection allows you to maintain your professionalism and authority while not embarrassing the other person publicly. If you know you look particularly young and these types of comments are likely to occur, it's a good idea to have your "pivot" ready and be prepared to talk about your desired topic instead of your age.

Confront It

If comments about your youth are happening over and over again with the same colleague or client—or worse, someone who reports to you—then you might decide to address the situation directly. Note that confronting the situation doesn't have to mean being confrontational. It's just that sometimes the only way to stop a behavior is to call it out. In some cases, you may even find that the perpetrator really doesn't mean any harm and would be happy to stop if asked. I'd pick a casual moment when you are alone with the person and say something like, "So I'm not sure if you even notice that you're doing it, but you've made a few negative comments lately in front of our team about my age. I'd really appreciate it if you could stop doing that."

If the comments persist, here is another tactic to try, again in a private moment: "I've noticed you're still mentioning my age in meetings and conference calls. I'd love your input on whether I'm doing anything that makes me appear young or inexperienced? I wouldn't want this perception to affect the entire team."

Remember to keep your requests short, polite, and nonaccusatory. A sense of humor usually helps, too. If the comments continue to persist, then I would take that as an indication that you are simply working with a jerk who probably makes negative comments about a lot of different things to irritate a lot of different people. If that's the case, then most people probably won't give this person's comments much weight and your best option to is to go back to ignoring them. If the comments become aggressive or offensive, or begin to compromise your ability to get your job done, then a discussion with your HR department, boss, or board is also an option.

Your Personal Leadership Brand Checklist

Now that we've talked about the big picture of your leadership brand, let's dig into the details. As Tom Peters wrote in that famous *Fast Company* article:

> Everything you do—and everything you choose not to do—communicates the value and character of [your] brand. Everything from the way you handle phone conversations to the e-mail messages you send to the way you conduct business in a meeting is part of the larger message you're sending about your brand.

Everything is a little broad, so let's break it down. For the rest of this chapter you'll get set up with the offline elements of your personal leadership brand, and in the following chapter we'll address your online image.

Personal Brand Checklist, Part 1: Your Offline (In Real Life) Brand

Of course you always want to be authentic and bring your unique approach to each element of your personal brand, but here are some overall guidelines for managing your IRL image:

A Strong Self-introduction

Also known as a thirty-second pitch or an elevator pitch (because you should be able to deliver it in the length of time of a short elevator ride), your self-introduction is especially crucial when you're in a leadership role because it immediately establishes your confidence and authority. I'm not a big fan of memorized canned self-intros, but I do recommend that you take some time to practice describing yourself so you make a great first impression in introduction-requiring situations such as client meetings, job interviews, and professional conferences. Make sure to clearly say your first and last name (it makes you appear young only to provide your first name), your job title, and your company, and speak at a normal pace (people tend to talk really, really fast when introducing themselves).

If your job title is uncommon or confusing, or your organization is not well known, I'd also recommend including a brief description in layman's terms of what you do. If you have a significant professional activity outside of your full-time job, you have more than one job, or you run a side business, in some situations you'll want to mention that, too. Remember that it's perfectly fine to introduce yourself differently depending on your situation. Here are two examples:

Introducing yourself at a meeting with a potential fund-raising client:

> Hi, I'm Tiffany Jones. I'm the manager of institutional development for Kansas Kids, which is a nonprofit organization that helps needy children in our state. I'm in charge of raising money for our great work from corporations and foundations like yours.

Introducing yourself at a local young professionals networking event:

> Hi, I'm Tiffany Jones. In my day job, I'm the manager of institutional development for Kansas Kids, a nonprofit that helps needy children in our state. I'm also active in the local classical music scene—I play violin in a chamber orchestra and teach private lessons as well.

MORE, PLEASE: THIRTY SECONDS' MORE ADVICE
ON #ELEVATORPITCHES

Since self-introductions are very personal, I wanted to provide a
diversity of advice on this topic. So I asked my Twitter followers
for their favorite tips to share with you:

- @ShimritMarkette: Smile! Put nerves aside and demonstrate
  your enthusiasm for what you do (and the chance to talk about
  it) with nonverbal cues.
- @Keppie_Careers: Make sure your intro addresses the target's
  needs. Think about what he/she wants to know about you and
  pitch that.
- @MattLaCasse: What's the thing you want that person to remember most about you? Focus on that and ask to follow up.
- @Glenderful: Your elevator pitch always has to have a "call to
  action" for the other party. "Since I work in HR, I'd love to know
  about . . ."

A Confident Handshake

In many situations, your self-introduction will be accompanied by a
handshake. Promise me you will not wimp out on the shake. This
is one of the easiest things to get right and the worst to get wrong.
Leaders, and business leaders in particular, tell me all the time that a
weak handshake is a huge professional turnoff.

A good handshake is firm, includes direct eye contact, and en-
closes the other person's full hand (not just the fingers) so the web
between your thumb and forefinger touches the other person's web.
If you tend to have sweaty palms, think ahead and keep a tissue in
your pocket to wipe your hand before shaking someone else's. If you
suspect you have a weak shake, ask someone you trust to practice

with you a few times until you get stronger. This seriously matters, especially if you don't want to come off as young or inexperienced.

A Level-Up Wardrobe

The definition of a leadership-appropriate wardrobe will vary widely depending on your specific profession and workplace, of course, but my strong belief is that if you want to be a leader you need to look the part. Particularly if you are young (and even more so if you *look* young), you can use your wardrobe to build your authority and command some immediate respect.

I think about this a lot in my field of professional speaking and consulting, where I am often standing and presenting in front of large groups of people. I try to dress one level up from the level of my audience. So if most of my audience will be dressed in business casual, I'll wear a suit. If most of my audience will be in suits, I'll wear a suit plus some nice jewelry to look a bit more dressed up. If my audience will be in jeans and T-shirts and I know the office environment is very casual, I might wear jeans and a blazer.

I'd apply the same rule of thumb for leaders: get in the habit of dressing one level up from the people you manage. You might not do this every day, but it's a good way to stand out and, I think, to show respect for your position. Even if everyone in your office wears hoodies, then as the leader you should wear the nicest, least wrinkled hoodie.

If you dislike thinking too much about your appearance, then consider the approaches of leaders like Steve Jobs or Hillary Rodham Clinton. Each one adopted a uniform—he wore only black turtlenecks and jeans; she wears only pantsuits—to keep people's attention away from their clothes. Even if you love fashion and dressing up, keep in mind that as a leader you never want people's attention more on your clothes or accessories than it is on you. Do your best to avoid distractions (clangy jewelry, chipped nail polish, excessive hair gel, too tight or too short anything, stained or wrinkled clothes) and develop a style of dressing that expresses your personal style but still gives you the authority you want. Not sure if a particular outfit is leadership-appropriate? Take a quick selfie, send it to a few trusted friends (or your mom), and ask for their opinions. When in doubt, change.

Business Cards

I believe that business cards are going to be obsolete in a few years, but today you still need them, especially if you work in a baby boomer–heavy industry. At their essence the job of business cards is to provide people with your contact information, so that's what your card should do. Now that we have so many communication options, a business card can guide people to your preferred method, which is different for everyone these days. If you want people only to call your mobile phone, then only list that number on your card or list it before or above your landline. If you want people to e-mail you instead of calling, then make sure your e-mail address is the most prominent call to action on your card (for example, place it in a larger font than your phone number and directly under your name). If you love interacting with people on LinkedIn, then include your LinkedIn profile URL right on your card. And keep in mind that many people already operate paperlessly, so it's possible your business card may end up forever lost at the bottom of their purse or pocket. This means it's always smart to send a quick e-mail the day after you first interact to say, "It was great meeting you." And of course provide a full e-mail signature with all of your contact information below.

If you're an employee of an organization it will probably provide cards for you and you may not have a choice as to what information is included, although it never hurts to ask if there is contact information you can add or delete. But what if you also work for yourself, have a side gig, or are starting a new venture? Then you need to create separate business cards sooner rather than later. Go to your local Staples or FedEx Office (Kinko's), or check out online business card design and printing sites such as Vistaprint.com or Designyourowncard.com.

If you want to have a professional logo designed for yourself or your business, take a look at 99designs.com. You can name your design concept and price, and then professional graphic designers will compete to design a logo within your budget.

When making your own cards, my advice is to opt for the highest quality paper and printing you can afford. I recently spent a small fortune on letterpress business cards printed on super heavy card stock, and the investment pays off every time I see the impressed reaction of anyone to whom I hand my card. Even something as small as a business card is an extension of you—make it count.

Personal Brand Checklist, Part 2: Your Personal Personal Brand

One of the most significant workplace changes of the past ten to twenty years is the blurring of the line between the professional and personal aspects of our lives and reputations. This means that part of being a leader in the workplace is being ethical and responsible in one's personal life as well.

Lori High, chief sales and marketing officer, Group Benefits, for The Hartford, who manages more than four hundred people, told me: "If you're wise in your personal matters, people have so much more confidence that you are wise in your business matters. Leadership includes emotional balance, financial balance, and family balance. There is no longer a private world and public world. For individuals who forget that, it causes problems." Most millennials agree. According to The Hartford's 2013 Millennial Leadership Survey, nearly nine in ten millennials (88 percent) say that one's personal life has a somewhat to significant impact on one's ability to lead.

Let's look more closely at some of the personal qualities that will contribute to your success as a leader. First comes your financial health, because it's hard to focus on leading other people and accomplishing big things professionally if you are constantly worrying about money or fearing that an accident could destroy your finances.

(This is particularly important if you are one of the two-thirds of millennial college graduates with student loan debt.) Here are some of the keys to building financial stability in your twenties and early thirties, so you have the peace of mind to focus on your leadership:

A Basic Budget

One of the first steps to managing your finances at any age is to get your head around where your money is really going. Start a document or note in your phone or a small notebook and write down absolutely every penny you spend for a week. At the end of the week, highlight any money you spent that wasn't essential or didn't make you happy and try to eliminate those expenses the following week. A good rule of thumb to aim for is 50/30/20 in terms of how much you should spend on needs (50 percent of your after-tax income), wants (30 percent), and set-asides for savings (20 percent, including short- and long-term savings). CEO of MoneyZen Wealth Management Manisha Thakor says that this simple formula is the financial version of the food pyramid. You'll want to tailor it to your specific situation, but it's a good reality check. For instance, if your rent and car payment alone are chewing up 50 percent of your take-home pay, you'll know you have a problem, as there's no room left for other necessities like food.

THERE'S AN APP FOR THAT: MINT

If the word *budget* gives you hives, you are not alone. I know it's daunting to take an honest look at your finances and try to get your head around every penny that comes in or goes out. Fortunately, there is Mint, a free budgeting software and app at Mint.com that will help track your finances. It works best if you primarily use a debit or credit card, but no matter what it will give you excellent insight into your spending—and where you can do a better job of saving.

Good Credit

Your credit report is now an element of your personal brand. I know this sounds pretty invasive, but it's true. Almost half of employers now use credit checks when making a hiring decision. While some states have passed laws to end this practice, it is still highly common and something to be aware of.

Emergency Savings

It's exciting to have your first *big* paycheck as a leader, and I totally support indulging a bit, but you need to be smart about saving, too. According to Thakor, you should start off by aiming for at least $2,000 in an emergency fund (as this is the average amount of unexpected expenses that tend to pop up in a year). As your career develops, you'll want to work toward building the gold standard of an emergency fund: three to six months of living expenses.

Retirement Savings

While it might feel strange to think about retirement when you're twenty-five and your parents are still contributing to your rent, it's never too early to start planning and saving. If you work for a company that offers a 401(k) retirement savings account, sign up immediately. Some companies will even match a portion of your own contributions, which means you are receiving free money. I'll say that again: *free money.* You'd be crazy to turn that down. Retirement contributions will generally be deducted from your before-tax income, so you'll be saving for your future without feeling it each month.

If your company doesn't offer a retirement savings plan, your best option, according to Thakor, is to open up a Roth IRA at a financial institution specializing in low-cost mutual funds, such as Vanguard or Fidelity. As of this writing, you can contribute up to $5,500 a year in a Roth IRA and it will grow tax-free for decades. Just be aware that Roth IRAs are taxed before contributions, so taxes are still involved. They also have income caps, so once you are making more than $100,000, you'll want to talk to your tax preparer or financial advisor about whether a traditional IRA is right for you.

Disability Insurance

I've learned a lot about disability insurance in my work with The Hartford, and my biggest takeaway has been this: as a young professional, your ability to work is your greatest asset; you need to protect it. Think of disability insurance as a safety net while you're recovering from an off-the-job injury or illness, such as a broken leg from a winter ski trip. The Hartford's 2012 Benefits for Tomorrow Study found younger workers without disability insurance would likely dip into their 401(k), get a loan from family, or move in with relatives if a health issue kept them from working. Disability insurance only costs an average of $250 per year when you get it at your workplace. In my mind, it is essential for peace of mind.

Note that disability insurance may be offered by your employer as what's called a voluntary benefit, which means you agree to pay for this coverage during your benefits enrollment period. If, like me, you are self-employed, a freelancer, or a consultant, you should check with associations, unions, or guilds that you belong to. They might offer disability insurance (along with other types of insurance and benefits) at group rates to their members. I receive mine through a terrific organization called the Freelancers Union.

Life Insurance

Most people know that life insurance is a must-have if you are the primary breadwinner in your family. (If you have children, it is also wise to speak to an attorney about creating a will to put in writing all of your wishes about their future, such as the division of your assets and guardianship if anything happens to you.) What many millennials don't know is that single young professionals should consider this coverage as well. For example, The Hartford's research has found 10 percent of millennials have a parent relying on their paycheck. If this describes your situation, what would happen to your mom or dad if the unthinkable happened? And many people don't know that if a parent cosigned your student loans, he or she will still be responsible for paying back those thousands of dollars if anything happens to you.

I know that all of the above is worst-case scenario, but life insurance provides some day-to-day benefits as well. Some life insurance policies offer additional features, such as ID protection and travel insurance. Plus, it's less expense to buy life insurance when you are young and healthy, and easy to buy it at work through payroll deduction.

Renter's or Homeowner's Insurance

These insurance options, which can be purchased through an insurance agent or directly from insurance companies, will cover you if anything happens to your apartment or house, and they often cover other valuable items like your laptop or smartphone as well. If you insure your car and apartment through the same company, you can often get a discount. Thakor adds this money-saving tip: "When you're just starting out, one thing you can do to lower your premiums is to opt for the largest deductible you can afford. Your renter's or car insurance may go down dramatically as you raise the amount you will pay out of your pocket (the deductible) before insurance kicks in. The key to this plan is to have an emergency fund big enough to meet the deductible if the need arises."

Now let's talk about your physical health. You limit your leadership potential not only when you are worried about money, but also when you are exhausted, starving, stuffed, hung over, sick, or stressed out. Of course these things may happen sometimes (and my husband could tell you a few horror stories about my own occasional hangriness), so I'm referring to your general state of wellness. You have to be at your best to lead people to be their best. I'm sure you can name a few successful people who defy this statement, but I wonder how sustainable their leadership will really be.

Sleep

Let's start with sleep. I know there are leaders like Marissa Mayer and Bill Clinton who claim they need only four or five hours of sleep a night, but they are the exception. Most of us need to sleep seven or eight hours almost every night to function at our best. I definitely do.

Arianna Huffington, the founder of *The Huffington Post*, calls herself a "sleep evangelist" and has made it a personal crusade to encourage more shuteye. In a commencement speech at Smith College in 2013, she drove this point home to an audience of future leaders by advising them to "sleep your way to the top"—meaning sleep in the literal sense. "Right now, the workplace is absolutely fueled by sleep deprivation and burnout," she said, sharing a story of how her own lack of sleep led to a dangerous fall, a broken cheekbone, and four stitches in her right eye. Sleep deprivation is also "affecting your creativity, your productivity, and your decision making," she continued. "The *Exxon Valdez* wreck, the explosion of the *Challenger* space shuttle, and the nuclear accidents at Chernobyl and Three Mile Island—all were at least partially the result of decisions made on too little sleep."

Have you noticed that it's become the norm to say how exhausted we all are? Let's make it part of the millennial leadership revolution to change this. I know it won't always be possible for you to get eight hours of sleep every night if you're launching a start-up, running for Congress, planning for a big client meeting, or—ahem—finishing a book deadline, but do your best to make a good night's sleep a priority in your life. As Huffington pointed out, it's not cool to be tired. It's unsustainable, it's painful, and it's a serious hazard to your own well-being and other people's.

Stress

The other wellness issue to address is stress management. I know it myself: the more stressed I feel, the less productive, effective, and successful I am. And the more likely I am to snap at one of the people I manage, which is not the kind of boss I want to be. People deal with stress in different ways, and we each need to find our own best stress relievers. My strategy consists of exercising, practicing yoga regularly, and trying to limit my sugar intake (which is really hard since I have a serious sweet tooth). No matter what strategies work for you, as a new leader you have to take this issue seriously or you'll burn out before you really begin.

TREND WATCH: MILLENNIAL MALAISE

I doubt you'll be surprised to learn that stress is particularly prominent among members of the millennial generation. Much of that stress is due to the lingering effects of the Great Recession, which has left millions of young people unemployed or underemployed. According to the American Psychological Association, in 2013, 39 percent of millennials said their stress had increased in that year, and 52 percent said it had kept them awake at night in the past month. Furthermore, more than any other generation, millennials report being told by a health-care provider that they have either depression or an anxiety disorder. The Hartford's claims data shows that behavioral health, such as anxiety, is one of the top three reasons that people in their twenties file a disability claim. Of course other generations struggle with stress as well. The World Health Organization has deemed stress the "health epidemic of the twenty-first century," and it's been estimated to cost American businesses up to $300 billion a year in lost employee productivity.

If you're looking for ideas, here are some suggestions for destressing outside of work: hiking, walking, biking, jogging, team sports, weight lifting, singing, dancing, listening to music, gardening, driving, playing with kids or pets, creating art, cooking, meditating, talking with a therapist, talking with a friend, cleaning, building something, playing video games, reading, watching movies or TV, taking a bath, getting a massage.

Here are some suggestions for destressing in the middle of a busy day so you don't rip someone's head off: taking five deep breaths, walking around the block, IMing with your best friend, spending five minutes looking at videos online, drinking tea, stretching, hanging upside down (seriously—Rosie O'Donnell swears by it!). And if you work for Arianna Huffington, you could even take a nap. In her Smith commencement address she mentioned that she created two nap rooms at *HuffPo*'s New York office.

In this chapter we talked about the ways to build your leadership brand in real life, both professionally and personally. Now let's move on to the way your leadership reputation extends online. In today's world, these elements are equally important.

CHAPTER 3

Be.com

Ego-googling, Hunting Moose, and Making Time to Tweet

I n organizing this book, I struggled with whether to talk about your Internet image before your live one, since it's probably more likely today that someone will check you out online before meeting you in person. This includes media outlets seeking experts to interview, conference planners seeking speakers, nonprofits seeking board members, awards panels seeking winners, clients, potential clients, bosses, colleagues, investors, and anyone else you want to impress. Your online image can make or break an opportunity you don't even know exists yet.

That said, online personal brands do matter more in some realms than in others. If you're a leader in politics, for example, you will need to have a strong online presence and absolutely everything you say and have ever said online will be scrutinized. If you are an accountant or lawyer at a big firm, you probably won't need (or, perhaps, be allowed) to tweet very much. But I cannot think of a profession where you would escape the reality that someone somewhere is going to google you. If you want to be a leader in any area, you have to pay attention to what people find when they search your name online. And you have to ensure that what they discover about you on the Internet is consistent with the you they encounter in person.

VOICES OF MILLENNIAL LEADERS

Today, leaders need to know all of the effective methods of communicating. For example, writing a great blog can help create a leader. Having a strong online identity is critical for leadership in the new workplace, and keeping it consistent with your real life actions is even more essential.

—Kevin Grubb, career and social media expert

As a leader, you also have to be mindful that you are representing more than just yourself. Every time you post to a social media site, you are also building (or tarnishing) the organization or community in which you hold a leadership position. As Julie Daly Meehan, executive director of Hartford Young Professionals and Entrepreneurs (HYPE), a four-thousand-member organization in Connecticut, told me, "It's a lot scarier to be in a leadership role today. If something goes wrong, your name can be plastered all over the Internet in ten seconds. If I do get worried about that, I remind myself that I am following a carefully crafted [social media] plan for my organization, and that I'm mindful of what I put out through my own accounts. Whenever you post, you have to remember that people perceive things so differently. They can blame your organization for something you personally posted. I'm not willing to hurt my organization just because I'm fired up momentarily about an issue."

In this chapter, we'll explore all of the ways you can use social media to enhance both your own personal brand and the brand of the organization, community, constituents, or services you represent.

Scrub First

I'll never forget the first few moments of my college experience: I breathlessly climbed the three flights of stairs to my freshman dorm room, ascending to what was sure to be the launch of my adult life, the dawn of my future career, the starting point for lifelong friendships and unforgettable experiences. I opened the door, stepped over the threshold, and . . .

The room was kind of a dump.

I am a proud Yalie and hate to badmouth an institution that has given me so much (and, I am happy to report, this particular building underwent a beautiful renovation several years ago), but there is just no other way to describe that room. The paint was peeling, the windows were dingy, the mattress on my bunk bed resembled a Wasa cracker, and the entire place was covered in a thick layer of dust.

After recovering from the initial shock, I dashed off with my brand-new roommates to get our student ID cards. An hour later, we returned to find all of our mothers surrounded by rolls of paper towels and various cleaning supplies, vigorously scrubbing every available surface. My roommates and I rolled up our sleeves and joined in.

Yale did, of course, turn out to be the launch of my adult life, the dawn of my future career, the starting point for lifelong friendships and unforgettable experiences. It just needed a really good scrub first. The same goes for your online presence: social media can be an enormously important component of successful leadership, but, as your unofficial leadership mother, I feel an obligation to make sure you are starting from a clean base. And it all begins with your name.

How (and Why) to Clean Up Your Online Presence

If you've never googled yourself, aka ego-googled, you're long overdue. Simply type your name into Google or another search engine and don't stop reading until the results run dry. You absolutely must know what information is available about you online.

There are a few reasons for you to review and monitor your online presence. First, if someone says or has said something positive about you or a project you're involved with, you will want to know about it so you can thank the person. On the flip side, if someone says or has said something negative about you, you'll want to know about that, too, so you can address it or correct it if possible.

THERE'S AN APP FOR THAT: GOOGLE ALERTS

Monitoring your name is a practice you'll need to continue on an ongoing basis. If you haven't already, immediately set up an e-mail alert that will let you know if your name is mentioned anywhere on the Web—in the news, on a blog, in a video, or on any social media. The best free options for this name monitoring service are Google Alerts (Google.com/alerts) and Talkwalker Alerts (Talkwalker.com/alerts).

If your name is difficult to spell, like mine, then you might also consider setting up alerts for the various spellings of your name (for instance, the correct spelling of my last name is "Pollak," but it's frequently misspelled as "Pollack," so I have alerts for both). If your name is very common, then you might want to include another identifying word or phrase, such as your company name or your particular area of expertise, but frankly I'd rather you receive the occasional update about another John Smith than miss an important mention of yourself online.

As a leader, your goal should be for the first few results on Google (or Yahoo or Bing) to reflect the professional presence you most want to project. For most people, I believe this should be your LinkedIn profile because it is 100 percent professional and 100 percent in your control. (Much more on LinkedIn later in this chapter.) Depending on your situation, other ideal listings to have in your top five might include:

- Your bio on your organization's Web site.
- Your Twitter, Tumblr, or other social media profiles, if you are using them primarily for professional purposes.
- Your own Web site or blog or that of your organization.
- A positive, professional news story written by you or about you.

If you find, as many people do, that your personal Facebook profile is one of the first search results for your name, don't worry too much. Just make sure that you have tight privacy settings and that your main profile photo, which people might be able to see even if they cannot access the rest of your profile, is appropriate.

What if your self-googling reveals some un-leaderlike stuff, such as red-plastic-cup-holding college party photos or a curse-filled rant you once wrote about your cable company's horrible customer service? Make no mistake: negative online content can absolutely hold you back from achieving your leadership goals. According to one study, 70 percent of employers say that they've rejected a job candidate because of information they found about that person online. An inappropriate social media posting can damage your professional reputation even if you are not actively job hunting. The average young worker is connected on Facebook to sixteen coworkers.

The good news is that in many (but not all) cases, you can clean up a less-than-professional online reputation. Here's how:

Untag, Untag, Untag

Your first line of defense in cleaning up your online image is you. Most of the bad stuff I've seen about people is posted on their own social media profiles and could easily be removed with one click. Go through all of your profiles and view them with the eye of an employer, an investor, a voter, an employee, or whomever else you want to impress professionally. Some sites, such as LinkedIn and Facebook, even offer the ability to view your profile as if you were a member of the public, so be sure to do that once in a while. If you find any inappropriate photos, posts, or comments by you or your friends, delete them or untag yourself. As for what I mean by *inappropriate*, I'm tempted to quote United States Supreme Court justice Potter Stewart's famous line about determining what counts as pornography—"I know it when I see it"—but here are some specific examples: drunken photos (especially if anyone in the photo is underage), too-sexy photos, violent photos, photos of you doing anything illegal, racist or sexist comments, profanity, or comments about how much you hate your boss or employer. When in doubt, delete.

Pay Attention to Privacy Settings

The default setting on most social networks—Facebook, Twitter, LinkedIn, Pinterest, Instagram, Tumblr, YouTube, etc.—is that everything you share (and everything that people share about you) is public. So make sure that the privacy settings on all of your social networking accounts are as tight as possible just in case someone hacks into your account or a friend posts a photo you wouldn't want other people to see. Privacy settings are complex and change constantly, so I recommend scheduling a note in your calendar to check your settings once a quarter or so.

Request Removal

If someone else posted the offending photo or piece of content, you can and should politely ask the source to remove that content. Sometimes, especially if the poster is a friend, classmate, family member, or colleague, it's as simple as that. However, not all sources will be able or willing to remove what you ask. Most news outlets and government agencies, for instance, will not alter their content.

Build Better Content

If the source of any negative content is unwilling or unable to take down the damaging stuff, your next step is to get search engine competitive. This means building better content with your name attached to it so that search engines will find and rank these pages higher than the unwanted link(s). Dan Schawbel, author of *Promote Yourself* and *Me 2.0*, recommends posting positive content on several social networks and building your own Web site with your full name as the domain name (e.g., DanSchawbel.com—more on this at the end of the chapter). Examples of positive content creation might include writing bylined book reviews on Amazon; or writing articles for an industry association Web site, a young professionals blog, or on your own blog or Web site—as long as you are writing about professionally appropriate topics.

Become More Social

The next strategy is to build up a positive presence through participating actively and appropriately in social networks such as LinkedIn, Twitter, Facebook, Tumblr, Reddit, Pinterest, Google+, and others. "For the social network profiles," Schawbel says, "make sure you get vanity URLs for them. For instance, on Facebook you want Facebook.com/YourFullName and on LinkedIn, you want LinkedIn.com/in/YourFullName. Then, once you have your sites, link between them so that they will rank high in searches for your name." To find out if your name is available on any network, check its availability for free at Namechk.com.

Accept the Attention

When you raise your hand for leadership, you are, to a certain extent, opening yourself up to public scrutiny and criticism. I'll admit that sometimes I wish I didn't have to be so vigilant about what I post to Twitter or Facebook. It would be fun, once in a while, to dash off a snarky comment about a kvetchy client or poke fun at a ridiculous question from an audience member. But as someone who teaches the importance of personal branding, I know that I can't do that. And frankly, I'd probably regret being so mean anyway.

Young leaders are more conscious of this than anyone. In fact, some millennials have confided to me that they don't want to seek too public a leadership role because of the nonstop scrutiny that comes with it. For the record, I deeply hope that the idea of social media scrutiny doesn't deter you from achieving your dreams and becoming a leader in our society, which desperately needs you.

To gain more insight on this topic, I turned to a young leader in perhaps the most scrutinized world of all: national politics. Along with Aaron Schock of Illinois, whom you've already met, U.S. representative Tulsi Gabbard of Hawaii is one of the youngest members of Congress. When I had the opportunity to interview her, I mentioned that many young people are afraid to run for office because of the exposure and scrutiny and asked her how she personally overcame that.

"You have to know why you're doing what you're doing," she responded. "What is your motivation? The scrutiny is real. When people entrust you with their vote, you carry an incredible responsibility and are held to a higher standard. I first ran for and was elected to the state legislature when I was twenty-one years old; a lot of people told me that I was crazy; many people wrote me off, both during the campaign and after I won. When your motivation is centered around the opportunity and responsibility you have to serve your community, and you know it's not about you, then the critics' voices ring hollow, and the results of your work speak for themselves."

Bottom line: when it comes to building your personal brand online, if your intentions are genuinely good and you keep your focus on doing the best job you can for your *constituents* (however you define that word in your leadership role), then you should be fine. Just keep in mind that the boundaries for what is appropriate will depend on the world in which you operate. To be on the safe side, I've given you the most conservative advice possible. But if you are a leader at, say, a satirical Web site or an edgy nightclub, you can likely push the boundaries a bit more than the rest of us. The key is to just be smart about it—take a moment to think before you tweet.

MORE, PLEASE: WHAT IF IT'S *REALLY* BAD?

Sometimes, after I've given a speech and spoken to some of the attendees who've waited in line to chat afterward, I'll notice someone waiting patiently nearby, head down, staring at his feet or fiddling with her phone. After everyone else has asked a question and walked away, this person will sheepishly walk up to me.

"Um, can I ask you a sort of embarrassing question?" the person will ask.

"Of course," I will reply, guessing what's coming next.

"A few years ago I was, um, well . . . arrested . . . but not charged, I swear . . . and now when you google me, the police report is the first search result for my name. I've tried to build my social media presence and add good content, but nothing has worked . . ."

Sometimes the person has been arrested, sometimes it's an embarrassing article the person wrote years ago in a high school newspaper, and sometimes it's an inappropriate photo that won't go away. But the next question is always the same:

"Is there anything I can do about this?"

The answer is yes. But it might cost you. If you find yourself in a really tough situation regarding your online presence, fee-based services, such as BrandYourself.com and Reputation.com, exist to help improve your online image. These services will help you create professionally focused Web sites and articles, optimize this content for search engine rankings, and monitor your progress to push the negative content down and out.

Where Are Your Moose? Determine the Essential Social Networks for You

Once you've done your best to cleanse your online image of anything too negative, it's time to create a whole lot of positive. The first question to answer is: on what social networks do you need a presence? Last I counted there were approximately a bazillion networks to choose from (and new ones launching daily), so this is not an insignificant question. To answer it, I always think of something a former client used to say about marketing: "If you want to hunt for moose, then go where the moose are."

I have no idea why he chose moose for this axiom, but I've never forgotten the lesson: if you want to reach a certain audience, you can't expect them to come to where you are. You have to go where they are. And this is my advice when it comes to choosing which social networks will be most beneficial for building your online leadership presence. Decide which networks are most important in your industry, community, or other environment in which you want a following and build your presence there.

How to find your moose:

- Google some prominent people in your organization or industry and note on which social networks they are most active.
- Ask five to ten people you admire in your field which social networks they believe are the most important and valuable.

Based on my experience working with more than 150 organizations in a wide variety of industries, here are some of the most important social networks for a variety of industries. This is by no means a comprehensive list, but it will give you an idea of the trends. And don't just take my word for it; always check with the people you know, as trends change quickly:

Accounting: **LinkedIn.** For most traditional industries, LinkedIn is considered the most professional and appropriate for personal branding and networking.

Banking/financial services: **LinkedIn.** Same as above, particularly because the financial services industry is heavily regulated.

Entertainment: **Facebook, Twitter, YouTube, Instagram.** Whenever I give speeches in the entertainment industry, audiences remind me that entertainers want to entertain, so they gravitate to sites that allow them to demonstrate their talent.

Event planning: **LinkedIn, Pinterest, Instagram.** For any visual or experience-based industry, showing, not telling is essential. However, LinkedIn is still critical for connecting with vendors, clients, and potential clients in a professional way.

Health care: **LinkedIn.** Again, heavy regulation means that LinkedIn is the way to go.

Human resources: **LinkedIn.** More than anyone, HR professionals know how too personal social networking posts can get employees in trouble. Stick to LinkedIn if you want to be an HR leader.

Journalism: **Twitter.** Twitter is the network of choice for reporters and editors who love breaking news and trend spotting. If you're employed in this industry or even a freelancer, just be careful to note that your tweets are your own and don't necessarily reflect the opinions of any outlets you contribute to.

Media and publishing: **LinkedIn, Twitter, Facebook, Pinterest.** For book and magazine publishers, social networks allow you to connect with readers and to promote the content you are publishing. Many magazine brands do a great job of sharing their content through Pinterest and Twitter in particular. They also create reader panels through Facebook fan pages. When it comes to finding freelance writers, editors, fact checkers, designers, and photographers, LinkedIn is your best bet.

Nonprofit: **LinkedIn, Facebook, Twitter.** In the nonprofit world, "going where the moose are" means connecting with donors and potential donors. Since they can be anywhere, nonprofit leaders are generally active on multiple networks. If you find that your donors or supporters gravitate to certain networks more than others, then by all means stick to those.

Politics: **LinkedIn, Facebook, Twitter, YouTube.** Potential voters and donors could be anywhere, so politicians have to be everywhere. And it goes without saying to be cautious. Every word—or, um, selfie—you share can and will be used against you by the opposition.

Public relations: **LinkedIn, Facebook, Twitter, YouTube, Instagram.** As a publicist, you are required to know the media and know the trends for your clients, so you have to be knowledgeable about as many social networks as possible. Google Alerts for your clients will be crucial tools as well.

Recruiting: **LinkedIn, Twitter, Google+, GitHub, Reddit.** Recruiters need to become experts on where to find the most talented people in the industry for which they recruit. I've included GitHub, the code-sharing community, here because recruiters in the tech industry have told me that this is where they go to find talented coders. As for Google+, I once interviewed a recruiter for an open source software company in the Czech Republic. She told me that the most talented open source programmers in Eastern Europe like to hang out on Google+, so that is where she has built the biggest presence. That is a perfect example of knowing where your moose are.

Technology: LinkedIn, Twitter, Tumblr, Google+, Reddit. People working in the technology industry generally want to embrace the latest and greatest tools, so, along with all the other sites, the micro-blogging network Tumblr is a hot spot. And in this field more than any other, be sure to keep current on what new networks are becoming popular.

The Ultimate LinkedIn Guide for New Leaders

The reason that LinkedIn is the most important social network for the majority of industries is that it is completely professional (no cat photos or animated GIFs). So as I mentioned in the previous section, for those in the vast majority of industries, the ideal search scenario is for your LinkedIn profile to be the first, or among the first, listings when someone googles your name. (Full disclosure: I am a paid consultant and official ambassador for LinkedIn, but even if I weren't, it is a fact that LinkedIn is the world's largest professional online network.)

Given how important your LinkedIn profile is to your online personal brand, I'm going to walk you through a step-by-step process for building a leadership-worthy LinkedIn profile and building your overall presence on the site. Note that, like any social network, LinkedIn's features are updated frequently, so if you have any questions that aren't answered here or if you notice changes from the descriptions below, check out help.linkedin.com.

Step 1: Study the Best

As a longtime ambassador for LinkedIn, I've given a lot of people a lot of tips on how to use the site. And the advice I give most often is to study the LinkedIn profiles of the people you admire, especially those in your particular industry or company. This will give you an enormous amount of information about what should appear on your own profile. Ask these questions about the LinkedIn profiles of your role models:

- How do they describe themselves in their LinkedIn headlines?
- How do they write about themselves in the Summary statement section?
- What words and phrases do they include in their Skills and Endorsements section?
- Have they posted examples of their work to their LinkedIn profiles? If so, what type of examples and how many?
- What do they write about in their status updates?
- What groups do they belong to?

You might also notice that some very senior leaders have quite minimal LinkedIn profiles. In some industries—such as the heavily regulated fields of finance, insurance, government, and health care—professionals tend to avoid robust social media profiles. Beyond these industries, it's not uncommon for executives to feel skittish about sharing too much information about their career paths, clients, projects, or key achievements. Some people worry that it looks to their current employers that they are job hunting; others just don't want the world to know the details of their careers.

I believe this is often a generational difference, too. For baby boomers who built their careers in the pre-Internet days, it might feel strange to promote your achievements for the world to see. But today, most younger professionals have found that the benefits of having a professional LinkedIn profile—such as being discovered by a new client, contacted by a former classmate or colleague, or approached by a recruiter if you are, in fact, job hunting—far outweigh potential concerns. However, if you do find that the leaders you most admire have minimal LinkedIn profiles, you might want to follow suit and keep yours simple as well.

For the vast majority reading this book, my hunch is that you will be wildly inspired by the LinkedIn profiles of leaders you admire. The Internet gives you amazing access to the choices that successful people are making; use this information to motivate and guide you as you craft your own online presence. (Just don't "borrow" any full sentences or paragraphs from a career hero's profile. That's not flattery; that's plagiarism.)

Step 2: Impress with Your Profile Headline

I believe that your headline—the title or phrase at the top of your profile—is the most important piece of real estate on your entire LinkedIn profile. The reason is that people are very busy. They want a concise explanation of who you are and why they might want to know you. For many people, it's fine to use your current job title as your LinkedIn headline (and that is the default on LinkedIn if you don't type in an alternate title). But perhaps your job title doesn't adequately reflect your awesomeness. In that case, you can use your headline to help build people's perception of you as a leader.

There is no need to have a perfectly crafted phrase or title; it's fine to use several important words separated by slash marks, hyphens, or vertical lines. Your goal is to use words that a potential contact might type into a search engine to find someone with your specific skills or experience. These words are called keywords and they will be very important throughout your entire LinkedIn profile. Here are a few examples of LinkedIn headline makeovers.

"Meh" headline: MBA Student
Made-over headline: MBA Student/Marketing Major/Expertise in
    Brand Management and Consumer Packaged Goods
"Meh" headline: Career Coach and Blogger
Made-over headline: Certified Career Coach for Job Seekers and
    Entrepreneurs/Blogger at MichaelSmithCareerAdvice.com
"Meh" headline: Project Manager
Made-over headline: Technology Project Manager/Passionate about
    Big Data/Experience in Start-ups and Fortune 500 Corporations

As a general rule, the more information and keywords you can provide, the more opportunities you are creating for a recruiter, potential client, potential investor or other VIP to see your profile in search results. Later we'll apply this same principle to other sections of your LinkedIn profile.

Step 3: Post a Professional Head Shot

One of the most common questions I'm asked about LinkedIn profiles is whether the photo matters. It does. It's human nature that people are going to check out what you look like. And in my opinion, what you want to look like is a leader. If you can afford it, have a professional photographer take your head shot, or ask a friend with good camera and lighting skills. What you should wear in the headshot is what you would wear to a job interview or an important meeting. So if you're in politics or a conservative corporate career, you'll wear a suit. If you work in a start-up or other more casual environment, wear whatever you'd wear to dress up (even if that just means a clean T-shirt).

One tactic to consider is taking your picture in context, which is a nice touch for a leader, particularly if you're an entrepreneur. For example, have your company's logo appear in the background of the photo, or, if you run a retail operation, stand in front of your storefront or pose with one of your key products. If you are a media personality (or want to be), use a screenshot of you talking on television as your photo. I know a sports marketing executive whose head shot shows him standing in a suit in the stands of a baseball stadium. It's unique, it's professional, and it's memorable.

Step 4: Craft Your Summary

Most professionals have a résumé. Leaders also need a bio, which is the description of you that would appear on your company's "Our Leadership" Web page or a conference program for an event where you are speaking. This is also what LinkedIn asks for in its Summary section. Your bio should act as an overview or greatest hits version of your career—an expansion on the keywords you used to describe yourself in your LinkedIn profile headline and the key accomplishments you display on your résumé.

Although I frequently see Summary statements written in the first person (using *I* when you talk about yourself), my preference is for using the third person voice and describing yourself using your name. This is a more formal style, it makes it easier for someone to cut and paste your bio if they want to use it for, say, introducing you at an awards ceremony, and it's better for search engine optimization (SEO) purposes to associate your name with the skills and experience you describe in your Summary.

MORE, PLEASE: LINKEDIN PROFILE SUMMARY TIPS FOR ASPIRING LEADERS

How should you approach the LinkedIn Summary statement if you are not yet in a leadership position, or if you are job-hunting? In this case, your Summary should resemble the first few paragraphs of your best-written cover letter, describing where you are in your career now and then mentioning your career goals and outlining your qualifications for the next position you want. You should also include keywords and phrases that a recruiter or hiring manager might type into a search engine to find a person like you. Remember that the best place to find relevant keywords is by researching the job listings that appeal to you and the LinkedIn profiles of people who hold the kinds of positions you want to obtain.

In terms of length, LinkedIn (or any social network, for that matter) is not the place for long-form prose. Present your Summary statement in short blocks of text with lots of white space. Bullet points are great, too, especially if you don't consider yourself to be a strong writer. If you possess lots of diverse skills or you hold several roles at the same time (for instance, you are an HR consultant at a fashion brand and you also have your own stylist business on the side), you can present your Summary in two sections with an all-capital-letters heading above each one.

Step 5: Show, Don't Tell

If I had written this book a year ago, a written LinkedIn Summary statement would have been enough to tell your story and promote your skill set. However, things move fast today and now you need something more. LinkedIn, along with many other social networks, now offers the ability for you to share your professional accomplishments through visual examples. I believe one of the core competencies for leaders in the future will be the ability to show, not tell your professional story. Future employers deciding to hire you, boards of directors deciding if you should be CEO, investors deciding whether to give you funding—all of these audiences will want to see real-life examples of your work, not just a list of career highlights. This is already happening on Pinterest, where many people—particularly those in design industries—are creating artistic, infographic-like versions of their career stories. To see examples of this, go to Pinterest.com and type "resume" or "curriculum vitae" into the search box.

On LinkedIn, showing your story means including visual examples such as videos of your professional speaking, slide decks from presentations you've delivered, or PDFs of articles you've written or in which you've appeared. If you are a graphic designer, animator, architect, interior decorator, industrial designer, photographer, or work in any visual field, this will be even more important.

Step 6: Promote Your Skills

The next important section of your LinkedIn profile is Skills and Endorsements, which is the area where you choose keywords to describe your top talents and the people in your LinkedIn network have the opportunity to give you an endorsement (essentially a "like" click) for the skills they know you possess. You can enter up to fifty words, but I would shoot for about fifteen to twenty. The top ten terms that people endorse will appear in a vertical list and the rest will be bunched below. As I've mentioned, pay closest attention to the top three to five skills that people in your network endorse. These are likely the words or phrases that people most associate with you, and that is important information. By the way, don't be shy about including leadership among your list of skills. It's not boasting if you can back it up with real leadership examples throughout the rest of your profile.

Step 7: Customize

Beyond the standard sections of a LinkedIn profile that we've already discussed, there are optional sections you can add depending on what you want to promote as part of your personal leadership brand. Here are some tips on which sections you might want to add:

Honors and Awards

Add an award if the name of the honor is recognizable (e.g., a Fulbright scholarship) or if the meaning of the award is clear from its name (e.g., Salesperson of the Year). If you've won an award that is not clear from its name (The Joe Schmoe Award), then give a one-sentence description of the qualities the award recognized in you.

Projects

This is another way to show, not tell your accomplishments. If you've worked on a particularly big or exciting project—such as planning and executing a successful fund-raiser (in your day job or in a volunteer role) or designing and launching a new product, you can share that project as a sort-of case study on your LinkedIn profile. Companies share case studies on their Web sites all the time, so why not individuals? Just be sure that you have permission from your employer or any organizations or partners with whom you worked. Speaking of collaborators, LinkedIn invites you to link each project to those people's LinkedIn profiles, which is a great way to share credit and show that you are a team player.

Publications

In addition to posting examples of your writing (if they are relevant to your career and leadership plans), this section allows you to increase your credibility by featuring any books you've written, articles you've bylined, or blog posts you've created.

Volunteer Experience and Causes

Millennials are known for being a cause-minded generation, so you should promote any volunteering you do in this optional section. Most leaders I know, especially at the top levels, are committed to philanthropy and community service, so this section will be noticed. Just be sure to write about your volunteer work in professional leadership terms, detailing the skills you exhibited and, most important, the tangible results you achieved. For example: "Recruited and managed a team of six colleagues to renovate an inner-city elementary school playground."

More Optional Sections

Additional optional sections to consider adding to your profile include certifications, patents, test scores, and languages. To keep your LinkedIn profile as focused as possible, add only the sections that will best build your brand and leave off the sections that won't contribute to the leadership reputation you want to create.

Step 8: Crowdsource

Once you're happy with the state of your profile, ask a few trusted friends or colleagues to review it and share any feedback or suggestions they have. (You can show your gratitude by offering to look at theirs in return.) While you might not incorporate every recommendation, this input could help you discover a valuable new way to explain your job or highlight a strength you had never thought to emphasize. You'll also glean insight about what to delete from your profile. Perhaps you've been promoting an unimportant credential or a too-junior-sounding skill set that you're better off omitting (for example, your résumé and LinkedIn profile no longer need to promote knowledge of common programs like Microsoft Word or Internet Explorer).

Step 9: Update Your Profile Frequently

Finally, make sure that you continually tweak and add to your profile as you take on more responsibility, manage more people, accomplish more impressive feats, and participate in higher-level activities. Anyone who visits your profile will want to see immediately that you are someone who is on the rise.

The Ultimate Twitter Guide for New Leaders

Now that we've covered LinkedIn in detail, let's move on to another essential online branding outlet: Twitter. I know that this site has a reputation for being frivolous, but Twitter is not just a place for bored people to report on the daily activities of their pets or for celebrities to promote their movies and vegan diets. (Okay, it's a little bit of those things.) According to Twitter's own executives, the site is not a social network; it's an information network. I completely agree.

Twitter is an indispensable tool for new leaders to learn vital information and to build your professional reputation as a thought leader. It's like a combination of being a fly on the wall for your industry's most important conversations and having a 24/7/365 personal news ticker that allows you to follow and comment on all the conversations and happenings in your world (which might include your day job, a side business, and your nonprofit or political passions). If you follow the right sources, your Twitter feed will essentially curate the Internet for you. It's also an amplifier to help you build an ongoing reputation for being a newsmaker and conversation contributor yourself. Here is a step-by-step plan for using Twitter to build your personal leadership brand:

Step 1: Set Up a Professional Account

- Set up a Twitter handle with your real name or a close version of it. For example, mine is @lindseypollak. If you are already tweeting in a nonprofessional way (using a handle like @MetsFanatic or @LuvBug), you'll want to rename your handle or set up a separate, professional Twitter account.

- Post a professional headshot as your profile photo. It's fine to use the same photo as your LinkedIn pic if you'd like. On Twitter you can also post a background image, which could be the logo of your organization or another image that places you in the context of your professional leadership role. If you can't think of a great image to use, then just keep the background black.
- Create a short profile description that includes (as long as your organization allows it) your title and organization, or a general description of what you do that includes the fact that you are in a leadership role. For example, "Head of social media for a boutique marketing agency." Since Twitter has a looser vibe than LinkedIn, you can include a few fun facts as well, such as your love of travel, your addiction to coffee, or the fact that you're a cat person. Just keep it professionally appropriate.

Step 2: Follow

Next you'll start creating that personal newsfeed by following the right sources.

- Follow prominent leaders in your company and industry. (Remember that on Twitter you can follow people without their needing to accept or follow you back.)
- Follow your clients and potential clients to stay up-to-date on their news and what is important to them. This will provide you with ongoing opportunities to reach out and say congratulations, good luck, good job, or anything else. And it helps you stay attuned to the mind-set of your clients, customers, and prospects.
- Follow your competitors to see what they're up to.
- Follow reporters who write about your industry to stay on top of the news you need to know, and perhaps get on their radar screens as a future source for stories and expert commentary.

- Follow the people that all of the above tweeters follow. One of the things I like to do to expand my knowledge and network is to view the list of people followed by my role models. For instance, I really admire the business author Daniel Pink, so I might view all of the people he follows to find more authors and speakers that he values enough to follow on Twitter. If you are new to an industry, this is an effective way to learn who the major players are.

Step 3: Tweet

Notice that all of the above activity involved listening first. Especially if you are new to Twitter, or new to using Twitter in a professional way, this is important. Check out what people are talking about, how they compose their tweets, what types of articles they share, and what types of content they choose to retweet. This will give you ideas for what to tweet about yourself. Remember that your goal is to be a conversationalist in the Twitter community and not a self-promoter. Here are some tips on what and when to tweet:

- If you are in the process of building an online leadership reputation, I would recommend tweeting at least once every weekday and working yourself up to about three tweets per day. The frequency of your tweets is really up to you, but consistency is most important. For instance, you don't want to tweet fifteen times in one day and then stay silent for two weeks.
- Get in the habit of tweeting out articles that you are reading about your industry. Add a few words of your own commentary to each article link—e.g., "Great analysis," "Agree with this opinion," "What do you think?"—to add a more personal touch. This is an easy way to continually build your visibility and your credibility as a knowledgeable, thoughtful person in your field.

- React to other people's tweets to show that you are listening, especially to clients, colleagues, and industry leaders you want to build relationships with. This includes retweeting them and replying to their tweets by answering a question or wishing them luck with an upcoming event. Again, remember that Twitter is about having a conversation with your community, not just posting announcements about yourself.

- Take a breath before tweeting anything potentially controversial, catty, or cranky. If those 140 characters will cause you—or your organization—more harm than good, then resist the urge to tweet. The decision will depend on your industry, but the news is filled with stories of people who should have paused before tweeting.

- Keeping in mind the above caveat, Twitter is a network where you can show some personality and humor, too. The most popular tweeters tend to mix up their posts a bit, sharing lots of valuable, relevant information, but also posting the occasional funny story, random link, or comment on a movie star's Golden Globes dress. Just be sure you're always staying true to yourself and not crossing the line between funny and offensive.

How do you determine that line? I posed this question to Jimmy Lepore Hagan, director of digital media for fashion brand Nanette Lepore. It turns out that it all comes back to listening again. Hagan says, "My advice for trying to find that line is to look at people three or four years more experienced in your same space and see what they are doing. If they post something and it makes you feel uncomfortable—like posting a picture of their abs after a workout—then don't do that! Or, if you find people who are creating a persona you admire, then follow the guidelines or etiquette that person seems to follow. Basically, judge how you react to other people on social media."

THERE'S AN APP FOR THAT: BUFFER

When I talk about tweeting on a consistent basis, you might be wondering how anyone finds the time. The good news is you don't have to: there's an app for that. I use a free app called Buffer (Bufferapp.com) to schedule and post my tweets for me. Whenever I come across an interesting article that I want to share with my network, I click on my Buffer app, which then schedules my tweets into a queue. I can schedule tweets whenever I want and Buffer will then tweet them for me at three assigned times during the day. The app also provides some useful analytics so you can see how many people are reading, retweeting, or responding to each tweet you share.

Should You Have Your Own Web Site?

I have a confession to make. Before naming our daughter, my husband and I checked to see if the domain name was available. (It's not that we wouldn't have given her the name we wanted if the domain were not available, but it was nice to know that it was!) As someone who has owned my domain name, LindseyPollak.com, for more than fifteen years, I know how important this can be for one's personal brand, especially as an entrepreneur. (And if my daughter does choose to start her own business someday, she'll thank us for our foresight, right?)

But let's get back to you. Do you own your domain name? As we've already discussed, it's a smart move for a leader whether you have your own business or not. As the CEO of your personal brand, your name is an important asset to protect. My advice is to buy your domain name (ideally with a .com domain) even if you aren't sure whether you want to build your own Web site. This is relatively inexpensive (ranging from about $7 to $40 per year) and easy to do at a registration site such as GoDaddy.com or Register.com. If your name is common and already taken, try including your middle name or middle initial, or using an easy-to-remember version of your name, such as MarySmith1.com. (I would not recommend using your birth-date or year of your birth in your domain name for privacy reasons, or your city or state in case you move.) If you do choose to set up a personal Web site at your domain, you can build a simple site using inexpensive Web site design tools such as those at Weebly.com or Wix.com.

Another option for building your online brand is to create what is called a nameplate site. The most popular is About.me, which essentially serves as a one-page Web site to share your contact information and provide links to your social networking profiles and any other sites you want to direct people to. About.me will also provide you with a short custom URL that you can include on business cards or in your e-mail signature line. And to come full circle to the advice at the beginning of this chapter, nameplate sites can help push positive content about you to the top of your Google rankings as well.

Now that we've spent an entire chapter focused on social media, let's step away from our screens and talk about some other key communication tools for new leaders. Remove your earbuds and get ready to do some focused listening.

PART II

Lead

CHAPTER 4

Listen

Choosing Your Method, Knowing Your Audience,
and Becoming a Master of Meetings

Words matter.

(And I'm not just saying that because my dad was an English teacher.)

The words we use (and don't use) can make or break our reputations, our projects, our relationships, and our organizations. Communication is critical to career success. For leaders, the stakes are even higher: one comment from a leader can cause elation, confusion, or panic among your ranks. This is especially true at the very top. As Liam E. McGee, chairman and president of The Hartford, said, "Nothing prepares you to be a CEO. The buck truly does stop with you. You have to be careful of what you say. People take what the CEO says differently."

This chapter is all about being careful with your communication: using the right words at the right time to send the right message, including when you are talking, e-mailing, texting, IMing, conference calling, Skyping, leaving voice-mail messages (sorry, but you still have to do that sometimes), and, most important to all of the above: listening.

How to Communicate Like a Leader: Five Essential Rules

Let's start with some big-picture advice and then we'll get more tactical about how to handle common communication challenges (aka opportunities) you are likely to face as a leader today.

Rule 1: It's Not About You

A fascinating study by researchers at the University of Texas at Austin found that leaders use the word *I* less than nonleaders, dispelling the commonly held belief that leaders are self-centered or egotistical. According to the researchers, "There is a misconception that people who are confident, have power, have high status tend to use *I* more than people who are low status. That is completely wrong. The high-status person is looking out at the world and the low-status person is looking at himself."

This is where I often see an opportunity for improvement among new bosses. Instead of saying, "I believe this is the right strategy because . . ." simply say, "This is the right strategy because . . ." Or, even better, "We need to implement this strategy because . . ." Remember that as the leader of a team (or a company or a nonprofit or a community), you are still a member of that team. *We* is one of the most powerful words in your leadership vocabulary.

HOW TO SAY IT: SHARING CREDIT FOR SUCCESS

Perhaps you're wondering, "I understand it's not all about me, but if I'm the leader it's still partly about me, right?"

Yes, it absolutely is. So how do you communicate your work, your team's work, and the difference between the two without sounding too selfish or too selfless? According to com-

---

munications expert Jodi Glickman, president of Great on the Job, "The goal is to make your team look great and show how proud you are to be part of such a high-performing team. Then you highlight your own accomplishments, but do it within the context of the greater good."

Here are two sample scripts.

Example 1:

> I'm thrilled to be a part of the ABC Client team. We've increased our revenue share with the client by 8 percent this year and we've established ourselves as a trusted advisor to their senior leadership. On a personal level, I'm really proud of the fact that I was able to bring in the business and build momentum for significant growth in the account.

Example 2:

> Our team did an amazing job putting on the corporate sponsor dinner last month. It was a lot of work and everyone really pulled together. From a management perspective, it was a great opportunity for me to take the lead on an important initiative and show that I have the ability to successfully execute an event of that size.

The goal, according to Glickman, is to "give yourself props and show how great you are, but balance your self-promotion with some humility and real acknowledgment that no one in business succeeds on their own. The strength of the team is always more powerful than the abilities of one single person."

Rule 2: Know Your Audience

One of the biggest lessons I've personally learned about communication is that you can't have a one-size-fits-all communication style.

You have to be adaptable based on the situation you're in and the person or people you're speaking to. We all know this intuitively—it's why we tend to talk in a slower, more high-pitched voice to small children and why we use formal language when testifying in court.

But we sometimes forget this in the busy day-to-day work of being a leader. Whether you are leading three people or three thousand, you have to remember that they are each individuals with their own individual communication preferences. When deciding how to communicate a message, you should think more about how the other person wants to receive the message than about how you personally want to deliver the message. I don't mean to suggest that you should send three thousand individually customized e-mails to announce a new initiative, but it does mean that when making a big announcement you need to think about the various members of your audience. What different types of people will be listening? What will their concerns be? What other questions will they have? The more you can address these questions in your original communication, the more successful it will be.

You also need to know how the members of your audience prefer to consume information. For instance, just because you like to make an argument using a lot of numbers and statistics doesn't mean everyone else does. People learn in different ways and they hear in different ways, too. In a one-on-one or small group communication, you should make your choices based on the individuals you will be speaking to (for example, if you are presenting a business plan to your finance team, you'll want to tell your story in numbers and spreadsheets). If you are presenting to a large group, you'll want to offer your information in a variety of ways, including your voice, visual images such as a PowerPoint presentation, and a written handout.

This is a generational issue as well. People tend to be comfortable with the communication style they grew up with and can be intimidated or uncomfortable with the way other generations express themselves. As Sofia, a graduate student, pointed out to me, "Millennials are used to asking the question 'Why?' a lot. We want to understand everything. That clashes with older generations who see it as insubordination and a challenge to their leadership." So when I'm presenting workshops to millennials, I make sure that I take time to explain *why* each topic I'm discussing—personal branding, networking, managing generational differences, etc.—is important to their individual success.

Finally, knowing your audience is an emotional issue. It's important to think about the emotional state of the people you are communicating with. Will they be happy to hear your news? Upset? Indifferent? Do you need to consider potentially negative reactions to the information you are about to share? And if you misread a situation and incorrectly predict the emotional response of your audience, can you adjust in the moment? One of the questions I like to casually ask people arriving for one of my workshops or speeches is, "What brought you here today?" Sometimes people will say, "I'm really interested in your advice on managing different generations" or "I saw a poster for this and I know I have a lot to learn about this topic." Then I'll know I can dive right into my content. Other times, the majority of people will avoid eye contact and say something like, "My boss made me come." Then I know I'll have to do some extra work to win over the room.

Rule 3: Overcommunication Trumps Undercommunication

My brother and sister had a high school marching band instructor who was known for his strictness and meticulousness (and also for his amazing success, winning championships and performing in national college bowl parades year after year—not a coincidence). When it came to arriving for their many practices, the band instructor would warn his students: to be early is to be on time, to be on time is to be late, and to be late is to be unforgivable! (Pretty harsh, but it worked—no one would dare arrive one minute tardy.) I mention this because it's a good parallel for your communication strategy: as a leader, to communicate an amount you think is enough is too little. To communicate what you think is too much is probably the right amount. And not to communicate is unforgivable.

According to a recent survey of HR managers by Accountemps, "lack of open, honest communication" topped the list of issues that can erode staff morale—above micromanagement, excessive work-loads, and even fear of job loss. The survey also found that "better communication" topped the list of ways a leader could boost morale, beating out recognition programs, team building exercises, and even more time off. Let's hear that again: people crave good communica-tion from their leaders more than they crave additional vacation time! Give your people what they want and communicate as frequently, honestly, and thoroughly as you possibly can. There is no greater ac-tion you can take to improve the motivation of the people you lead.

If you're not sure what people want to know with all of this com-munication, go ahead and ask them. Host focus groups or create sim-ple employee surveys to learn what information people desire, how they want to receive it, and in what ways your current communica-tion might be lacking. Use a simple survey tool such as Google Forms or SurveyMonkey.com or try one of the more expensive and robust services that can benchmark your team's responses against similar organizations' results.

Rule 4: Actually Listen

My grandfather used to say, "There's a reason you have two ears and one mouth. Listen twice as much as you talk."

Wise advice, for sure. In fact, I had Grandpa's words in mind when I titled this chapter "Listen." Over and over again in my interviews with leaders of all ages, the importance of listening arose. Here's how Julie Daly Meehan of Hartford Young Professionals and Entrepreneurs put it, "Communication is half listening. If you are just thinking about the next thing coming out of your mouth, you are missing a lot of key information—not only what other people are saying, but how they are feeling about it. When I'm more actively listening, I'm able to recognize the holes in the information I'm receiving and ask questions, rather than getting back to my desk and realizing I'm missing something."

How can you become a better listener? Here are some valuable tips from Angela Lee, an assistant adjunct professor at Columbia Business School, who teaches a course called "The Leader's Voice":

Start with Your Audience

What is their perspective? Taking five minutes to ask yourself about your audience's objectives, goals, and biases will prime you to listen.

Be Open

Release your agenda. In other words, don't listen for what you expect to hear; listen to what the other person is actually saying.

Strive to Understand

If they disagree with you, do you know why? When someone disagrees, this is the time to listen even more carefully. Maybe they have different information or a helpful perspective. Don't forget to pay attention to body language, volume and tone of voice, and other visual and auditory cues to understand what they might not be saying out loud.

Respond

Paraphrase and use the other person's vocabulary. When you respond, use his or her language (e.g., *member* vs. *customer*) to show you were listening, and summarize the person's points to make sure you understood.

Pause

Don't rush to fill the silence. The final element of good listening is to pause and think before you respond. This moment to think may save you from blurting out something you regret later, and it shows your conversation partner that you are letting his or her words sink in.

Rule 5: Your Method Matters

There is an episode of *Sex and the City* where a guy breaks up with the main character, Carrie Bradshaw, by writing her a message on a Post-it note.

A Post-it note! Can you imagine a worse way to get dumped?

Communication method matters. This truth is complicated by the fact that today we have more communication methods than ever, and the nuances among them are complex and frequently changing. Here is an example of the kinds of intricate questions I'm asked by young professionals when I give speeches about communication: "Is it okay to provide feedback on a private Microsoft Word document using the track changes tool, but too passive-aggressive to post feedback as a comment in a shared Google Doc?"

Now is a good point to remind you of Keith Ferrazzi's adage, "Little choices make big impressions." When it comes to communication, the nuances mean everything. (By the way, my answer to the track changes question was that it depends on the type and tone of your feedback. If you are making positive suggestions, then it's okay to post to the shared doc. If you are providing criticism that might embarrass the person, then stick to a private document or send an e-mail message with your comments. If the writer is your boss or you are at all in doubt about how the person will receive your feedback, then err on the side of caution and stick to the most private method.)

Katharine Golub is a recent graduate of Bucknell University who served as president of both her junior and senior classes. One of her top pieces of advice to her fellow young leaders is to choose your communication methods carefully, especially if, as in her experience, you are leading a group of peers: "In my senior class congress, I had three girls who were in my sorority. I knew if I played favorites with my friends, the other people would become unmotivated. You have to be fair to everyone and treat everyone equally. For example, don't e-mail information to some people but text it to your friends. Group text it to everyone."

TREND WATCH: TECH TALK

For most young leaders, communicating through technology will come so naturally that you might not think to use the phone or walk over and talk to someone. (And in the not-too-distant future, you may find that members of the next generation are using technologies with which you're not totally comfortable.) If you're not sure how to communicate with members of different generations, older or younger, the best way to learn is through observation. Start to pay attention to the methods by which other people communicate with you.

For instance, if a member of your staff always calls you instead of e-mailing or uses very formal language, then those are signs that she prefers that style of communication from you as well. I know it may seem counterintuitive (or even annoying) that you have to adapt your communication style when you are the boss, but it's about getting your message through. You simply won't be able to achieve your goals if you are not communicating in a way your team members will respond to.

To Text or Not To Text: How to Choose the Right Communication Method

How do you determine which communication tool is appropriate for which situation? Remember that it's not always the tool that feels the most comfortable to you; it's the tool that will best communicate the information to your listener and will achieve the outcome you desire. Every communication is unique and nuances mean everything. As mentioned in the previous section, different people have different preferences, but sometimes the choice of method will be up to you first. Here is a guide to help your decision making:

In Person

If the information is extremely positive, negative, sensitive, serious, or confidential, or if you don't want a word-for-word record of your comments to exist, then your best option is an in-person communication. Of course nothing today is truly private—anyone can tweet any piece of information in a heartbeat—but it is still safest to communicate eyeball-to-eyeball about sensitive issues. In-person communications also give you a better chance to defuse heated situations. For example, if you are reprimanding someone who has made a damaging error (more on how to do this below), the person may become angry and start threatening to sabotage the project or accuse you of being unfair. If you are looking this person in the eye and can remain calm and collected, you'll be more able to handle such a reaction than if you are talking on the phone and can't read the person's body language and energy.

You'll also score some points for choosing the most difficult communication method. It's not easy to confront someone face-to-face, with no time to plan your responses or reactions. I believe you garner respect—particularly as a young professional raised on technology and particularly if you are confronting an older colleague—

by stepping away from the computer screen and facing a situation (literally) head-on.

On the positive side, it's much more fun to share good news in person!

E-mail

E-mail has become our default communication for almost everything these days, but it's not always the most effective tool. For instance, it's not a good option for highly time sensitive issues because you can't guarantee when your message will be read or responded to. E-mail tends to be best for nonurgent communications that are short ("Would you like to meet for coffee next Wednesday morning?") or longer ("Here are the follow-up actions determined on today's team conference call . . .").

One of the huge benefits of e-mail is that you can really think about what you want to say and craft the right language. For moderately sensitive or complicated communications, it's often the right tool, especially if you want a written record of what's been discussed. Likewise, in your role as the boss, you'll want to be sensitive to the fact that the people you manage may want some time to digest and respond to the messages you send.

E-mail has also become the best tool for reaching out to someone you've never met. For instance, it's my method of choice for contacting a potential interview source for an article or pitching my keynote speeches to a new client. In these cases, a phone call would be too intrusive and would put the other person on the spot.

Phone

A major advantage of e-mail is that it can be carefully crafted and provides a written record of your words. This is also a major weakness: e-mail can be carefully crafted and provides a written record of your words. There are many times when you can't speak in person and don't want an electronic trail of exactly what you've said, such as during a negotiation, when written comments could even have legal ramifications. It's safer to pick up the phone. Plus, there are times when you won't want the other person to have the time to craft an e-mail response. For example, if your printer is late with an important order, calling that person on the phone is a much more effective way to find out when your order will be ready and argue for a faster delivery if necessary.

The phone is also somewhat of a novelty now. I admit that I often become so mired in my e-mail inbox that I completely forget the phone is a communication option. Phone calling is even less common among millennial professionals, so use this to your advantage. If you are constantly e-mailing back and forth with an important client, higher-up, or other VIP, you can stand out from the crowd by reaching out by phone. Not to mention the fact that a quick call is often a far more efficient way to solve a problem or make a decision. I know a lot of people don't like to make phone calls anymore, but never forget it's an important and effective tool in your leadership arsenal.

Voice Mail

I know, I know. Millennials absolutely despise voice mail. It's time-consuming, it's inefficient, and there are so many better ways to leave someone a message. (I once worked with a vendor who, if he couldn't reach me, would leave me a voice-mail message and then also send an e-mail saying the exact same thing. It drove me absolutely nuts.) But here's what I want you to know about voice mail: like the phone, it is a tool that has a purpose. The purpose of voice mail is that it is valuable in situations where the tone of your voice is essential to your message, and you are not able to reach a person directly. For instance, if you need to apologize to a member of your team—say, for making an overly critical remark on a conference call—and the person is not answering his phone, a genuine apology by voice mail in which the recipient can hear the honesty in your voice is better than a well-written e-mail.

Instant Message

IM is the best tool for quick, specific, and nonsensitive communication, particularly yes/no answers: "Free for lunch in 10 mins?" "Are you coming to the budget meeting?" "Can I offer ABC Corp a 5 percent discount?" In some offices, particularly when lots of people work wearing headphones or headsets, the majority of communication happens by IM. If this is true in your world, just be careful of the spontaneity of IM: don't dash off a message too quickly that you might later regret. And don't default to IM for performance issues— such as reprimanding someone for a missed deadline—that deserve more gravitas than a quick informal message can provide.

Text

It feels funny to give advice on texting, but it's probably the realm in which I see the most professional mistakes. Text is, of course, one of the fastest ways to provide information, but—and I hope this is not news—it's not always professionally appropriate. For instance, if you're running late for a meeting with an important client, it's more polite to call and apologize than to text (unless it's a person you've texted with in the past). When reaching out to superiors, you'll also want to err on the side of formality. Overall, I would never text any professional contact unless that person has texted me first. Texting is usually okay with a peer, but, as with IM, remember not to address sensitive or serious issues through such an informal medium. Be aware, too, that your professional colleagues may not have your cell phone number programmed into their phones, so identify yourself by name the first time you send them a text.

MORE, PLEASE:
WHEN THE AUDIENCE IS *YOUR* BOSS

The exception to any of the above guidelines is if the person you report to (your manager, board chair, investor, etc.) has expressed other communication preferences. Your relationship with your direct supervisor is one of the most important to your leadership success, so your communication with this person is crucial. Handling this relationship is known as "managing up."

In his excellent book for first-time managers, *The First 90 Days*, Harvard Business School professor Michael Watkins recommends having a "style conversation" with any new boss. This conversation should clarify such issues as, What form of communication does he or she prefer? Face-to-face? In writing? By voice mail or e-mail? How often? What kinds of decisions does he or she want to be consulted on and when can you make the call on your own?

In addition to the above questions, you might also want to ask anyone you report to:

- When, if ever, should I text you (e.g., when running late for an off-site meeting)? This is a particularly important question for members of older generations who may not feel that texting is professionally appropriate.

- Do you tend to prefer long e-mails or short e-mails? For instance, if I have three pieces of information to share, should I send one e-mail with three bullet points or three separate e-mails?

- Is it okay to pop into your office frequently or do you prefer that I schedule specific time with you?

- Do you have any communication pet peeves I should be sure to avoid (emoticons, writing in all capital letters, too much

IMing)? While moderating a panel discussion once, I asked a group of managing directors at an investment bank to share their e-mail pet peeves with the audience of entry-level bankers. One panelist piped in immediately with, "Exclamation points. Young people in particular use them way too much." He went on to give one of my favorite communication tips ever: "If you are going to use an exclamation point with a managing director of a bank, it had better be *really* good news."

P.S.: Tell People the Best Way to Communicate with You, Too

One of the perks of being a leader is that your direct reports should be having the "style conversation" with you. If the members of your team have not asked how you prefer to communicate, it's okay to initiate this conversation yourself. Simply say, "Let's have a chat about communication style to make sure we're on the same page" and then outline your most important dos and don'ts.

HOW TO SAY IT: COMMUNICATING YOUR COMMUNICATION STYLE

You can share your communication preferences with contacts outside your organization as well. For instance, if you are introverted and feel more comfortable interacting with new contacts by phone before you meet in person, you have every right to respond to a meeting invitation by saying, "Thanks so much for the invitation to meet. My schedule is quite busy at the moment— can we set up a thirty-minute phone chat first? Let me know what days and times are most convenient for you."

> Julie Daly Meehan provides polite, respectful information about her communication preferences in her outgoing voice mail greeting. After saying her name and inviting people to leave a message if they'd like, she says: "Please note that the fastest and most reliable way to reach me is by e-mail." Then she says—and, most important, spells—her e-mail address.
>
> Is it rude to tell people what to do? Not if you do it respectfully and with genuine care for their needs. "I know I am not in my office that often," says Meehan, "so if a matter is urgent, I don't want the person to be upset that they can't reach me." (Note that many voice-mail providers, including Google Voice, provide the option of translating your voice-mail messages into e-mails, so you can consider opting for that service as well.)

Fourteen Secrets of Great Communicators

Keeping those five big-picture communication rules in mind, here are fourteen in-depth tips and tricks of leaders with stellar communication skills. When absorbing this advice, remember that the goal is to be your authentic self, but to project the authority, confidence, and clarity that people want in their leaders.

1. They Get the Basics Right

As I've already mentioned, my name is difficult to spell. Is it Lindsay Pollack? Lyndsey Pollock? Lindsay Pollak? Lindsey Pollak? Really, the only way to get it right is to look it up or pay close attention to a message from me. So when someone spells my name right, I know they've taken the time to check. And I like that person a little bit more. I can't help it—my name matters to me! As our friend Dale Carnegie wrote in *How to Win Friends and Influence People*, "Remember that a person's name is, to that person, the sweetest and most important sound in any language." Never guess how to spell a person's name, even if it seems obvious (as any Mathew, Stefanie, or Jenifer will tell you). The more senior you are, the more impressive it is that you take time to notice the details.

Be careful with gender, too. There are both women and men named Kelly, Alex, Chris, Ryan, Jamie, Blake, and Taylor, among hundreds of other gender-neutral names. Always check a person's gender before writing "Mr." or "Ms." or using a masculine or feminine pronoun when talking or writing about that person. Thankfully, a quick search of LinkedIn can usually offer a photograph that answers the question.

In person or on the phone, you also need to pay attention to pronunciation. The millennial generation is the most multicultural in American history, so this is not a minor issue. It's totally acceptable—and encouraged—to ask someone how to pronounce his or her name. I appreciate when people ask how to pronounce my last name, rather than guessing at a pronunciation, usually the incorrect "POE-lack." (The correct way to say it is "PAH-leck.")

Spelling and pronunciation are also important when it comes to discussing current events or news in your company or industry. You'll lose a lot of credibility if you mispronounce the name of a competitor company's CEO or a major donor to the nonprofit on whose board you sit. In fact, a recruiter from a German bank with a difficult-to-spell name told me that she is able to toss dozens of résumés she receives because the applicants have misspelled the company's name in their cover letters.

THERE'S AN APP FOR THAT:
PRONOUNCENAMES.COM

Too nervous to ask or just want to learn more about names? Check out the Web site PronounceNames.com, which dubs itself the "dictionary of name pronunciation." For prominent names associated with current events, check out Pro•nounce at names.voa.gov, a government-sponsored service that will teach you how to pronounce a variety of names and places from all around the world.

2. They Eliminate Filler Words

Nobody will even notice your pronunciations if your sentences are filled with *ums* and other filler words. Even though these are common speech tics or signs of nervousness, people tend to interpret your use of words or phrases such as *um*, *like*, and *you know* as a sign that you're unsure of what you're saying. *Like*, in particular, makes you sound very, very young. To eliminate your filler words, here are two suggestions. First, recruit your friends and family to help. Ask them to (politely) point out instances when you use those words in everyday conversations. Awareness of the habit is the first step to breaking it. Second—and this sounds simple, but it works—is to take one breath before you answer a question or respond to a statement. In that breath, gather your thoughts so you won't find yourself thinking while speaking. Sometimes we use filler words simply because we're talking too fast.

Filler words also include any word that lessens your authority or impact. A phrase I hear often that waters down people's confidence in you is *kind of* (or, more likely, *kinda*). Adding this phrase before a statement about something does not make you sound humble; it makes you sound hesitant. This filler word is an even bigger faux pas than others because it calls your credibility into question. Do you *kinda* know something or do you really know it? Be sure to clarify that for yourself so you can speak firmly. (Other, similar filler words include *just*, *actually*, and *almost*.)

3. They Avoid Upspeak

We've talked a lot about words; don't forget to think about your tone as well. The biggest error I notice with young leaders' tone of voice is what many call upspeak—ending statements on an upward inflection so they sound like questions.

Read this sentence aloud: "I need the report by Friday."

Now read this sentence aloud: "I need the report by Friday?"

That second example is upspeak, when declarative statements come across as questions. If you notice yourself committing the up-speak slipup, envision in your mind the sentence you want to say with a period at the end and consciously lower your tone at the end of your sentences. It may feel (and sound) weird at first, but it's far better than committing upspeak. And if you're actually not sure you want to make a statement, it's best to reframe your thought into a true question instead.

4. They Limit Clichés

Sometimes, in an effort to sound important, new leaders use words or phrases that they *think* a leader should say. This habit can be even worse than using filler words or upspeak because it comes across as inauthentic. Here are some of the most common—and irritating—examples of business clichés:

"Let's take this offline."
"Lots of moving parts."
"Low-hanging fruit."
"Run it up the flagpole."
"Push the envelope."
"Drink the Kool-Aid."

And my all-time personal pet peeve is: "Can I pick your brain?" This one tops my list of worst clichés because (a) it sounds gross; and

(b) it implies that I will receive absolutely nothing from our interaction and wind up with a picked-over brain. Ew.

The thing about clichés is that people become immune to them and stop listening to what you're actually saying. You might as well be the teacher in *Peanuts* saying "wanh-wanh-wanh." When you use more original language (or just say precisely what you mean), people are far more likely to pay attention.

5. They Are Concise

In today's faster-and-faster-moving world, attention spans are becoming shorter and shorter. (Think about it: Are you doing something else while reading this book? Watching TV? Listening to music? Scanning tweets?) When it comes to communicating as a leader, you've got to be concise to be effective. According to Soojin Kwon, director of admissions at the Stephen M. Ross School of Business at the University of Michigan, one of the attributes she looks for in aspiring MBA students is "the ability to boil things down into easily digestible, compellingly presented ideas . . . More communication happens now in sound bites, 140 characters, and well-designed graphics. Today's leaders need to understand that and have the ability to communicate in that way."

Conciseness is particularly important in written communications. Whenever I'm composing an e-mail, I always go back, reread what I've written, and remove as much filler as possible. No one likes a rambling e-mail and, in my experience, people are much quicker to respond to shorter messages. E-mail was never meant to be a long-format communication method anyway. Plus, conciseness (as long as it's grammatically correct and professionally appropriate) is a sign that you have been thoughtful and precise about what you want to say. As Mark Twain supposedly quipped, "I would have written a shorter letter, but I did not have the time."

How do you know you're going on too long? If you're communicating in person, you can tell by the fact that your conversation partner has stopped making eye contact or is not making any active listening or agreeing motions like a nod or "mmm-hmm." If you're communicating by e-mail, a sure sign is when people respond to your very long e-mails with very short responses. Consider such responses a not-so-subtle hint to start editing yourself.

6. They Show, Not Tell

Once you've gotten your tone and length right, one of the best ways to engage an audience is to provide real-world examples to make a larger point. This establishes the depth and breadth of your knowledge and makes your information truly come alive. For instance, if you are trying to raise money for a nonprofit that fights childhood hunger, anyone can rattle off a bunch of statistics about how many kids go to bed hungry. Great communicators say, "The number of hungry children in our community could fill the Rose Bowl. Twice."

7. They Make Eye Contact

This is especially important when you first greet someone, but it's also crucial to hold eye contact throughout a conversation and also with various audience members in a big crowd. It shows people that you are confident in the words you're speaking. Studies show that anywhere between three and five seconds of eye contact at a time is the right amount to make without initiating an awkward stare-down, and you should aim for making eye contact about 50 percent of the time during a conversation. It's most important when the other person is speaking, to show that you are engaged. If you're sitting at a large table, perhaps in a boardroom, consciously point your toes toward the person you're addressing or listening to, which will square your shoulders to face that person. I've started to do that and it really works to build more connection and authoritative presence.

8. They Stand (and Sit) Tall

On the topic of boardroom tables, be mindful of the fact that strong leaders don't slouch. This is especially important if, like me, you're on the shorter side. If you're standing up, especially when you're giving a presentation, consciously think about keeping your shoulders back and your head up. And I know it can feel really weird, but I remember from my acting days in high school that the most natural place for your hands when you're giving a presentation is simply at your sides. Crossing your arms makes you look closed-off and withholding, and placing your hands behind your back or in your pockets gives the impression that you're hiding something. Gesturing is great to make a point, but moving your hands around too much can be distracting and take away from your authority.

When you're sitting, keep your posture strong and lean forward instead of backward to show you're engaged with the conversation at hand. And try to avoid touching your face, playing with your hair, or tapping your hands or pen on the table. Of course you want to stay a little loose to avoid looking robotic, but avoid a too-relaxed posture that gives off a defensive or lazy attitude. Overall, be sure not to "shrink your space," as coach and blogger Tara Sophia Mohr calls it. "Take up room, uncross your hands or arms, sit tall, and make eye contact," she advises. "Basically, *be noticed*." You have every right to be in the position you are in, so make sure your body language shows it.

You should follow all of these tips while talking on the phone as well: sitting with strong posture will make you sound more authoritative. Sometimes I'll even stand up when I'm on an important phone call or when I'm leading a teleconference or webinar to project more authority.

9. They Don't Have All the Answers

One millennial leader recently asked me, "I feel like I have to know it all or, at least, pretend that I do. How do I approach a situation where people are looking to me for the answers when I might not have them all?"

First and foremost, I told him, remember that nobody has *all* the answers. In fact, I believe that one of the most important characteristics of a leader is acknowledging what you don't know. But strong leaders do have to know where, how, or from whom to get the information they need. Never say, "I have no clue," "I have no idea what you're talking about," or "I'm not good with that sort of thing." Instead, you can try one of the following alternatives.

Refer

One of the perks of leadership is having a team of people who have different types of knowledge, so don't hesitate to refer questions to members of your staff. "I am not an expert on that topic, but I'd like to refer you to my colleague Maria, who can get you the right answer. Here is her contact information; please tell her that I sent you."

Defer

It's completely acceptable to say, "I'll get back to you." Just be sure to give the person an exact time and method by which you will provide the information. For example, "I need to look into that. I'll e-mail you by the end of the day with an answer." Then keep your promise.

Infer

In some cases, you might not have an answer because you don't have enough information. It can be helpful to gather more data by saying, "Can you tell me a bit more about what you need?" Then you'll either determine an answer or can use one of the above approaches instead.

10. They Are Discreet

For better or worse, one of the most universal languages around the world is gossip. Everyone knows we shouldn't do it, but we all fall prey to the urge sometimes. And the urge might only intensify the higher up you rise in your organization or community because you'll be privy to bigger and juicier secrets. I'm constantly amazed at the confidential information people divulge to me in business situations—who is getting fired, who is secretly dating, who makes what salary—even if they don't know me that well. I actually love it when this happens, not because I care so much about the gossip, but because it's an easy way to determine which people I can truly trust and which people I can't. In a world where every whisper can be tweeted to millions of people, discretion has become more rare and more valuable than ever.

Discretion also includes being cautious when and where you talk about sensitive business issues—this includes restrooms, elevators, airplanes, coffee shops, and other places where people might overhear you. During the writing of this book there was a news story about a guy who overheard a former National Security Administration official conducting a media interview on his cell phone while riding on an Amtrak train. The eavesdropper happened to be a blogger and he tweeted every detail of the overheard conversation along with a photo of the NSA official, who had repeatedly told the interviewer that his comments needed to be anonymous. Yikes! The bottom line: always assume that someone is listening, and that that person might share your comments with the world. (Or, as I do, just sit in the Amtrak quiet car where cell phone use is not allowed. It's better to be safe than sorry!)

11. They Always Have an Ear to the Ground

One of my personal observations about the best leaders is that they are always well read and curious—not just about their own subject areas, but about a wide variety of other topics as well. We live in an information economy, so information is the currency of great leaders today. Leaders have to know the buzz inside and outside their organizations to stay current and, ideally, ahead of the competition.

Having your ear to the ground also means that your leadership role is always in the back of your mind, even when you are off duty and doing something completely unrelated to your work. Jeremy Lade, U.S. Paralympian in wheelchair basketball and coordinator of wheelchair athletics and recreation at the University of Wisconsin at Whitewater, told me that he is constantly seeking new ways to build the team atmosphere for the basketball players he coaches. "I get ideas from everyday life," he says, "from surfing the Internet, talking to people, watching commercials. I look outside of wheelchair basketball. I'll watch football or soccer practice or talk to the leader of a fellowship of Christian athletes. You can always find some kind of benefit from every experience or conversation. My athletes give me a hard time because I always come to practice with some story about seeing a play on *Monday Night Football* that gave me an idea for us. My wheels are always turning about being a leader."

12. They Face Conflict

Becoming comfortable with conflict has been one of the more challenging communications skills for me personally to master. The first time a boss yelled at me in a professional situation I cowered wimpily and apologized over and over again. I had missed a deadline, but from my over-the-top reaction to my boss's reprimand you would have thought she'd caught me committing a felony. Needless to say, cowering and profusely apologizing were not an effective communication strategy. I'm sure that boss had little respect for me, and my reaction certainly didn't stop her from yelling at me again in the future. (This boss was pretty mean, but that's a personality type we all face at some point in our careers, so it's one we all have to learn how to manage.)

At the time, I was so afraid of confrontation that I would have done anything to make it go away. Now, many years later, I know that facing conflict is a skill that can, and needs to be, built. My confrontation education began with another boss—we'll call her Pam. Pam was the executive director of a small nonprofit and spent her days dialing for dollars to secure grant and sponsorship money for our operations. She was a fantastic salesperson and afraid of nothing. Whenever a conflict arose with someone—a dissatisfied donor, a sponsor threatening to cut support for our programs, a late child support payment from her ex-husband (hey—it was a small office so I heard everything)—she would say, "Okay, let's deal with this," and pick up the phone to address the issue.

Pam wasted no time letting a conflict fester or trying to solve a problem with a back-and-forth e-mail chain in which words or tone can be misinterpreted. She'd simply call up the person and say something like, "I hear we have a problem. Let's figure it out." Then she would ask question after question to really understand the issue (and show the other person she really cared about his or her point of view on this issue) and find a way to resolve it. No anger. No cowering. No drama. Just lots of listening and an attitude that everything would all work out in the end. With Pam's blessing I listened in on as many of these calls as I could and learned to be less afraid of the inevitable clashes that occur when you're a leader. I wouldn't say that I relish conflict now, but I no longer shy away from it.

13. They Have a Sense of Humor

On the flip side of conflict is humor, which, believe it or not, can be just as much of a struggle for some leaders. It's hard to be funny if you're a naturally shy or serious person, but it's important. In fact, when I recently polled my online community about what they seek in a leader, "sense of humor" was among the top responses. You don't have to be a comedian to be a good leader (although Twitter CEO

Dick Costolo did stand-up before launching his corporate career), but a little levity goes a long way toward building morale. Let kids throw pies in your face at the company picnic. Hire a speechwriter to draft a few light jokes for your next pitch. As career and social media expert Kevin Grubb commented to me, "I like a leader to remind me that we don't always have to be serious to be effective."

14. They Show Their Passion

Finally, whether you are a nonprofit board member, an entrepreneur, a school principal, or a corporate vice president, one of your jobs as a leader will be to persuade people to support your vision and strategies. You will have a much easier time doing this if people can see and feel that you truly, deeply believe in what you are advocating. In other words, they want to see your passion.

There has been some controversy in recent years as to whether "follow your passion" is valuable career advice, or if it sets up false expectations that everyone can achieve his or her dreams. My personal feeling is that following your passion is great advice as long as you combine it with hard work and real skills. And I feel the same way about passion in leaders: if you are working hard and doing your job as a leader, being passionate can put you over the top. People crave leaders who are deeply committed and have a true calling for the work that they do. The best leaders let this authentic passion shine through.

Baseball's Terry Francona is a great example of this. He led the Boston Red Sox to their historic 2004 World Series championship and was named Manager of the Year in 2013 while leading the Cleveland Indians. He has said, "I love the players, I love being around them, and I don't really want to hide the fact that I do . . . You know, everybody's different, but you've got to be true to your own personality. I'm not a big yeller or screamer. I think you can talk to players. I think if you have an atmosphere where guys want to do the right thing, more often than not, you're going to be okay."

Like Francona, don't be shy about telling people, especially the ones you lead, that you love the work that you do. Perhaps you ran for office because you were tired of the corruption of many of the politicians who served before you. Maybe you took over an automotive parts business from your dad and want to bring his American dream to fruition while also jazzing up the place. Maybe you launched a start-up making plus-size clothes because you could never find anything that fit right. Integrate that passion into your daily communications and you'll inspire as well as lead—and probably have more fun, too.

VOICES OF MILLENNIAL LEADERS

I have several indicators I use to determine if someone is a good leader. One of them includes how well they are able to get my attention. If they are talking and I find myself no longer taking notes and putting my pencil down to just listen, I would say that person is captivating (a good trait). If they are able to grab my attention like that I would say they are also passionate about what they talk about (another good trait).

—Sara Hutchison, recycling and surplus coordinator,
Western Kentucky University

Become a Master of Meetings

Now let's shift gears and dig into the nitty-gritty of leading in various communication situations, including meetings, conference calls, and formal presentations. The overall rules of communication remain in place, but some tweaks are necessary. My objective with the following tips is that you become so good at these various situations that people actually *enjoy* attending the meetings that you chair, they *look forward to* your conference calls, and they *never reach for their phones* while you are giving a speech. If you think I'm being overly optimistic, read on.

Meetings in particular are often perceived as the biggest time wasters in life and are despised by some otherwise very friendly people. I want your meetings to rise above! When you are the leader of a meeting, consider it your chance to shine, inspire, encourage, and achieve. It's your show. Become the meeting master. Take control and make every meeting the very best it can be every time. I know this sounds Pollyannaish, but I promise the results will be phenomenal: when people actually want to attend your meetings, you are far more likely to achieve top results during and after those get-togethers.

Cancel It

Yep, you read that correctly. The first way to be a meeting master is to cancel as many meetings as possible. There is no rule saying you have to hold a certain meeting just because the previous boss always held that meeting. There is no law dictating that teams have to meet once a week whether there are issues to discuss or not. One of the first changes I made when I took over as board chair of She's the First was to cancel all regular committee meetings until we determined which ones really needed to be held. Cancel any meeting that is not absolutely essential and you'll find that the meetings you do deem necessary are far more productive.

Keep It Small

Following the same principle, when you hold a meeting, invite the minimum number of participants possible. Meetings (and conference calls and e-mails, too) are most effective when they are limited to only the people who need to attend. Take time to really think about who needs to be at the meeting rather than tossing the invite out to anyone and everyone. The fewer people in attendance, the more you'll accomplish. This may ruffle some feathers—some people feel offended when they are not included in meetings—so it's a good idea early in your leadership to explain to your team that you like to keep meetings lean so no one's time is wasted. If someone really makes a stink out of not being invited, you can offer to include that person on any follow-up e-mails. (Or just wait for him or her to get over it.)

Confirm

Send a shared calendar invitation or an e-mail confirmation within twelve to twenty-four hours of the meeting. This will avoid those "Hey—do you guys know if Laura is coming?" moments.

Set a Clear and Realistic Agenda . . . and Stick to It

Even if the meeting is short and even if the agenda is informal and scribbled on an index card for your eyes only, make sure you have a written plan for the topics you want to discuss and the outcomes you need to achieve. For larger, more formal meetings, you'll want to send an agenda out to all meeting attendees twenty-four hours in advance so that everyone can arrive prepared (or at least not blame you if they are unprepared). Then it's your job to stick to the agenda and gently guide the conversation back on-track if necessary. Remember, it's your meeting: own it and don't let anyone else hijack your program.

Start on Time

As a general rule, I always start meetings and conference calls on time. If I absolutely can't do that (for example, a crucial person is missing), I'll thank the people who arrived on time and let them know exactly how late we will be starting so they'll know how much time they have to check e-mail, use the restroom, or twiddle their thumbs. The very few times someone has questioned my exactitude, I've always made it about my meeting attendees rather than my own type-A-ness: "I respect everyone's time too much to start the meeting late. And of course, if we start on time, we can end early." People respect leaders who are in control, and that includes being in control of what time your meetings start. I also feel strongly that if people are late, it's their responsibility to catch up. You'll just bore everyone else in the room if you take time to provide a court-reporter-like review of what's already been said for the benefit of the latecomer. (Obviously, you should use your judgment for that last tip. If the latecomer is your company's CEO or your largest client, you will make an exception.)

Keep Up the Energy

It's also in your power to set the tone of the meeting, and that includes keeping the pace moving forward. Be conscious of when the energy in the room is fading and do something to fix it. If, for instance, one person is droning on and on, you can jump in and say, "Thanks so much, Matt—I'd love to get a few other perspectives on this point, too. Olivia?" If you sense that the meeting is just running too long, the room is too hot, or you've crammed too much into your agenda, then suggest a break or suggest that you end the meeting and connect one-on-one with people about the remaining topics. Better to end a meeting without accomplishing all of your goals than to push forward and achieve lackluster results that will just require another meeting anyway.

Stop the Smartphones

If people become totally distracted by with their devices, it's up to you to make a rule about checking them. You might say, "Let's all put away our phones for fifteen minutes so we can focus on this issue." Or, if things get really crazy, you can set a rule that smartphones are not allowed during meetings at all. I've heard of people at lunch meetings making a rule that everyone has to put their devices on a stack in the middle of the table during the meal. The first person to cave and check his or her phone has to pick up the bill. As a version of this, you could try requiring that all devices be stacked in the center of the meeting table. It would probably be a great way to ensure a short meeting! (P.S.: You as the boss really set the tone on this issue. If you are constantly scrolling through your messages, others will do the same.)

Assign a Note-Taker if Necessary

For important meetings in particular, don't rely on your meeting attendees to take accurate notes. Assign an intern, an admin assistant, the most junior person in the room, or ask people to take turns taking notes. For efficiency, make sure the person takes notes on a laptop or tablet so he or she doesn't have to convert written notes to a digital format later.

Provide (Truly) Clear Next Steps

Pretty much every meeting ends with someone saying, "Okay, let's talk about next steps." But how often do those next steps actually occur? Ask the note-taker to be in charge of sending any follow-up assignments to the people in the room and request that the note-taker list each person's follow-up assignments and deadlines right in the body of his or her follow-up e-mail, not just in an attached document. As the leader, it's also your responsibility to put a note in your to-do list to make sure all assignments were completed as planned, or—even better—to delegate this responsibility to someone on your team.

End Early

Completing a meeting earlier than scheduled will make people happy in the moment and will encourage them to look forward to your meetings in the future. Remember how much you loved the teacher who let you out before the bell rang? Be that.

Change It Up

As a final suggestion, why not consider meeting differently once in a while? If it's a beautiful day, suggest a field trip and meet outside. If you only have a few items to discuss, challenge yourself to have a stand-up meeting where no one is allowed to sit down (superefficient former New York City mayor Michael Bloomberg was a big fan of the ten-minute stand-up meeting). Or surprise your team with a little treat like cupcakes or beers if the meeting is late in the day. Contrary to popular belief, meetings don't have to be soulless conference room affairs. Don't be afraid to shake things up a little.

How to Lead a Nonboring Conference or Videoconference Call

Sometimes I think the real reason I wanted to write this full-length book was to have an excuse to teach people how to make conference calls less boring. You have to agree that the majority of them are mind-numbingly awful, right? Someone always enters the wrong dial-in number, everyone talks at the same time, half the attendees are actually reading e-mail or shopping on Amazon, and the awkward silences are excruciating. It's in your hands to make conference calls—and videoconference calls—better. Follow all of the above guidelines for in-person meetings and then add these tips:

Check Your Tech

Even if you've used them a million times before, double-check the call-in line and your headset, headphones, or microphone before leading a conference call. Make sure (or have an assistant or intern make sure) that people will be able to hear you clearly and that everyone's been provided the right dial-in info. If your organization has a shared conference line, check that you've booked it properly and won't enter into someone else's call (this embarrassing snafu has occurred multiple times when I've joined a conference call initiated by someone at a start-up or small organization). And of course make sure you're in a quiet enough spot. If at all possible, never lead a conference call from your car, a cab, a coffee shop, or any other venue where you can't control your environment, your barking dog, or your Wi-Fi signal.

Call in Early

You lose credibility and irritate people when they call in on time and hear that robotic voice repeat over and over again, "The host has not yet arrived." Don't be late to your own party.

Channel Your Inner Radio Host

Introduce each agenda item with some of your own comments and then ask individuals for feedback by name. This is similar to how a radio show host handles guests who are not physically in the studio: "We're talking today about potential ideas for the new social media campaign. Danielle, can I ask you to weigh in with some thoughts?" And then, when Danielle is finished speaking, "Thanks for the great ideas, Danielle. Steve, what are your suggestions?" This will avoid having people talk over each other. To make sure everyone has had a chance to talk, you can always say, "Who else wants to jump in on this point? Derek, how about you?"

Make Virtual Eye Contact

During a videoconference remember that you need to look into your device's camera rather than looking at the person you are talking to on the screen. This can feel awkward, but it's vital when giving a presentation or making a lengthy comment. Otherwise it will appear to your listeners that you're actually looking downward and they'll lose interest quickly. Likewise, look into the camera when another person is speaking so it doesn't appear that your attention is wandering.

Be Unbiased

If you're in a situation where some people are attending your meeting in person and some are attending by videoconference or teleconference, do your best to treat the people on the screen or phone as if they are actually in the room. It's natural to focus your attention on the people breathing right next to you and even to make side comments to them, but it's unfair to the virtual participants. They may have trouble catching your attention, so tell them at the beginning of your meeting that you'll be sure to ask for their input on each discussion topic, and then stick to your promise to do so.

How to Give a Killer Presentation

Finally, let's discuss situations in which you are on stage as a formal presenter. Even if you're speaking for only five minutes, you would be smart to think of any presentation as an opportunity to promote your leadership brand and win support and respect from the people in the room. Many leaders are terrified of public speaking (as one of my colleagues used to say, "Most people would rather be in the coffin than delivering the eulogy"), so this can be a huge differentiator if you excel at it.

Here are my best presentation tips, based on more than fifteen years as a professional speaker:

Be Smart About Structure

The classic advice about structuring a presentation is still the best: (1) Tell them what you're going to tell them. (2) Tell them. (3) Then tell them what you've told them. People want to know that you've organized your talk in a meaningful, logical way, and this structure proves that you have. You should also provide audiences with the purpose of the presentation so they know what's in it for them. For example, you'd begin by saying, "Over the next ten minutes I will give a progress report on three of our key clients. The main purpose of this presentation is to make sure each of you knows what projects we have remaining with each client by the end of the year so we can be sure to reach our performance goals. Please save your questions until the end." Next, you would spend a few minutes talking about each of the three clients. Finally, you would conclude by saying, "As promised, that was an update on our progress with client A, client B, and client C. What questions do you have?"

Keep Time (Quietly)

As demonstrated in the previous example, tell people up-front how long you plan to speak and when they will have the opportunity to ask questions.

Once the presentation begins, it's 100 percent your responsibility as the speaker to keep track of time and stick to what you've promised. You can certainly ask a colleague to give you a five-minute warning, but other than that no one in the room should have to watch the clock. This is especially important if you know that you are running out of time. One of my pet peeves is when a speaker says, "Well, it's getting late so I'm going to have to skip ahead a bit . . ." There is no need for anyone else to know if you are cutting out information, even if you need to bypass a few presentation slides. It makes people feel nervous for you and annoyed that you didn't manage the time better.

Try to determine in advance which of your slides or topics are skippable if the clock is ticking or if the event or meeting is running behind schedule through no fault of yours. As a general rule, give yourself a cushion by always preparing a bit less content than you think you'll have time to deliver. (Most people err in the opposite direction and prepare way too much.) If you finish with time on the clock, you can always take more questions, or you can simply end early, which will probably make your audience love you forever.

You *Are the Presentation—Not Your Slides*

When it comes to visuals, less is more. "I just love dense Power-Point slides!" said no one ever. So why, oh why, does everyone use them? Personally, I show mostly visual images on my slides and use bullet points only when they are absolutely necessary, usually to denote key takeaways. One of my speaking mentors advised me never to have more than sixteen words in any slide. I cheat sometimes (usually when sharing an expert quotation), but otherwise that's a great rule of thumb.

In general, your slides should be additive to your presentation, not central, and you should be able to deliver your entire presentation without slides if necessary. Paul Smith, an executive at Procter & Gamble, learned this lesson when he was pitching a new market research technique to the company's CEO, A. G. Lafley. Smith carefully prepared more than thirty PowerPoint slides for this incredibly important presentation. When Lafley walked into the room, he turned his back to the screen and stared directly at Smith through the entire presentation, never glancing at a single slide. Smith said of the incident, "I felt like maybe I hadn't done a very good job because he wasn't looking at my slides like everyone else. It didn't

occur to me until later that he did that because he was more interested in what I had to say than in what my slides looked like." Yep.
Everyone is.

Practice, Practice, Practice

People often ask me if I get nervous before my speeches. My honest answer is no, because I would never stand up to give a formal
professional speech without practicing it many, many, many times
first. Public speaking is a learnable skill, and the more you practice
the better you become. (By the way, the same goes for negotiating,
giving feedback, firing people, and lots of other situations that many
people fear, but more on those topics in the next chapter.) Whether
you practice in front of a few trusted people or just stand and talk in
front of your mirror, every time you speak your content out loud you
become a little better. Never stand in front of an audience—especially
an important one, like investors, donors, voters, or potential clients—
without practicing as much as possible first.

Even if you are invited to give a presentation on very short notice,
take whatever time you have to organize a few thoughts before you
open your mouth. I was once sitting in the audience of a conference,
listening to one of my biggest consulting clients give a speech, when
out of the blue he asked me to come join him on stage and say a
few words. Instinctively, I grabbed the only piece of paper I could
find—my own business card—and quickly jotted down a few things
I wanted to say. I continued writing as I walked up to the stage and he
handed me the microphone.

To be fair, I give speeches for a living and am more comfortable
with public speaking than most people. If the thought of needing
to give an impromptu talk terrifies you, rest assured that all of the
preparation you've put into your formal speeches will help you tremendously in short-notice situations as well. Alternatively, you can
fall back on the questioning technique. Most people find it easier to

answer questions than to formulate their own ideas from scratch, so if you are put on the spot you can turn your time into a Q and A session. For instance, "I'd love to tell you about the project my colleague was describing and I want the information to be most relevant to you. What questions do you have that I can address?"

Press "Record"

Bar none, the best form of presentation practice is to rehearse in front of a camera. As horrifying as it can be to watch yourself on video, the best speakers record themselves and learn from what they see. This is the quickest way to notice if you have any weird habits, like clicking a pen, twisting your hair, or rocking back and forth. (Watching myself on video early in my speaking career led me to the alarming realization that I had a tendency to tilt my head to the side, Valley-girl style. Once I was aware of it, it was easy to correct.) If you already consider yourself a good public speaker, watching yourself on video will show you areas where you can become even better. Studying great speakers on video (TED.com is my favorite inspiration) can help you become even better, too.

Plan a Great Ending

Even for the shortest presentation, you always want to finish strong. Many novice speakers ruin a great presentation by trailing off with something lame like, "Okay . . . I guess that's it . . ." I like to conclude with an inspirational statement or a word of thanks. Using our earlier example of the client presentation, a strong ending would be, "Thank you for listening to this overview, and I would love to hear your thoughts. But before I take questions, I wanted to remind everyone that our clients are some of the best in the business and their feedback on our work has been stellar. You are a great team, and I deeply appreciate your hard work. Thank you."

———————

Okay. . . . I guess that's it . . .

(Kidding!)

We've spent a lot of time talking about a variety of communication skills because how you communicate is one of the most important contributors to your success as a leader. Next, we'll dive into another crucial element of your leadership journey: managing people.

CHAPTER 5

Manage

Driving the Truck, Giving Out Trophies,
and Closing Your Door Almost All the Way

As you'll recall from the introduction, my first official management stint lasted three short weeks. But even that limited tenure was enough time for me to learn one of a new boss's most important lessons: succeeding as an individual contributor is *not, not, not* the same as succeeding as a manager.

Being a great salesperson does not automatically make you a great sales manager. Being a great actor does not make you a great director. Being a great councilmember does not make you a great mayor. And for me, being great at developing marketing partnerships with women's professional associations did not make me remotely competent at managing my first-ever direct report, Alex, to do the same. While I did a fairly good job of teaching him the importance of these relationships to our company and how they would ultimately benefit our customers—the professional women accessing career advice on WorkingWoman.com—I continued to do all of the work I'd been doing previously, such as negotiating agreements and reaching out to new potential partners, myself. I assigned Alex a few administrative tasks, but I kept all of the important stuff for myself and wondered why he didn't seem all that busy while I was more slammed than ever trying to manage him and do all of my work, too.

What Got You Here Won't Get You There

I couldn't resist stealing the title of this section from a book by executive leadership coach Marshall Goldsmith: what got you here won't get you there. It's the perfect way to instill the outrageously important message that I myself failed to grasp and legions of new managers have struggled with as well: while being a great employee got you promoted, being a manager is a totally different position requiring a totally different skillset and a totally different mind-set.

Don't just take my word for it (or Marshall Goldsmith's). Google it.

In 2009, Laszlo Bock, senior vice president of people operations at Google, launched an empirical study to figure out the differences between the best and the worst bosses at Google (which, by the way, consistently ranks as young professionals' most desired employer). The company had always believed that because they hired really smart people, all a boss at Google had to do was leave people alone and provide technical wisdom when requested. Well, they couldn't have been more wrong.

Bock and his team's study, dubbed Project Oxygen (and comprising, in true Google style, more than *ten thousand* observations about managers), found that technical expertise ranked last among the predictors of a boss's effectiveness. Instead, employees most wanted "even-keeled" bosses who made time for one-on-one meetings, helped them solve problems, and took an interest in their lives and careers. As Bock put it, "If I'm a manager and I want to get better, and I want more out of my people and I want them to be happier, two of the most important things I can do are just make sure I have some time for them and to be consistent. And that's more important than doing the rest of the stuff."

Michael "Dr. Woody" Woodward, PhD, an organizational psychologist and author of *The You Plan*, agrees. "When you are going into a role that requires people management," he told me, "the key is your ability to operate through other people. And it's not always fun! Your natural inclination is often to fall back on your expertise and do what you do well, which is being an individual contributor. Any new manager struggling to get the result they need will tend to jump in and do the work themselves. You'll find yourself in the trenches with the people you are supposed to be leading. Then you need to ask yourself who is leading if you are trying to do the work yourself?"

Welcome, Freshmen!

As Dr. Woody pointed out, stepping up into management can be a tough transition. As much as you want to be a leader, you might not want to relinquish your status as a star employee or the aspects of your job that got you noticed and promoted in the first place. If you're in sales, you might not want to turn over your top client relationships to one of your team members. If you're in customer service, you may be convinced that no one can placate an angry customer the way you can. If you're an entrepreneur, you might dread handing over your baby to someone else for the first time ever. You may find yourself missing your old role or even feeling envious of your employees.

Many new managers also experience feelings of inadequacy and that impostor syndrome we talked about in chapter 1. This is entirely normal and to be expected. After all, while you are certainly moving forward when you assume a leadership role, you are also moving backward. Think about it: you're shifting from a level of mastery in your individual contributor role to a level of beginner in your management role. Don't underestimate how hard this can be, no matter how smart, successful, or supported you are.

It reminds me of the transition from senior year of high school, when you're on top of the food chain, to freshman year of college, when you're back down on the bottom. As a resident advisor I witnessed this difficulty on a regular basis. My advice to my often overwhelmed and frustrated freshman advisees was to dive in headfirst to their new reality. When you're immersed in the work of your new environment, you think less about your old one. I'm not saying to gloss over any emotions you're feeling—it's certainly normal and healthy to acknowledge any feelings you're experiencing and discuss them with a supportive friend outside of the office—but when you're at work, you cannot wallow or reminisce. Get busy becoming a master of your new people management responsibilities as soon as possible.

This means there will be times when you'll have to do things you are not yet good at (or have never done before), such as delegating responsibility, interviewing and hiring, or even demoting or firing. So how do you become a great leader from day one?

You don't.

Unfortunately, some things cannot be fast-tracked, and management experience is one of them. You can and should read as much as possible about how to be a good manager (and hopefully this book and this chapter in particular will give you a strong start), but you just can't become a master manager in a day, or a month, or even a year. You'll have natural strengths and strong instincts to leverage (such as giving great motivational pep talks or showing compassion for people's mistakes), but you simply can't excel at every nuance of management when you've never had experience doing it. There are a million situations where you'll have to lead before you're totally ready. That is perfectly okay. Lead anyway.

Lead anyway means mustering up some confidence based on your trust in the people who promoted you to a management role, or in your own instincts that guided you to launch your own venture. *Lead anyway* means googling "How to interview a CFO" an hour before the prospective candidates come in to meet with you. *Lead anyway* means doing the very best you can every day and correcting bit by bit from there.

Of course I'm still going to share every secret I can to help you feel as prepared as possible . . .

VOICES OF MILLENNIAL LEADERS

A few months into my first "big-girl job" I was training newbies who had no idea how nervous I was. I bet that most great leaders hide their anxieties and insecurities.

—Elizabeth Lotto, editorial assistant in book publishing

The Three Essential Laws of Twenty-First-Century Management

A question I asked every person I interviewed for this book was, "What skills do today's leaders need that are new or different from the skills that past leaders needed?" I found that their answers fit into three overarching themes that will permeate many of the specific situations you'll face as a boss today and in the near future:

1. Adaptability to Rapid Change

There is no question that we are living in—and you will be managing in—turbulent times. Economies, companies, countries, technologies, and career paths are morphing and changing faster than ever before. Stéphanie Villemagne, director of the MBA program at INSEAD (dubbed "the business school for the world"), cited "adaptability to rapid change" as one of the most important qualities a twenty-first-century global leader will need, and many other leaders agreed. "It's about being at ease with uncertainty," she told me. There are a few areas in particular in which you will need to be adaptable in your leadership and management:

Technology

"No one talks much about specific technical skills anymore," said Ville-magne. "It's about being able to adapt as new technologies arise." This may seem easy today when, as a young leader, you're likely at the forefront of current technologies like new operating systems and wearable tech. But what about tomorrow when the *next* generation comes in with their virtual reality headsets and personal 3-D print-ers? It is easier than you think to fall behind or to start avoiding new tools. In the "old days" when e-mail was brand-new, it was common for executives to have their assistants print out each message so they could still read their correspondence on paper and file it all in alpha-betized cabinets. Don't let that be you! Commit to keeping up with technology no matter how busy you become. If you don't have a basic understanding of the technologies your organization uses today—security encryption programs, customer relationship management (CRM) software, shared document services, etc.—set up a meeting with a member of your tech team and get up to speed. As I tell my baby boomer and Gen X audiences as well, it is no longer acceptable to say, "I'm just not a tech person."

Employee Tenure

At no time in human history have people changed jobs and careers more often than now, and this trend will continue to grow. Accord-ing to the U.S. Bureau of Labor Statistics, the average worker today stays in a job for just 4.4 years. For members of Gen Y tenures are closer to three years, which means that an average twentysomething will hold fifteen to twenty jobs in the course of his or her career. That also means you'll be leading teams with frequent changes in talent. "Historically, you hired people from beginning to end," says Lori High of The Hartford. "You now have to hire talented people who come in and out and be comfortable with the changes in culture that that creates."

This is perhaps the only trend over which you do have a modicum of control. If you want to keep your best talent longer, you can be a better boss. Study after study (including Google's Project Oxygen) have found that the single greatest contributor to how employees feel about their jobs—and whether or not they stay in them—is their relationship with their direct manager. People don't usually quit organizations; they quit managers. The more approachable, fair, and supportive a manager you are, the less frequent turnover you are likely to see on your team.

Time Lines

Almost everything happens faster today than ever before. This is true on a minute-to-minute basis, but also with longer-term thinking. As Lori High commented to me, "The historical way of looking at things long-term was an eight- to twelve-year plan. Now, a 'long-term-plan' is probably five years, with the need to adapt to changing market forces in a moment."

By no means should you change your strategy or management style with every passing fad, but the pace of change today requires extreme agility and open-mindedness. It's not all that dramatic these days to say: adapt or die. Case in point: in 1958, a company could expect to stay on the S&P 500 (the list of the five hundred most valuable companies traded on the U.S. stock market) for sixty-one years. These days, the average is just eighteen.

2. Cultural Awareness

Adaptability to change also includes changes to the people with whom you'll be working. For traditionalists and early baby boomers, the majority of large institutions were led and dominated by white men. Then came the civil rights movement, the women's movement, the gay pride movement, the rise of the Hispanic population (which is now the fastest growing minority group in the United States), and other cultural and demographic changes. Millennials, as a result, represent the most diverse generation in American history, which means that millennials will need to cultivate a more inclusive leadership style than previous generations may have needed.

TREND WATCH: MULTIPLE MASH-UPS

You are becoming a leader at a moment of extraordinary change, with the baby boomers reaching traditional retirement age at the same time millennials are beginning to reach the age of thirty and stepping up to take the reins. Countries like China and India are evolving into global economic powers, and industries are rising and falling at a rapid pace.

These changes will profoundly alter our country and our organizations toward a more global, diverse, and technological (read: millennial) way of operating, but right now and for the next several years we are smack in the middle of the mash-up. Leaders, marketers, product designers, entertainers, politicians, and anyone else wanting to succeed will have to understand and appeal to an incredibly wide range of people, cultures, work styles, and functional competencies. As Columbia professor Angela Lee noted to me, "Cross-functional leadership is not even listed as a job requirement anymore because we all have to do that now."

Dan Black, the director of recruiting at EY Americas, has been hiring young leaders for more than sixteen years. When I asked him what he looks for most in potential leaders, he mentioned diversity first and foremost: "We look for people who can exhibit inclusive leadership. We think this is an important predictor of future success given the shifts in the world. We look for people who embrace the value that differences bring, who understand that having a point of view makes you wildly successful, and that your approach is based on your specific background. It's about being able to appreciate other people's different thoughts and approaches, and being able to incorporate those."

How does a young leader or potential leader show evidence of an inclusive approach to leadership? Black says, "It's evidenced by the teams or organizations they select to participate in. Are you actively seeking out those that have a different opinion, skill set, or background from yours? For instance, if you're a student, when you are assigned a project in class, do you go to the same five or six people or do you actively seek out students with a different background, with a different major, or from another region of the country? What is your appetite for trying new and different things? Have you been abroad for any length of time? How aware are you of what is going on outside of your immediate world?" If your answers to these questions demonstrate that you haven't been particularly inclusive to date, now is the time to expand your horizons and expose yourself to some more diverse people and ways of thinking.

3. Transparency

When the U.S. Paralympic athlete Jeremy Lade was a kid, his baby boomer dad coached his basketball team. "There wasn't a lot of communication that went alongside any instruction," Lade remembers. "'Correct' or 'incorrect' was the feedback. And my dad told me that his own basketball coach was even tougher—'my way or the highway.'" Now that Lade is a coach himself, he is learning that the old "command and control" leadership style no longer works. "I don't get much out of the players by just saying what they are doing right or wrong. Much more communication is required," he explains. "The players want to know *why* we are doing a drill, for example."

According to the 2014 Deloitte Millennial Survey, "Across all geographies, millennials expect twenty-first-century leaders to be more open, transparent, and collaborative—departing from the baby boomer model of leader as distant and autocratic." Transparency is the third essential law of management for today's leaders, and, as Lade's story illustrated, it's a huge departure from the way previous generations managed people.

To be fair to previous generations, much of the reason we expect transparency is the Internet. We simply know more about everything now, so we want to know more about, and from, our leaders. It's not uncommon today for companies to publicly disclose the salaries of their leaders or to live stream previously closed-door events, such as board meetings or product development sessions. Even the president of the United States has participated in an "Ask Me Anything" session on Reddit. "Trust and transparency in communications are becoming ever more vital," says Jacqueline Broder, a millennial and director of marketing and communications for KG-NY Restaurant Group. "The digital age practically screams for it. People can easily find out more information on leaders and their personal lives than ever before. In fact, they can even see it now via video versus reading an article. They can focus on reading one's facial expressions, tonality, and character rather than decipher through text. It's easier to judge someone's credibility than ever before."

VOICES OF MILLENNIAL LEADERS

I think the biggest difference between leaders today and leaders of the past is the amount of transparency required. People are willing to accept faults, even in their leaders, but no one likes—or trusts—a liar or someone who's hiding something. A leader, even one with faults, is willing to show their cards and still be powerful.　　　　　—Alexis Odesser, vice president, Emanate

How to Manage People When You Have Zero Experience Managing People

We've now established that most first-time managers have no idea what they're doing and the role of a manager is more complicated today than ever. Unfortunately there is more bad news: very few organizations are good at teaching people how to be good bosses. Many don't provide this training at all, or they provide it way too late: the average age of first-time managers is thirty years old, but the average age of people in leadership training is forty-two! And millennials like you are becoming leaders at even younger ages because so many baby boomers are retiring and vacating management roles. According to millennial leadership expert Alexandra Levit, "At the same age as today's millennials, most baby boomers and Gen Xers were still in junior-level positions."

BY THE NUMBERS: READY OR NOT . . .

Of current millennials who are leaders, only 36 percent said they felt ready when entering the role.

—Deloitte Global Human Capital Trends Survey, 2014

There is a silver lining to our shared history of unprepared leaders: we can all learn from their experiences. I asked a variety of successful leaders to offer their suggestions from the new manager trenches. Here's what they want you to know:

Be Yourself

This advice comes from Alexandra Lebenthal, who is the CEO of financial firm Lebenthal & Co., the second-largest woman-owned financial institution in New York City: "Managing people can be a daunting task and a new manager might have preconceived ideas about all of a sudden becoming someone else, but the best leaders I have known are the ones who let their true personalities shine through by being open and approachable." She continues, "When I first became CEO of my company, I was young and felt that to get respect I had to act more authoritative. In doing so I made a decision and communicated it in a way that was far from my usual way of dealing with people. As a result, someone left the company. Had I handled it differently, she might have stayed. It was a real wake-up call for me."

Please don't interpret this advice to mean that you should share your every fear or insecurity with your team. That can cause twice as much fear and insecurity among your ranks, and is not at all appropriate. What Lebenthal is saying is that it's a mistake to put on a new "boss" persona that is not authentic to you. People will be able to see through that false front, and, as she points out, it can lead to serious fumbles.

How can you be authentic while maintaining your new authority? One technique I've used is rehearsal. While it may seem counterintuitive to practice being natural, it's a helpful strategy if you'll be having a lot of conversations you've never had before. It's hard to sound natural when you're saying something for the first time in your life. When I'm planning for a first-time moment (such as my first-ever nonprofit board meeting), I'll enlist the help of a supportive friend or mentor and practice what I want to say and the way I want to say it. (Note that this friend should not be someone you manage.) I've practiced whether I should be sitting or standing up and whether some of my language sounds too formal and should be softened. I've role-played the questions and challenges I worry I might receive so I have a plan for handling them. I wish I could tell you that every event I've rehearsed has gone perfectly, but that never happens. What I can tell you is that I learn a little bit from every situation and get a little better—and more natural—all the time.

Launch a Listening Tour

Most successful leaders I interviewed for this book talked about the importance of spending tons of quality time with your team members when you take on a new leadership role. The worst thing you can do is hide in your office; you have to go out and spend time with the troops. Politicians call it a "listening tour" and it's an essential strategy for a new leader's toolkit. Scott Davis, principal of Tisona Development, a real estate development company in the Houston area, says, "Work quickly to establish solid relationships with your employees or followers. When you learn what they are about and know them personally, it is much easier to encourage them to follow you."

VOICES OF MILLENNIAL LEADERS

Getting input from others is the single fastest way to build morale. Listening to what those you lead are saying will guide you better than any other resource ever could.

—Stephanie Jensen, coordinator of internships,
University of Central Oklahoma

Just be careful that seeking input doesn't turn into managing by consensus. As James Duffy, an employee representative in the food service industry, commented to me, "Leaders need to have confidence in their decisions. That is not to say they cannot seek feedback from their teams, but when a manager or leader wavers on every decision, the performance of the whole team quickly reflects that indecisiveness."

For example, let's say you've just taken over as leader of your department and a big budget decision is due. It's your first time submitting an annual budget to the CEO and you're nervous. You know that a good leader is decisive and you don't want your staff members to start worrying that they'll be losing their jobs, but you're really not sure what line items to cut and you want your first-ever budget to be a home run. It would be a mistake to call an all-hands meeting, announce your indecision about the budget, and ask everyone to share their suggestions. A better move is to meet individually with a few key advisors who have worked on budgets before and ask for their insights. There is no need to express to them your lack of experience or indecision; just ask for their expertise, listen to their suggestions, and say thank you.

Drive the Truck

If you've ever watched the TV show *Undercover Boss*, you'll know why this advice is important. On that show, CEOs put on disguises and work alongside their employees. They are often shocked to learn what it's really like to work at their own companies. To avoid this disconnect yourself, it's important to "drive the truck" as early in your leadership role as possible. I heard this phrase from one of my leadership mentors, Trudy Steinfeld, assistant vice president and executive director of the Wasserman Center for Career Development at New York University, who told me, "Even if you are going to be a leader of many people, you need to understand what it's like at every level of the company, what every job entails so you have some experience and understanding."

This used to happen naturally, as many companies—such as UPS and Walgreens—consistently promoted from within and the CEO likely began his or her career literally driving a truck or working behind a pharmacy counter. That's not as common today, so if you haven't risen up the ranks yourself, do your best to learn from each employee what his or her daily experience is and what changes would improve that person's productivity or results. It helps build rapport to be able to commiserate with an employee about a difficult assignment, or to fully appreciate when he or she has accomplished something really complex or time consuming. Not to mention the fact that if you don't know how to do simple tasks, such as saving a file to the network or refilling the printer ink, you'll feel (and look) helpless if the employee who usually handles that task is out of the office.

Just remember, as I learned while managing Alex, that driving the truck does not mean to do your employees' jobs for them. Dr. Woody warns that a challenge he's seen with many young managers is when they actually compete with the people they are managing. He even admits to making this mistake himself when he was promoted to a manager role at PricewaterhouseCoopers. We're talking about that individual-contributor-to-manager transition again. "As a new young manager," Dr. Woody says, "you still have the inclination to be that star player and outperform others. That can come at a great expense and cause a lot of resentment among your team members." Know how to drive the truck, but don't try to drive it better than your team member whose job that really is.

Secure Early Wins

While you're being yourself and bonding with your employees in your first leadership role, you also want to make sure you are making genuine progress. This is why presidents of the United States are obsessed with accomplishing so much in the first 100 days of their terms: people want leaders who can get things done. Early wins can be large or small, ranging from cutting an unpopular "required" report to announcing a new client or funder. (If you know you are on the verge of a promotion or new manager role, it's not a bad idea to save some good news for after you take on your new title.) It's a good use of your energy to ensure that a few positive, public changes take place early on. Two weeks into Marissa Mayer's leadership of Yahoo, she announced free food in all the cafeterias. Consider early wins an investment in future team morale and support.

Establish Key Performance Indicators

As a new leader, you also want to secure early wins for the people you manage, so that they can feel part of a winning team. To do this, it's essential to tie their individual contributions to the overall goals you have for the team, project, or organization you are now leading. One popular way to measure progress is to set key performance indicators (KPIs) for each person. KPIs are the results that matter most to your team or organization. For instance, if you run a tutoring service, your KPIs might include the percentage by which your students' grade point averages increase. If you lead a nonprofit that provides books to needy children, one KPI might be the number of kids you reach in a year. Setting KPIs will help your team members see the big picture of what you want to achieve and how they each will contribute. Check in on these KPIs on a regular basis to make sure everyone is pulling in the same direction.

Remember That Managing Is Your Job . . .

Particularly in the first few months of your new management role, you will spend an enormous amount of time handling people issues and, as with KPIs, helping other people succeed in their jobs. This can be frustrating if you are used to accomplishing a lot of tasks or producing a lot of work product in the course of an average day. Dr. Woody says, "I've found with a lot of new managers that they don't view the 'managing' part of their jobs as work. They feel like it is peripheral or adjunct to their role, but the reality is that it should be their main focus. Your role as a manager is to develop your players and lead them to success. It's about working *through* others by influencing action." If you have spent an entire day talking to your team members, meeting with your team members, and answering e-mails from your team members, rest assured you have been doing your job and you have accomplished a lot.

. . . But Do Make Time for the Rest of Your Work

Of course, in most management roles, you will also have reports to write, spreadsheets to review, deals to negotiate, clients to woo, and any number of other responsibilities in addition to leading your team. Even the most collaboration-minded, open-door-policy millennial leader still needs some individual work time. How do you get it all done? Kate White, former editor in chief of *Cosmopolitan* and author of the career advice book *I Shouldn't Be Telling You This*, recommends two specific strategies that she implemented successfully throughout her career. First, she told me, "In my magazine career, when I needed to really concentrate, I closed my door for an hour each day—or I should say *almost* all the way closed so people could see I was working rather than changing my tights or something." Second: "I always, always got in before everyone else. That, to me, is a key secret to success because it gives you a fabulous head start."

I'm with Kate on both of these points. You have to carve out moments in your day that are uninterruptable. If you are consistent about your boundaries, however you choose to set them, your team will become accustomed to your habits and will respect your need to get things done. If you simply cannot get a particular person to stop interrupting you, tell the interrupter that you'll meet him a few minutes later . . . in his office. Then you can complete whatever you're working on, visit the other person on your timetable, and leave when you want to. (By the way, if you ever need to fire someone, this is why you should do it in the other person's office and not yours.)

BY THE NUMBERS: WORKING FOR A WINNER

As much as your employees (or volunteers, constituents, or other stakeholders) want to ask you questions or receive your input, they also want you to be successful. Why? Because they want to work for a winner. According to a 2013 study by the Workforce Institute at Kronos released in honor of National Boss's Day (which is apparently October 16 in the United States and Canada—who knew?), when given the choice between a manager who is a high achiever but demanding, or a manager who is nice but ineffective, 75 percent of employees would choose the high achiever.

Quiz: What Is Your Management Style?

In the early chapters of this book, we discussed the importance of knowing yourself and solidifying your personal brand. Once you've been overseeing people for a while, your personal brand will evolve to include a management style, which basically means the way you interact with the people you manage. It's worth pausing for a moment to reflect on whether the management style you are forming is what you really want it to be.

Why does knowing your style make you a better boss? I posed this question to another of my leadership mentors, Carol Frohlinger, managing director of Negotiating Women, Inc. "The benefit to knowing yourself and having a management style," she told me, "is that it grounds you. It gives you a point of view. You will continue to encounter situations you haven't faced before, and your management style will give you a compass."

For example, if your management style leans toward asking a lot of questions and you find yourself facing a crisis situation, you can remind yourself that you do best when you do your research rather than jumping to conclusions. Your management style also hints at where you might face challenges. For instance, if you're the questioning type, you may find it difficult to stop asking questions and start making decisions. If you know this about yourself, you can limit this tendency by, perhaps, setting a deadline at which point you'll stop polling people and come to your ultimate answer. Knowing your style also helps you create the right team around you: when you know your tendencies, you can better determine which other types will best complement yours. (Think: introvert/extrovert, good cop/bad cop.)

What is your management style and how can that help you make decisions as a leader? Take this quiz to find out.

You need to decide whether to cut your company's holiday party or scale it back big-time in order to meet your budget. What do you do?

a. Cut it. Don't most people dread going to these things anyway?

b. Ask the resident office party planner to put together some ideas on how you can celebrate without breaking the bank. If you like her suggestions, the party's on!

c. Let your staff weigh in on whether they want a holiday party and will accept cuts elsewhere. Majority rules.

d. Delegate the decision to your second-in-command. He's much friendlier with the team and will know how the decision will affect morale.

When it comes to making tough decisions, you:

a. Always trust your gut. It never fails you.

b. Talk it through with your longtime mentor before making a move. She has a different background from yours and is always a great sounding board.

c. Ask at least three people what they think you should do.

d. Take your time weighing all of your options before coming to a decision.

You're the chair of a charity committee. One of the members often insults the others and has become difficult to work with. What do you do?

a. Ask him to leave the group. There's no place for negativity in charity work.

b. Have a conversation with him about how his attitude is affecting the other members. If he doesn't change his ways, give him the boot.

c. Hold a vote with the other members on whether or not to oust him.

d. Assign him to one of the more menial tasks with the hope that he'll get fed up and leave on his own.

As a boss, you want to be:

a. Feared.

b. Respected.

c. Fair.

d. The right balance of friendly and aloof.

You've got an extra ticket to an upcoming Beyoncé concert and two friends who'd love to go with you. How do you choose which person to invite?

a. You ask each one what he or she would be willing to barter for the ticket. The one with the best offer wins.

b. You give it to the one who is the bigger fan.

c. You flip a coin.

d. You let them fight it out. You're going to the concert no matter what.

You're thinking about starting a running group to help you stay motivated. What's the first thing you do?

a. Fire off an e-mail to the people you think would want to join, with a detailed schedule of where, when, and how long each workout will be.

b. Send out a feeler e-mail to gauge people's interest and then follow up with some ideas on how to get started.

c. E-mail your running friends and ask them if they've heard of any good resources for starting such a group.

d. Let your friends know that you'll be running at 7 p.m. each evening in the park if they want to meet up and work out together.

It's your mom's sixtieth birthday and your family decides to throw her a surprise party. What's your role in the planning?

a. What isn't? If it weren't for you, this party would never happen.

b. You've made a list of everything that needs to get done and then let your siblings choose what they want to tackle.

c. Decorations. Your brother is much better at the catering thing, so you'll leave that to him.

d. You're waiting for your sister to tell you. You let her take the reins.

When you delegate a task to a coworker you:

a. Don't delegate. Nothing gets done right unless you do it yourself.

b. Give him explicit instructions on how you want it done and leave him to it.

c. Let him know what you're looking for and that you're open to his ideas.

d. Give him the gist and let him take it from there. You don't micromanage.

Results

Although everyone is unique, management styles are typically divided into four categories. Based on your answers to the questions above, which one best describes you?

Mostly As

Your style is autocratic. Quite simply, you like to be the boss and make all the decisions. This style is efficient, but just be aware that it can sometimes alienate your coworkers and limit innovation and team morale. If you lean toward this style, you'll want to keep in mind that—as we've discussed—most people today prefer inclusive and transparent leaders. To be the strongest leader you can be, balance your autocratic nature by seeking others' opinions and allowing them to delight you with how capable they are of excelling at their jobs.

Mostly Bs

Your style is traditionally known as paternalistic, but I prefer to think of it as inclusive and compassionate. You still like to call the shots, but you carefully consider others' thoughts and ideas before you do. People are often loyal to you and feel like you are looking out for their best interests. If you are struggling with a decision and you fall into this style, remind yourself that you work best when you talk things out with a trusted sounding board.

Mostly Cs

Your style is democratic. You believe that everyone deserves to have his or her point of view heard and you like to ask a lot of questions.

If you consider yourself a servant leader, you likely identify with this category. While this fosters fairness, be mindful that it can also slow down the decision-making process. You've heard the analogy "too many cooks in the kitchen," right? If you lean toward this style, make sure you always set a deadline for ending your polling phase and moving on to action.

Mostly Ds

Your style is laissez-faire. You don't like to be micromanaged and won't subject others to it. You surround yourself with highly competent, intelligent people and let them do what they do best. This makes people feel highly valued, but if you are too far removed then your effectiveness often goes with you. Remember to acknowledge people for their contributions on a frequent basis and let them know you are paying attention to all that they do.

VOICES OF MILLENNIAL LEADERS

The toughest lesson I had to learn was that the type of management I like to receive isn't always the type of management someone responds to. I think it's a common problem for leaders to lead in a style that they themselves would respond to and not always take a step back to figure out whether they need to be more passive or attentive.

—Jada A. Graves, senior editor, careers, *U.S. News & World Report*

Personality Management 101

When I ask young professionals to share their biggest questions about leadership and management, the most common concerns revolve around problematic people issues—building authority with older employees, overseeing friends, handling higher-ups, managing difficult personalities, and just getting along with everybody on a daily basis.

What I most want to convey on this topic is that relationships with people, whether personal or professional, are often messy, frequently difficult, and never perfect. It's just the nature of being human, which we are even when we're at work. A lesson that I've learned over the years is that every potentially tough interaction—whether a negotiation, a performance review, or even a reprimand or dismissal—is never going to go perfectly, no matter how much you plan (although, as we'll discuss, you absolutely do need to plan). You may say a few things you wish you didn't or forget to say something you really wanted to express. It's okay. In most cases, as long as you didn't say something extremely offensive or potentially illegal, you should judge yourself on the overall outcome of the situation. And know that, in most cases, you can usually have another conversation and revisit any issues you failed to raise or didn't address the way you wanted.

While every interaction won't be perfect, here are some strategies to handle common people issues with grace and effectiveness.

How Do I Manage People I Don't Like?

Carol Frohlinger of Negotiating Women says, "One of the things that's really important for strong managers to realize is that not everyone with whom you work has to be your best friend. If they are competent [and that's a big if—we'll talk about managing poor performers below], then figure out how you can be pleasant with one another and focus on the outcome that you are trying to accomplish. You can sometimes expect too much: adjust your expectations to realize that you are not going to like everybody and that's okay. Don't beat yourself up about it! If you are fair and you are giving people the support they need to do their job, that's enough. You don't owe them friendship; you owe them guidance and fairness, and that is where the role of manager ends."

This is wise advice, but easier said than done, right? Especially if you work in a particularly casual or social environment. Or if the person you don't like is really eager for your attention and approval. Here are some more specific tips:

Treat the Annoyer as Your Teacher

This is my personal favorite trick for dealing with difficult people in all areas of life (from irritating relatives to rude store clerks), and it comes from a life coach I once worked with. Every time I get that pit-of-the-stomach feeling of annoyance with someone's behavior or words, I ask myself, "What can I learn from this moment?" Is it a reminder to be more patient? To remember that people communicate in different ways? To stop being so judgmental?

I know this may sound a bit new-agey, but the reality is that there will always be people in this world who bug you (and they will find oh-so-many different ways to do it), so you have to figure out how to deal. This is also an essential part of your growth as a leader. As my friend Christine Hassler, life coach and author of *Expectation Hangovers*, has written, "Any successful businessperson must learn to deal with a myriad of personality types and workplace issues. If rising to the top ranks is your goal, learn this lesson now. I would bet that the mental energy you are investing in being annoyed by [this person] is far more distracting and time consuming than her actual behavior, so stop the trash talk going on in your head."

Shift Your Perspective

What if you consider it a good thing that you are not in love with some of the people on your team? Some experts say this is actually better for overall performance. The employees you gravitate toward might be the ones who act nice, don't deliver bad news, and flatter you. It's often the people who provoke or challenge you that prompt new insights and help propel the group to success. "You need people who have different points of view and aren't afraid to argue," author and Stanford professor Robert Sutton has said. "They are the kind of people who stop the organization from doing stupid things." See if you can shift your perspective on annoying or difficult people from irritation to gratitude.

Focus on the Positives

If the annoyer is a good performer, but just happens to rub you the wrong way, then another potential strategy is to convince yourself to focus on his or her best qualities, particularly those that help your team succeed. For instance, if your social media manager is killing it for your product on Twitter and Instagram, but her cutesy chatter drives you crazy, can you let it go or tune it out? One tactic is to limit your conversations to the positives of her work and steer clear of situations (such as making small talk in the cafeteria) that bring out her annoying qualities.

A VIEW FROM THE TOP

Yes, I did have favorites. But they were always the people who did the best job—it was never a personality thing—and they got the compliments, the perks, and the raises.

—Kate White, former editor in chief, *Cosmopolitan* magazine, and author of *I Shouldn't Be Telling You This*

How Do I Manage People Who Don't Seem to Like Me?

Just as certain people will bug you, it's likely that you might bug other people. How do you deal with it when you sense someone on your team isn't a fan?

"First," says Carol Frohlinger, "I'd ask myself why. If it's one person that you feel doesn't like you, then that's one thing. If it's more than one, there may be a pattern that you might want to consider." Dr. Woody, who has coached numerous executives, agrees: "Good management begins with introspection. You really have to understand how others react and respond to you, and you need to seek out that tough feedback from the people you manage directly and from colleagues. You have to constantly be willing to hear that feedback and adjust. We can come across differently than we think we do, and that could be harmful to building team cohesion."

In other words, get into the habit of asking people, as former New York City mayor Ed Koch used to say, "How'm I doin'?" Just be sure to let them know that you are genuinely open to both positive and negative feedback and that there will be no backlash to any criticisms. "I have thick skin," you might say, "I'd love to know some areas where I can do a better job." (If you don't have thick skin, then perhaps say, "I know I can be a bit sensitive, so please be gentle, but I really do want to know how I can improve as your manager.") You don't have to accuse the other person of disliking you. Just ask for the feedback and listen with an open mind. You may receive some extremely helpful insight or you may even learn that the other person's dislike was all in your head.

THERE'S AN APP FOR THAT:
PERSONALITY ASSESSMENT TESTS

If you have trouble talking about personality issues, then consider taking a personality assessment. Dr. Woody, who is a big fan of such assessments, says, "They will give you some insight and put language around issues that are not easy to talk about."

His favorite assessment test is the Hogan Development Survey (HDS), which must be administered by a certified professional. The same is true of the well-known Myers-Briggs Type Indicator (MBTI), which I've found to be quite helpful in understanding my personality style as well as other people's. (I'm an ENFJ, by the way.)

To sample the world of personality assessments on your own, here are two recommended resources.

The 9 Personalities Test: Discover your Enneatype

This iPhone app, which has been downloaded more than one million times (itunes.apple.com/us/app/9-personalities-test-discover/id386312239), conducts a personality assessment that will identify your Enneagram type, one of nine specific yet interrelated personality types. Answer several multiple-choice questions, each with nine possible answers, and the app will tell you your type along with a description of your virtues, flaws, challenges, and motivations.

41 Questions. 1 Personality.

This assessment (41Q.com) is exactly as it sounds—forty-one questions with two-option answers, taking about five minutes to complete. The results are displayed in a format similar to that of the MBTI types, and you'll receive a description of your personality along with career choices that could be a good match. For a fun twist, the free report also tells you which famous people share your personality.

While it's smart to be attuned to people's feelings about you and to assess your overall personality, I would caution you not to spend too much time on this. At a certain point, you have to accept that everyone won't adore you or your style, and this is part of the deal as a leader. What's more damaging than being disliked is having too strong of a need to be liked.

I am among the many people who struggle with the need to please, and I've found this trait to be particularly prominent with women. Perhaps it's because girls are often socialized to be nice, quiet, and agreeable, or because we worry about being perceived as too aggressive and called the infamous b-word. Of course, many men are afraid of being disliked as well.

Setting aside the why behind any people-pleasing instincts you might have, what's important is noticing this tendency when you have it and nipping it in the bud. You simply cannot please everyone all the time and be an effective leader. (Believe me; I've tried!) By its very nature, leadership requires making some tough decisions. Becoming comfortable with this reality is part of the confidence-building process of transitioning from employee to leader. If you set a standard of being a pushover, it will be even harder to make those inevitable tough calls because you will appear inconsistent.

As clichéd as it is, I often have to remind myself, "It's not personal; it's business." This doesn't mean you have license to be a jerk; it means you as a person are not the same as the decisions you make as a leader. If you are regularly collecting honest feedback on your leadership and you genuinely believe in the decisions you are making and the actions you are taking, then don't overthink occasional frostiness or even outright anger from someone on your team.

How Do I Confront Conflict?

Since you can't avoid displeasing people sometimes, another reality of being a leader is that you'll have to become skilled at handling conflict. I've noticed that this is another particular challenge for a lot of young leaders I meet, both female and male. One of the results of growing up in a high-tech world is that you might not have much experience handling face-to-face conflict. Recently I've observed young leaders reprimand their employees by instant message, get into major strategy debates by text message, and even quit their jobs by e-mail. I'm concerned that these practices will become the norm as more and more millennials step into leadership positions in the future. But right now, the more important issue is that you will lose credibility quickly with your Gen X and baby boomer colleagues if you are unable to have difficult conversations in person or by phone.

So how do you become more comfortable with conflict? Here are a few recommendations:

Take Your Time

While you may never feel 100 percent ready to have a potentially heated discussion, you have every right to prepare yourself and gather your thoughts and confidence. Advises Trudy Steinfeld of NYU, "Give yourself permission to say, 'I haven't thought it all through yet' and take some time. Then think about the person with whom you have a conflict, such as her personality and how she has reacted in your prior dealings with her. You really have to think about her style and her ego." When I am nervous before any conversation, I'll jot down some notes, say them out loud a few times, and make sure I'm feeling calm. The conversations I later regret usually take place when I've picked up the phone in anger rather than stopping to think through my response first.

If you're in the habit of engaging in difficult conversations by e-mail or another written method, I again want to encourage you to start taking these conflicts offline. Phone calls and in-person discussions can be uncomfortable, but they are almost always more effective, more efficient, and more capable of solving whatever problem has occurred. Refer back to the tips in chapter 4 on how to handle difficult conversations (you'll recall that I improved my skill by observing the techniques of a highly skilled boss).

Bring Solutions

Your goal in addressing any professional conflict is not to win a fight but to end up with a workable solution to whatever the problem is. In other words, think of a difficult conversation as a negotiation and not a rant. Suggesting solutions will not only bring the conversation to a conclusion more quickly, but it also has the benefit of garnering respect from the other person.

Be a Broken Record

This advice came from my mother when I was on the verge of breaking up with a boyfriend many years ago. It's a particularly good approach when the other person is being unreasonable or doesn't want the same outcome that you do (in this case, I wanted to break up and he didn't). The idea is to come up with your most important point or most compelling argument and repeat it no matter what counterarguments the other person makes.

To give a professional example, if a junior employee you oversee has been spending too much time texting her friends and online shopping during business hours, your broken record phrase might be, "Spending so much time on personal activities is not acceptable and it's hurting your reputation with the senior staff." Don't yell or become angry, just make the point clearly and memorably. Keep making your point, even if she says, "But you check Tumblr sometimes!" or "I was texting my mom about my dad's heart surgery!" or "But I am getting all of my work done!" You can briefly acknowledge each point if you'd like (e.g., "I'm sorry to hear about your dad") and you certainly want to have a conversation and not *literally* sound like a broken record. But do not waver from your main message. The key is to be firm in your argument, not get caught up in details or tangents, and continue repeating your bottom line.

Bookend

This is another great tip from my mom (who, as you may have guessed, is not just my mom but also a small-business coach). Before and after having a difficult conversation, bookend it with a supportive friend or colleague (or your mom). This means that you'll call or talk to your support person before heading into a confrontation to build up your confidence; have the interaction; and then call that support person afterward to debrief. If you are nervous, it's really helpful to know that someone is out there cheering you on and will be there when you're done.

As you advance in your leadership you'll likely not need the above tricks anymore, but once in a while they'll still come in handy.

Managing Your Mom (Or Someone Old Enough to Be Your Mom)

One of the management issues that is unique to the millennial generation is that you will likely be managing people who are older than you are, sometimes many people, and sometimes those who are older by a generation or more. As we've discussed, this is simple demographics: baby boomers are staying in the workforce longer and millennials are stepping into management roles earlier. There is nothing inherently problematic about managing someone older than you are, but it's an issue about which many millennials express discomfort. So let's demystify it.

BY THE NUMBERS: YOUNGER BOSSES

Thirty-four percent of U.S. workers say their boss is younger than they are, and 15 percent say they work for someone who is at least ten years younger.　　　　　CareerBuilder.com, 2012

Don't Assume Age Is an Issue

Don't assume that someone is uncomfortable with your age or thinks you're young and inexperienced if they show no signs of feeling that way. The workplace is in such a state of flux right now that most people have learned to go with the flow and expect that they will work with members of all generations. So make sure you do the same: don't assume that older employees fit common stereotypes such as being less technically savvy or clueless about pop culture. If you don't want to be judged by your age, be careful not to judge your colleagues by theirs.

Earn Respect by Showing Respect

When I've asked workers of all ages what they most want from their colleagues, people from age eighteen to eighty mention the desire for respect. For example, older workers want respect for their years of experience and younger workers want respect for their technical skills. Even if you feel that an older employee's skills are slow, outdated, or old-fashioned, you can still show respect for his or her longevity in your organization (often referred to as institutional knowledge) and other assets. You can show your respect by making older colleagues feel valued: ask for their opinions, request their help, praise their well-informed ideas, tell them you appreciate their perspective. A little humility goes a very long way, especially because the millennial-shaming media has cast today's young people as entitled, ungrateful, and skeptical of anyone who doesn't love technology. When you show other generations that you value them, they will almost always respect you in return.

Friends with Salaries: How to Manage Your Peers

Another common concern among young leaders involves managing people with whom you were once on the same level, or those you know socially. In other words: how do you become the boss of your friends?

Lori High of The Hartford has a lot of experience with this

potentially sticky situation. "Having gone from being a peer to leading all of them," she told me, "my advice is to acknowledge that that relationship exists, but to be aware as a new leader that everything has changed and to own that change.

"Your peers," she continued, "will tend to make the relationship the same because that's what they're comfortable with. The reality is that the relationship *isn't* the same. You have to respect the relationship you had before, but as a new leader over a former peer group, you are now held responsible and the decision making is yours. The person who promoted you believes in your decision-making ability. When everything is said and done, you are going to be held accountable.

"For example, if you attend a holiday party with a bunch of your friends from work who report to you, there is a point the social gathering could become 'messy.' Know when it is best to exit and be aware that you are always representing the company. That means now is not the time to divulge info to your friends or be involved in behavior that could later affect you and your relationship with them or the company."

So how do you follow High's advice and exit such a situation gracefully? You can say something like this: "I would love to go to the afterparty with you guys, but unfortunately I won't be able to do that because of my job. I don't want to see or hear anything I shouldn't. You understand, right?" Now that you're a leader, you have to be aware of when it's inappropriate for you to be part of a conversation or activity. Even if you're just sitting there quietly, by virtue of being the leader of the group you are implicitly condoning whatever behavior is taking place.

Zoë Ruderman, deputy director, style & beauty at *People*, adds this advice about managing friends: "Be comfortable with your position and authority. As tempting as it is, never say things like, 'I don't know why I got this job' or 'I'm so underqualified,' because it could give the sense that you're nervous about the position, that you still feel the need to prove yourself to your own manager, or that you are in competition with others." It's okay to feel these emotions, but, while you might have discussed such feelings with your friend when you were peers, now that you're the boss you need to keep your feelings to yourself. It will sap your credibility and also make it harder to give your friend/employee directions and feedback in the future.

MORE, PLEASE: SHOULD YOU FRIEND YOUR EMPLOYEES ON FACEBOOK?

The issue of being real-life friends with the people you manage is tricky enough. It becomes even more complicated when you add in the issue of being friends on Facebook or other online networks. What are the right boundaries when it comes to work relationships and social media?

This question is further complicated by the fact that work cultures vary widely, as do industry norms, generational styles, and individual personality types. You may work at a start-up where everyone follows everyone else's Instagram and it's no big deal to write a Tumblr post in the middle of the workday. Or you may work in a conservative financial services firm that blocks employees' access to social media sites and you'd never even consider friending anyone in your department. If you do feel comfortable connecting with your team on Facebook and elsewhere, just remember that you are still the boss. Your professional reputation will be affected (for better or worse) by the photos and information you post, and you may discover information about your employees that you might not have known (or wanted to know) otherwise. Tread carefully.

If you have any hesitation about how to handle this issue—particularly if you manage people of other generations who are not as social media savvy as millennials—then the safest, most

ethical course of action is to do your best to ensure a level playing field for the people who report to you. Fairness rules. If you
are going to connect on social media with some of your direct
reports, then you should make that option available to all of your
direct reports. If you are very private and don't want any of your
employees to be your Facebook friends, then you should share
this preference with people so they don't feel rejected if you
ignore their connection requests.

Here's a truth about managing friends that many young leaders
learn the hard way: even if you do everything right, some of your
former peer-level friends may never be comfortable with your rise
above them. If you sense this situation with someone and want to
do something about it, you'll need to have an honest conversation.
The conversation should take place on neutral ground, such as a
coffee shop, rather than in the workplace, and all you need to say is,
"I'm getting the sense that you are not comfortable with my being
the leader of our team. Can we talk about it?" You might discover
that you're not as humble a leader as you think, or you may find that
your friend didn't realize how he was behaving. In the end, if this
person is a true friend, he should understand the requirements of
your new role and change his behavior during work hours. If not,
then maybe the friendship wasn't that strong to begin with.

The Feedback Frenzy: How Much? What Kind? What For?

Feedback is a hot topic in the world of workplace theory right now.
How much is too much and how much is not enough? There is a lot
of concern among boomer and Xer leaders that today's young pro-

fessionals received too much praise as children and now require pats on the back simply for showing up to work every day. "These millennials want nonstop feedback!" is a common complaint from my corporate consulting clients.

Based on my experience working with and studying millennials for the past fifteen years, I tend to agree with my clients on this one. Far more than baby boomers or Gen Xers, millennials have received more coaching and praise from parents, teachers, professors, and coaches throughout their lives, so they enter the workplace expecting the same attention and encouragement from their employers.

And, as I tell my clients—often to shocked reactions—I think this millennial characteristic is fabulous.

Employees who want feedback are showing that they want to improve. They want to contribute. They want to do a good job. We should celebrate this and give millennials the feedback that will help them to do that! While other generations might not require the same amount of attention, most everyone wants to know how well they are doing at work, so why not give everyone more feedback while we're at it? If you agree with me, then you'll want to become an expert on giving feedback to the people you manage, no matter what generation they are. Here are my top tips:

How to Give Positive Feedback

My favorite approach to positive feedback comes from *The One Minute Manager*, which recommends that managers pay close attention to the work of the people they manage in order to "catch them doing something right." Then, when you make that positive observation, you immediately give a "one-minute praising" by looking that person straight in the eye and telling her precisely what she did well. Finally, tell her how good you as the manager feel about what she did so well. Even if this particular person is not thriving in every aspect of her job or acing every project, she will know that you are in the habit of praising good work when you see it. It shows that you are paying attention and you care, and it will inspire her to do better in other areas as well. This strategy is particularly effective with new employees or those who are struggling through a difficult assignment. And as promised, it only takes a minute.

Another key element of a worthwhile praising is to be very specific in your feedback. "Great job!" is a nice thing to say, but that sort of generic reaction does not help someone develop and grow. Specific praise is far more meaningful and effective. For example, "I'm really impressed by the creativity of your end-of-year sales plan. I particularly like the social media outreach and follow-up methods you proposed." When your praise is specific, the recipient is more likely to remember it and apply it in the future.

Finally, when it comes to positive feedback, I'm not opposed to praise that is accompanied by something tangible, such as a reward or—wait for it—a trophy. (Trophies are, of course, a fraught topic for the millennial generation, who are stereotyped as coddled kids who received trophies for merely participating as children—playing on a soccer team, attending ballet class, or even visiting the dentist.) While you don't want to go overboard and make recognition meaningless, do consider small ways to recognize achievement, such as quarterly awards, gift cards, flowers, a team lunch in the person's honor, or even something as simple as a personal handwritten note from you (Jack Welch was famous for acknowledging employees' success with personal notes when he was CEO of GE). What's most important is that the trophy is meaningful and enjoyable to the person receiving it, so give serious thought to a reward that the successful employee would truly value.

> **BY THE NUMBERS: WHERE TO PRAISE**
>
> When giving feedback, what you say matters. Apparently, where you say it matters too. According to a 2013 study by the Workforce Institute at Kronos, most employees would rather receive positive feedback in private than in public:
>
> • 43 percent prefer direct individual praise from their manager.
> • 25 percent prefer praise in front of their peers.
>
> This means it's wise to ask your team members for their preferences or observe their body language when you praise them in a particular environment to learn where they will most benefit from your kind words. To an extremely shy person, for example, a public praising may feel more like a reprimand whereas a private nod and smile might make that person's day.

How to Give Negative Feedback

Giving positive feedback is enjoyable for most leaders. But what about giving negative feedback for poor performance or inappropriate actions? When giving feedback that is critical or correcting, you'll achieve the best results when your genuine intention is to be constructive. If you truly believe, deep down, that you are giving negative feedback to help someone (and not just to vent), then there is a much greater chance that your message will be well received and improvement will occur.

The trick, of course, is making sure that your team members feel that your negative feedback is genuinely constructive. Liam E. McGee of The Hartford says that leaders need to create an environment where feedback and coaching are routine. You also have to walk the walk, especially as the top boss. McGee routinely undergoes 360-degree assessments (which include feedback from his direct reports, his fellow board members, and a self-evaluation) and shares high-level results publicly at all-employee town halls.

As with positive feedback, when sharing criticism you want to be specific and, most important, only criticize the issue at hand rather than implying that everything the person does is wrong. You also want to be mindful of criticizing the behavior and not the person. For instance, if you are an editor and need to give negative feedback to a writer for handing in an article with several typos, you'll want to say, "I was disappointed in your story. There were several mistakes." You don't want to say, "You are so lazy!"

HOW TO SAY IT: GIVING NEGATIVE (I.E., CONSTRUCTIVE) FEEDBACK

According to communications expert Jodi Glickman, if someone you manage does something subpar, you've first got to highlight what went wrong or what didn't live up to your expectations. Be careful of becoming accusatory or argumentative; just state the facts. Next, give specific guidance about how you would like things done differently going forward, or how you would have done it differently yourself. Finally, make it clear that you are giving feedback (aka constructive criticism) because you care, you want the other person to succeed, and you believe in his or her talents and abilities. You are sharing your feedback because you want the person to improve, not because you want him or her to feel bad.

Helpful phrases to include in your negative feedback include:

- "I'm telling you this because I know you can do better and I want you to be successful."
- "My mentor (or former manager) told me something similar early in my career and I've never forgotten it—it really helped me excel at my job."

By the way, it's okay to be nervous about giving negative feedback. One Fortune 500 CEO shared with me that he often can't sleep when he knows he has a negative performance review to deliver the next day. But here's why he knows the insomnia is a sign of good leadership: "It means I care."

Finally—and this can be challenging when you're really mad or disappointed in someone—when the reprimand is over, let it go and move on. Life is too short and the workplace is too busy to hold a grudge. Once you've given your feedback and it has been heard, it's over. The more people see that a reprimand doesn't affect your overall working relationship, the more open they'll be to your constructive feedback in the future.

The Virtual Manager

Another situation you will face as a modern leader is managing employees who don't work from the same location or during the same hours that you do. As a virtual leader, you'll be able to apply many of the same tactics and strategies we've already reviewed in this chapter. But other virtual management situations will require a different approach, and as I've thought about an overarching theme for this approach, the word that keeps coming to mind is *empathy*.

Empathy—the ability to understand the feelings of another person—is one of the characteristics I most admire in leaders (or any professionals, for that matter). I admire people who recognize that their colleagues are busy and have jobs to do and personal lives to lead, and who can put themselves in their employees' shoes. When managing people you don't see face-to-face on a regular basis, it can be too easy to neglect those people's feelings, opinions, and contributions. To succeed as a virtual leader, you cannot let this happen.

Sometimes the empathy required of a virtual leader is big-picture, such as setting policies to ensure that remote or flex-time employees receive the same feedback, benefits, opportunities, and mentoring as other employees. Sometimes it's in the small details, such as remembering that people are participating by phone during your weekly team meeting, and directing some questions to them. My advice on being a strong virtual leader will focus on the smaller details because they are the easiest to implement and can make a difference very quickly.

TREND WATCH: HOW TO MANAGE A ROBOT

It can be challenging enough to learn to work with different kinds of people, especially if they are virtual employees. In the near future, you'll most likely be managing employees who are literally virtual: robots. If you pose questions to Siri or make flight reservations by talking to a computerized customer service rep, you're already well on your way to embracing this trend.

Not convinced? If you know any kids attending school in Southern California, they may be learning from robot teachers already. Thanks to a grant from the National Science Foundation, tabletop robots are now teaching healthy lifestyle habits to Los Angeles kids. And if your elderly relatives need a caretaker to provide the right medicine dosage or just someone to talk to, robots are now doing that, too.

It's only a matter of time before humanlike robots with high intelligence (and even a sense of humor) become more commonplace at the office. Whether you find this sci-fi-sounding future scary or exciting, you must begin to prepare for it. The baby boomers adapted to computer-based work lives. Millennials will inevitably adapt to robot-based futures, too.

Columbia Business School professor Angela Lee uses the term *other-oriented* to describe the empathy a virtual leader needs. The goal of being other-oriented is to think about communication from the other person's vantage point and to remove as much ambiguity from your communications as possible. The goal is not only to avoid uncertainty or miscommunication with your virtual team members, but also to elicit the best performance from people you do not see in person on a frequent basis. Here are some tips for becoming more other-oriented:

Set Extremely Clear Expectations on What Needs to Be Accomplished

In my observation, most millennial bosses don't care as much how people get their work done as long as the final product is excellent. (This, of course, is quite different from previous generations of managers who cared about face time.) However, since you won't have the chance to even minimally observe a virtual employee's work while it's in progress, you'll need to be extra specific about exactly what that person needs to get done and what level of quality you expect. You can do this by scheduling more frequent check-in calls or deadlines on large-scale projects and by encouraging virtual employees to always request clarification on anything they are uncertain about.

Explain Your Time Management and Communication Style

It can be difficult for people who don't see you on a daily basis (and can't pop in to your office) to get your attention, so let them know the best methods and times to reach you and what your communication expectations are of them. Proactively offer guidance on such questions as:

- What is generally the best method to reach you—cell phone, text, e-mail, IM?

- When do you expect the virtual employee to be available and by what methods? How will you most likely reach out?
- What is usually the best time of day to reach you? Is it okay to reach out after traditional business hours in your time zone?
- How quickly can virtual employees expect to hear back from you if they send an e-mail or leave a message?
- Are there any times you are absolutely *not* available?

Setting boundaries can be particularly tough for younger leaders, who tend to want to be as accessible and collaborative as possible. I believe this tendency is an asset, but as a busy leader you'll likely find that you do have to set some limits on your time and accessibility. You also need to be aware that team members of different generations might be thrown off by a "feel free to e-mail me 24/7" style. Here's an example of what can go wrong:

Dr. Woody told me the story of one of his clients, a top executive, who would send e-mails to his staff members whenever an idea occurred to him, which was often late at night or on weekend mornings. He had no expectation that anyone would respond right back; he just wanted to capture his ideas when he had them. Of course his staff members, eager to impress their boss, would scramble to respond right away whenever they received an e-mail from the executive and often complained of stress and burnout. Lots of drama could have been avoided had the executive explained that he didn't expect immediate responses to his off-hours messages.

So if you are a night owl and love answering e-mails at three a.m., just be sure that your team knows that about you and won't panic when their phone buzzes with a new message in the middle of the night. Tell them that you don't expect a response until business hours. This is even more important with instant messenger: tell your staff members to set their status to offline if they don't want to be messaged by you at certain times of the day.

When you're traveling, particularly to different time zones, be other-oriented by ensuring the people who report to you know your basic itinerary (including when you'll be in the air and likely unreachable, although with inflight Wi-Fi this is becoming less of a problem) and when or if you will be available by e-mail, text, or phone throughout your trip. If you're planning to be in meetings all day and checking your messages in the evenings, inform people that they may receive a flurry of messages all at one time—and clarify when you expect responses back.

Adapt to International and Cultural Differences

If you are managing people from other countries, it's especially important to take time to learn about how they prefer to conduct business as well as any other cultural nuances. For example, as Stéphanie Villemagne of INSEAD says, "Understand that, based on how you write it, one e-mail can be interpreted differently by ten different people." (This is true here in the United States too, of course.)

Villemagne recommends that you do a bit of research on the countries where your international team members are located. For instance, you may learn that in one particular country, employees will never disagree with their bosses in front of other people. So if you want honest feedback from an employee of that nationality, you'll always need to ask for it one-on-one. In other countries, people will be highly offended if you don't engage in some pleasant chitchat before getting down to business. How do you learn this kind of stuff? Just ask. "People are extremely happy to tell you about how business is done in their countries," Villemagne told me. "Just ask simple questions, such as 'What is it like?' or 'How should I address someone older than I am?' People are usually quite happy to share this type of information with you."

On an even more basic level, always know the time zones in which your international employees are based, as well as the public holidays they celebrate that Americans do not. Try to vary your conference

call times so your Southern hemisphere colleagues aren't always joining calls in the middle of the night.

MORE, PLEASE: BEING BILINGUAL

The apex of other-orientation is to speak in the exact language
of the person you are communicating with. When doing business with someone from another country, there is no greater
sign of respect and desire to connect. I'm not saying you can't
be an excellent leader without being multilingual, but as one recent international study found, "The ability to work in a number
of languages can differentiate the effective executive from the
merely capable one."

Since English is now considered the dominant global business language, I think it's even more impressive when Americans
speak (or even know a few words of) the languages of our clients
and partners. Of course, as China, India, and other countries
continue to rise in power, the dominance of English may decline
(which is why fancy private schools now offer Mandarin language
classes to kindergarteners). Even if you are not fluent in another
language, you can and should learn the customs, communication practices, and etiquette of your international colleagues.

For more on international business practices, check out the
book *Kiss, Bow, or Shake Hands* by Terri Morrison and Wayne A.
Conaway, which also comes in special editions for Asia, Europe,
and Latin America.

Motivation Nation: Eight Ways to Inspire the Troops

Wherever your team members are based, another of your leadership
responsibilities is to build and maintain morale. Liam E. McGee of
The Hartford says, "I believe everyone shows up every day and wants

to do great work. It is the responsibility of the leader if they don't. Great leadership is the ability to inspire and motivate people to do what they don't think is possible." Here are eight ways to do just that:

1. Do the Opposite of Every Bad Manager You've Ever Had

Most all of us have had bad managers in the past, and this is good news. Now we all know what we absolutely should not do as leaders ourselves. For example, Trudy Steinfeld of NYU once had a manager who would claim authorship for all of her work, so Steinfeld is particularly careful to share credit with employees who contribute to her department's success. As for me, here is a list of some of the things my worst bosses did:

- Sent instant messages making fun of the way other employees sitting in the same office were dressed or how they spoke on the phone.
- Often decided at the last minute not to attend a meeting and sent whatever employee was available, with no preparation whatsoever, to meet with the unsuspecting person.
- Asked me how much I weighed and then said, "Oh, good. I weigh less than you." (Seriously!)
- Invited meeting attendees to brainstorm ideas and then dismissed their various suggestions as "awful," "terrible," and "the worst idea ever."

    I hereby commit to never, ever doing any of that as a boss. I'm all for revenge-minded management, as long as your intentions are positive.

2. Manage by Walking Around

This motivational concept, nicknamed MBWA, traces back to executives at Hewlett-Packard in the 1970s and was made popular by our friends from chapter 0.5, Tom Peters and Robert Waterman Jr., in their book *In Search of Excellence*. It is also one of the late Steve Jobs's claims to fame (although, to be honest, most people praise Jobs for his vision and power more than for his people skills). When Jobs was planning Pixar's headquarters, he designed the building to have a central atrium that all employees had to walk through to get anywhere else, including the coffee bar and the bathrooms. His goal was to encourage spontaneous conversations that would lead to more innovation and better ideas. It worked. One Pixar producer said, "I get more done having a cup of coffee and striking up a conversation or walking to the bathroom and running into unexpected people than I do sitting at my desk." The same will likely be true for you. If you want to motivate people, you have to see them, chat with them, and understand their day-to-day experience. If your employees work virtually, MBWA might mean having frequent Skype chats or IM exchanges throughout the day.

3. Explain the Why

As we've addressed, notable characteristic of millennial employees is the desire to know *why* they have to accomplish a given task. They want to know how their specific contribution—be it a spreadsheet for a client, a leaflet drop for a political candidate, or a day of follow-up calls to potential sales leads—affects the larger organization. Some boomers and Gen Xers complain about this tendency, considering it a form of millennial entitlement ("Who do they think they are? No one ever told me why I was doing grunt work. 'Because I said so!' was the only reason I ever got . . ."). But in my experience, members of other generations actually like to know the why, too. Everyone wants to feel that his or her work is making a difference. I know it takes time to explain the connection of every task to a larger goal, but it builds tremendous goodwill. If you want to be a better motivator, then continually educate your staff on your big goals and how each person is helping to accomplish them.

4. Show Interest in Each Person's Self-development

Another common trait among millennials is the desire for self-expression and personal development at work. As a leader, you can motivate your fellow Gen Ys by helping to support and encourage this. (Again, you'll find that most boomers and Xers care about self-expression at work, too, they just aren't as vocal about it.) As Zoë Ruderman of *People* told me, "The one boss I've had who's a millennial is very supportive of me focusing on myself in my job and trying to get the most out of it I can. She's also open to me working on outside projects. I definitely respect and support this self-focused attitude in members of my team as well."

Showing interest in people's self-development means asking that classic job interview question, "Where do you see yourself in five years?" and genuinely wanting to know—and support—the answer. (Some progressive companies now offer internal coaches to help employees make career decisions, even if that means the employee will leave the organization.) It means taking the time to understand what each person's top strengths are and giving them more work at which they can excel. It means supporting people in their desire to take training courses inside or outside your organization to build their skills. As millennial leader Katia Beauchamp, co-founder and co-chief executive of the beauty company Birchbox, tells her employees, "This is your life. This is your career. I'm here to set you up for success, but you are driving."

5. Motivate Different Individuals in Different Ways

Of course supporting each employee's personal development doesn't mean taking your attention away from the success of the group or organization you are leading. Strong leaders find creative ways to correlate each individual's goals with the bigger picture. Jeremy Lade does this in his role as a coach of wheelchair basketball players. He says, "I need to figure out each individual's strength to get the most out of them to best help our team. This takes a lot of communication. Before each season, I sit down and have a conversation with each of the players. They will tell me what is best for them. Some will say, 'My coaches always yelled at me and I respond to a little bit of fire.' Others respond better to a private conversation on the side." As Lade points out, motivating people is a lot like communicating with them: you have to know your audience.

And keep in mind that other people may not be motivated by the same rewards that personally motivate you. One issue I see frequently with my finance industry clients is that baby boomer bosses, who launched their Wall Street careers in the 1980s, tend to view money as the be-all, end-all motivator to work hard. When they started their careers, they were willing to forgo their personal lives to make more money. Their youngest employees, however, don't always feel the same way. Many Gen Y investment bankers tell me that they would happily give up some of their salary or bonus to work shorter hours or have more time off. This is absolutely baffling to their older colleagues. Frankly, if you can no longer assume that money is the top motivator for young Wall Street bankers, then all bets are off when it comes to knowing what motivates people in today's workplace. Always ask.

6. Encourage Excellence

One of the best motivators I've come across is also one of the simplest. It comes from millennial leader Jess Lively, whom I met when she was a student attending one of my workshops at the University of Michigan several years ago. At that time, Lively had her own jewelry business, which she began when she was a freshman in high school. Now she runs a business teaching people how to design their lives and businesses with intention. When I asked for her best motivational tip, she shared a single sentence she uses with her employees. Whenever she assigns a project, she says, "Make it as awesome as you want."

According to Lively, this small invitation to excellence works magic. For example, she told me, "I wanted to have an itinerary for my traveling workshops, so I asked one of my employees to create an itinerary for everything I need when I travel—and to make it as awesome as she wanted or as awesome as she could. In addition to providing clear information on flights and hotels, she color-coded all of my transportation and packing lists and designed everything according to my overall brand. I loved it. If you give someone ownership, it's amazing what they will accomplish."

7. Provide a Safety Net

A quick way to lose motivation is to fear getting yelled at if you make any sort of error. So assure your employees that it's okay to ask questions and occasionally mess up. "It's important to be approachable," says Julie Daly Meehan of Hartford Young Professionals and Entrepreneurs. "You can set up expectations and give clear deadlines, but people need to be comfortable approaching you if they have questions, not fearful that your reaction will be negative. Set people up for success and help them get there."

James Duffy, the employee representative for a large food service company, told me, "I often hear, regardless of their age, that employees still want what I refer to as 'supported autonomy.' They want to feel empowered but know that there is a safety net that is available in their leader or manager."

At SIB Development & Consulting, the company's leaders hold an ice cream party when an employee makes a big mistake (on that employee's dime, of course). What's the rationale? Founder and CEO Dan Schneider explained about one particular party thrown in honor of a staff member who forgot to back up his hard drive and lost a significant client project, "I realized that if I yell at everybody, they're just going to figure I'm a jerk. But if we're all sitting around eating ice cream, everybody knows why we're eating ice cream—it's because this guy screwed up. That will set in and they'll remember it and then just maybe they'll think, Oh, yeah. We had ice cream last week. Maybe we should back up our work."

8. Change It Up

Do you remember that surge of pure joy you felt when you walked into a classroom in school and saw one of those rolling carts with the TVs on top—the ones that meant your teacher would be showing a movie that day? Why not provide the people you lead with a few surprises like that? Random, unplanned perks can be fantastically motivating in all sorts of situations. Consider surprising your team with a half-day Friday before a long weekend, or taking everyone to see the newest blockbuster movie in the middle of the day, or hiring an ice cream truck to give out free cones in the parking lot on the first beautiful spring day (even if no one forgot to do a backup). A little fun can go a very long way.

MORE, PLEASE:
HOW DO I MOTIVATE VOLUNTEERS OR
PEOPLE WHO DON'T REPORT TO ME?

This question may be on your mind if you lead a student organization, membership association, nonprofit, or other team with volunteer staff. My answer is that because you don't have any direct authority—you're not paying them or formally assessing them—you might need to be more creative in figuring out what is going to motivate the people you're managing. Determine your answer

---

to the question, "Why should they listen to me?" and communicate your reasons to your team. Don't assume they will follow you just because you have a title or tell them what to do.

Some reasons or rewards that might motivate volunteers include:

- A title they can include on their résumé and LinkedIn profile, such as committee chair, board member, or editor.
- Taking charge of a project, leading a team, or participating in a project they wouldn't otherwise experience.
- Access to people who will become part of their professional or personal networks.
- Professional recommendations or referrals.
- Awards or honors for the work they've accomplished.

Tammy Tibbetts says, "At She's the First, our volunteers are able to exercise their creative muscles and have opportunities to manage other people. They get practice in project managing and being able to make decisions. We don't pay them, but they receive tremendous experience for their portfolios, and I've given many recommendations for volunteers citing the projects they've done for us. And in some cases, these experiences and recommendations helped them land great full-time jobs."

Ten Evergreen Management Tips That Are Evergreen for a Reason

To conclude this chapter on management, here are some final reminders of classic management tips to consider as you lead. They may seem clichéd at times, but these old adages still hold true for a reason: they work.

"Take One for the Team"

While you don't want to get in the habit of covering up any major problems in your ranks, there's no doubt that shielding your staff from the anger or criticism of a higher-up is a good morale builder. For example, if your group misses an important deadline, take responsibility and tell your superiors that it won't happen again. There's no need to point out which employee didn't deliver. She'll be grateful not to be called out and will likely work twice as hard next time.

"First In, Last Out"

Workers of all levels (even your fellow millennials who don't care much about face time) do tend to make a mental note of who's at their desk when they arrive and leave for the night or who is answering the phone after five p.m.—and who isn't. This doesn't mean you have to set up an air mattress in your office, but when you're in the middle of a big project, or are prepping for an important meeting, plan on putting in some extra hours alongside your staff. Your team will appreciate that the boss isn't eating bonbons while the minions toil.

"Hire People Smarter Than You Are"

When you have a say in hiring decisions, it's always wise to recruit talent that complements your natural skills and abilities. It's common for inexperienced leaders in particular to feel intimidated or threatened by people with stronger skills or lengthier résumés, but it's worth a bit of discomfort to have those strengths on your side.

"Practice What You Preach"

If you constantly nag your team about being accessible to customers, don't blow off your scheduled shift working the customer support line. If you can't stand grammatical errors, make sure you spell-check every last e-mail. If you don't live up to your own standards, you can't expect anyone else to do so.

"Think Outside the Box"

The overuse of this particular phrase is cringe worthy, but there is something to be said for people who can come up with fresh, creative ideas and solutions. (How about we start by thinking outside the box to come up with a new way to describe the ability to think outside the box?)

"Do Your Homework"

You can never be too prepared—and this is true whether you're interviewing for a new manager job or have been in your current leadership role for years. Knowing the answers before anyone asks the question is a highly valued skill.

"It Is What It Is"

Sometimes, whether we like it or not, we just to have accept that a situation isn't going to change. Knowing when to move on, instead of wasting time trying to fix it or complain about it, will serve you and your team well.

"It's Better to Apologize Later Than to Ask Permission First"

Obviously this depends on the situation (if $10 million is at stake, you may want to get an okay from someone other than yourself), but higher-ups, clients, and other stakeholders don't always want to be bogged down with details. They're interested in the outcome (preferably a good one) and if you can make effective decisions, they'll come to see you as someone who can handle even greater responsibility and trust.

"You Have to Pay Your Dues"

Chances are your boss didn't start out as the head of your group and she can remember what it was like to attend every client meeting and spend weeks on end negotiating deal points in windowless airport hotel conference rooms. In other words, you aren't getting much sympathy. But, if in between your grunt work, you offer to take on a project for your manager (preferably one she didn't even know she needed done) or offer up an innovative solution to a budget problem, your superiors will soon see that your skills are suited to even higher ranks.

"Go the Extra Mile"

If your significant other had dinner ready and waiting for you after a long day at the office, you'd be grateful, right? And maybe more inclined to sit through a OneRepublic concert, even if you can't stand their music? The same is true at work. On occasion, go out of your way to delight the people you work for and the people you manage. Ask yourself that question I recommended asking your employees, "How awesome can I make this?"

As you have seen, managing people is a complex, nuanced, and ever-changing art. If you have a management question that was not answered in this chapter, you can submit it on my blog at LindseyPollak .com/blog and I'll do my best to answer in a future blog post. In the next chapter, we'll talk about managing something even more daunting than people: a resource you can't motivate, negotiate with, or hire more of. I'm talking about . . . time.

CHAPTER 6

Prioritize

Running the Marathon, Delegating Undictatorially,
and Handling Stress Like a Buddhist Nun

In the old days (like, twenty years ago), most people had dial-up Internet, we used fax machines to crank out documents page by page, and we waited three days to receive an important item in the mail. The only instant communications were the phone and tapping someone on the shoulder. There were very few cell phones, so if you commuted to and from work, you usually listened to the radio in the car or read a book on the train or bus. If you wanted to get work done over the weekend, you went back into the office.

Believe it or not, people thought they were busy then.

Today we are regularly sending, receiving, and processing information by e-mail, text, IM, phone, voice mail, messenger, overnight mail, FTP, LinkedIn, Twitter, Facebook, blog comments, live meetings, teleconferences, videoconferences, Skype, shared folders, wikis, and whatever technology is invented tomorrow that I'll be annoyed didn't exist in time to make it into this book.

Plus, when you're the boss you're exposed to the stress and busyness of all the people you oversee in addition to your own. Managing your team's priorities is now part of your job description.

How do you lead in a world where the pace of work is so much faster, the amount of information is so much greater, and everyone's stress levels are constantly increasing? This chapter addresses time and energy management for the busiest and most stressed-out generation in history (yep, that's you). We'll talk about handling an endless workload, integrating your work and personal life, prioritizing when everything is a priority, coping with other people's stress, and much, much more.

Busy Is Not a Badge of Honor, and Five More Time Management Mantras

When I first started my career, I remember being really impressed by people who were "slammed," "buried," "overloaded," "getting killed," or "completely maxed out." "They must be so important!" I thought, as I chugged my third Diet Coke of the morning and tapped away on my PalmPilot. But now I know better, and you should, too. Being busy is not a badge of honor. Yes, the world moves much faster today, and yes, leaders have a lot to deal with. But managing it all is part of your job. If you are a leader and you are "slammed" all the time, then you are: (1) not delegating enough, (2) not organized enough, or (3) being dramatic. I've had the opportunity to know some very successful people—surgeons, judges, national politicians, celebrities, activists, and Fortune 500 CEOs—and, as busy as I know they all are, they rarely show it and they certainly don't complain about it.

I'm not saying that you won't ever feel too busy; the trick is learning how to manage a very full schedule without losing your cool. And as you become more and more successful in all areas of your life—friends, family, pets, hobbies, travel, philanthropy, and your career—you'll need time and energy management strategies even more. Here are five of my favorite reminders:

Leadership Is a Marathon, Not a Sprint

This is advice I received about parenting, but I love it as career advice, too. If you're truly committed to being a leader in any realm, then you know that you're in this for the long haul. Remember that one bad day will not break you, not finishing your daily to-do list is not the end of the world, and one accidentally missed meeting will not destroy your reputation (trust me; I overslept for my very first conference call with one of my biggest-ever clients. How did I recover? I apologized quickly and authentically, and then I worked my hardest to overdeliver on every assignment for that client from that point forward). You won't be perfect every day, and when you stop trying to be perfect, you'll end up better in the long run.

Take Care of the Big Rocks First

Management guru Stephen Covey tells a famous story about a teacher giving a lecture about time. As he begins, he places a wide-mouth gallon jar on the table in front of him. He adds three fist-size rocks to the top of the jar and asks the students if the jar is full. They say yes. He then reaches under the table and pulls out a bucket of gravel. He dumps the gravel into the jar and the gravel fills all the spaces left by the big rocks. Again, he asks if the jar is full and the class says yes. He brings a bucket of sand, which fills in the gaps between the rocks and gravel. Now the class is on to him and says no when he asks if the jar is full. Finally, he brings out a pitcher of water and pours water into the jar as well.

What is the lesson of this exercise? Many of the students think their professor is trying to demonstrate that you can always fit more into your day. He's not. The real lesson is: If you don't put the big rocks in first, you will never get them in. If you want to accomplish big things in your life—building a sustainable company, having a happy family, launching a new product, or writing the Great American Novel, you have to schedule the steps related to those big things before anything else. When you plan the big things, you are so focused and committed to your major goals that the smaller things tend to fall into place.

Laura Vanderkam, author of *168 Hours: You Have More Time Than You Think*, agrees. "People are always looking for ways to save time here and there," she says. "Maybe they're e-mailing more effectively or ending meetings earlier, or running their errands in a way where they only make right-hand turns. There's nothing wrong with these ideas, but they're all about playing defense. That's necessary to play the game of life, but it's not sufficient to win. Play offense with your time. Build the life you want. Put in the things that are meaningful and important to you, your organization, and the people you care about first, and then time will save itself. When you're working on a project you find compelling, leading people to great results, it's amazing how little time you spend on random e-mails."

An Ounce of Planning Is Worth a Pound of Work

This may sound counterintuitive, but on your truly crazy days— when you have back-to-back meetings, a huge deadline, staff members knocking down your door, and five urgent fires to put out— the most important action you can take is to stop in your tracks and make a plan. I learned this from Dan Black, who is not only the director of recruiting at EY Americas, but also the current president of the National Association of Colleges and Employers, a husband, a dad, and a volunteer fireman (so, you know, he has *actual* fires to put out). "On the busiest days," he says, "I have to determine what the real priorities of the day are. That can take fifteen minutes that, in the heat of the moment, I don't think I have. I think, 'I've just got to go, go, go.' But instead, I spend those fifteen minutes and say, 'This is clearly a crazy day that is going to drive me over the edge if I don't plan.' Planning is time so well spent and time people often don't take because of that instant response of needing to answer an e-mail or phone call. No matter how urgent everything seems, you can't lose out on the critical step of thinking meaningfully about what really needs to get done."

The former editor in chief of *Cosmopolitan*, Kate White, offers similar advice. On her busiest days, she says, "I triage the way medical personnel do in big emergencies. I figure out what has to be dealt with immediately and what can wait and what can't be saved anyway so it can be ignored . . . Also, I learned this from a cop who deals with crises: you often have more minutes than you realize to address the situation, so step back and give yourself a bit of time to really think what the best course of action is."

This means that sometimes you'll have to leave an important e-mail unanswered for a few hours in order to attend a crucial new business meeting, or leave a stuck employee frustrated overnight while you head to the hospital with your mom, who is having an important medical test. Part of being a leader is making tough choices about where your attention is most needed at any given moment. In the words of Stephen Covey, "Most of us spend too much time on what is urgent and not enough time on what is important."

Never Check E-mail in the Morning

This is the title of a book by the organizing guru Julie Morgenstern and also one of the most popular e-mail-specific productivity tips you'll come across. I can probably count on one finger the number of times I've actually not checked e-mail in the morning, but I do try to follow the underlying concept, which is that you should complete the single most important task of your day when you first arrive at your desk and not get caught up in busywork. You likely have the most energy in the morning, you're less likely to be disturbed by urgent issues that arise later on, and you'll feel such a sense of accomplishment after writing the difficult e-mail or finishing the design specs that you'll have a spring in your step the rest of the day. If you choose instead to procrastinate on that important work, you'll have it hanging over your head all day and will probably end up staying late in the evening to do it.

Stress Is Not Actually Contagious

Contrary to popular belief, being surrounded by stressed-out people does not have to affect your anxiety level. You are in control of your emotions and reactions, and you can and should remain as calm as possible when the people you manage are stressing out. Controlling stress is easier said than done, but I am inspired every day by my daughter's preschool teachers. They remain completely placid in the face of temper tantrums, biting, "I want mommy!" meltdowns, and more. As one of the teachers remarked to me, "It's easy to stay calm when you know the moment will pass eventually, and the kids need the safety of knowing there is a grown-up in charge."

As a leader, you are the "grown-up in charge" (no matter how old your employees may be), so you need to model the behavior you want your team to exhibit. Hysteria is a waste of your time and can cause your team members to become even more anxious and concerned, which wastes even more time and energy.

Quiz: What's Your Time Management Style?

Now that we've looked at some overall time management and prioritization concepts, take a few minutes to explore your specific relationship with time so you'll be aware of your potential strengths and vulnerabilities. Here is a simple quiz to help:

You're standing in line at your favorite lunch place. When it's your turn at the counter you:

a. Quickly rattle off your order and ask how long it'll take to be ready.
b. Interrupt the call you're on to order lunch, then go right back to chatting with your friend.
c. Tell the person behind you to go ahead. You're still mulling over the options.
d. Ask the cashier what he thinks of the butternut squash soup. Is it better than the spinach salad?

You join a study group for a big test you're taking next month. At the first meeting you:

a. Come prepared with a specific outline of the material you want to go over. There's a lot to cover and not much time to do so.
b. Study a few pages from each section of your test booklet. You learn better if you digest the information in small bursts.
c. Spend a lot of time helping the other group members get caught up.
d. Focus on one chapter at a time. Once you know it cold, then you can move on.

On the weekend you usually:

a. Hit the gym when you wake up, run errands, then meet up with friends if you have time.

b. Sleep in, and then see where the day takes you.

c. Get roped into helping a friend with some task. You just can't say no!

d. Make some time to work on your latest project.

You're supposed to meet a friend for coffee at three o'clock. It's 3:15 and she's nowhere in sight. What do you do?

a. Leave. Her time isn't any more important than yours is.

b. Give her a few more minutes. It's a miracle you're on time.

c. Text her to see if she's okay and let her know that whenever she arrives is fine.

d. Call and text her several times. Maybe you got the meeting place wrong?

Your greatest strength is:

a. The ability to stay focused.

b. Coming up with unique ideas.

c. Your willingness to put others before yourself.

d. Your attention to detail.

Your boss just tossed you a big project. The catch: she needs it done by tomorrow. You:

a. Get to work. You thrive on tight deadlines.

b. Call a coworker to brainstorm some ideas before you get started. You have all night.

c. Gladly take it on despite the fact that you've told three other coworkers you'd help them with their projects.

d. Have an inner meltdown. How can she possibly expect you to get this done in one day?

You could never work with someone who is:

a. Habitually late.
b. Close-minded.
c. Selfish.
d. Impulsive.

A 4
B 2
C 0
D 2

An appointment got canceled so you have time to kill before your next meeting. What do you do?

a. Sneak in an extra workout.
b. Sit down with a cup of coffee and your favorite magazine.
c. Call your mom.
d. Catch up on all of the work that you're behind on.

Results

Salary.com, the popular compensation and job search tool, breaks down time management style into four categories, from which I've adapted the following descriptions. Determine which style best describes you, and take note of the advantages and potential disadvantages you might experience based on your type.

Mostly As

Your time management style is direct. You make decisions quickly and efficiently and don't like to waste a moment. While sticking to a strict schedule allows you to accomplish a lot, you may miss some of the spontaneity that can spark creativity. As a leader of people who won't always share your style, you may risk alienating people with your potential lack of tolerance for other people's indecision or procrastination.

Mostly Bs

Your style is free-spirited. You happily juggle many things at once, you're creative, and you love to brainstorm your next big idea. You can become easily distracted, however, and often take on new projects before you've finished old ones. As a leader, be aware that deadlines and decisions can be a challenge for you, but some of your direct reports may thrive on them.

Mostly Cs

Your style is considerate. It's no wonder you have so many friends: you're extremely generous with your time and often put others' needs above your own. While admirable, your inability to say no can sometimes backfire, leading you to make promises you can't keep and set unrealistic expectations for what you and your team can really accomplish.

Mostly Ds

Your style is systematic. You're an excellent, conscientious worker—when you're given enough time and direction to complete a task. Sometimes you have a tendency to get bogged down in details, which means tight deadlines or unexpected requests can throw you into a tailspin. To overcome this tendency, give yourself permission to occasionally not proofread a document for the fourth time and rest assured that your overall industriousness will carry you through.

How to Handle Stress Like a Buddhist Nun

For years I've saved a magazine clipping of an Oprah Winfrey interview with Pema Chödrön, a Buddhist nun and author of several bestselling books on spirituality. Born Deirdre Blomfield-Brown, the mother of two, and an elementary school teacher, Chödrön decided after her second divorce to convert to Buddhism and move to a monastery in Canada to pursue her spiritual path.

Winfrey, as she so often does, asked Chödrön the exact question I wanted answered: "Can a well-known Buddhist nun ever have a bad day and get ticked off at people?" Chödrön replied:

> You mean can I afford to, because my reputation is at stake? Well, as much as I value my teacher [Buddha], I value my children, my family, and an old friend because they don't regard me as this big deal . . . Recently, my son very sweetly said, "Mom, tell me honestly: what does your Buddhism have to do with the fact that you get so uptight about things?" I just roared with laughter. I said, "It has nothing to do with my Buddhism at all, except that I don't flagellate myself for it."

I loved reading that even a Buddhist nun cannot always be as calm as a . . . Buddhist nun. Which means those of us trying to lead teams and organizations in today's 24/7/365 global world really have our work cut out for us. Here are various stress-management strategies—some micro, some macro—to help you handle the inevitable strain:

"Don't Flagellate Yourself for It"

Just as Chödrön said, the Buddhist way of handling stress is to accept it and not waste precious energy trying to resist it. Feeling irritated or angry about feeling stressed will only make your anxiety worse and delay any of the actions that would calm you down. (Try not to flagellate yourself for anything, for that matter. Getting angry or frustrated with yourself in any aspect of life just creates more anxiety and compromises your ability to lead.)

Cut Down on Decisions

I cannot tell you how relieved I felt when I learned there is such a thing as decision fatigue. After a typical day of making choices large and small—what to wear, which images to use in my new speaking deck, which calls to return first, whether to take the subway or a cab to the downtown meeting, which contract points I'm willing to negotiate, which Web hosting plan to choose, which sentences to delete from an article draft, etc., etc., etc.—I often become completely incapable of making even the smallest choices, like deciding what to eat for dinner. Thankfully, I am not alone.

According to research reported by the science columnist John Tierney, "No matter how rational and high-minded you try to be, you can't make decision after decision without paying a biological price. It's different from ordinary physical fatigue—you're not consciously aware of being tired—but you're low on mental energy. The more choices you make throughout the day, the harder each one becomes for your brain." This is why President Barack Obama says he wears only gray or blue suits and why has an assistant order his lunch each day: so he can focus his energy on far more important decisions.

Even if you're not the president of the United States, you can cut down on stress and decision fatigue by routinizing a few trivial choices. For instance, have the same meal for breakfast every weekday, lay your clothing out the night before, check e-mail at the same designated times, or, like the president, have someone else choose what you'll eat for lunch.

TREND WATCH: DIGITAL DETOX

According to Experian, U.S. smartphone owners aged eighteen to twenty-four send 2,022 texts per month on average—that's sixty-seven texts on a daily basis! Another report found that a whopping 81 percent of workers surveyed say they check

work e-mail on the weekends. This constant connectivity may
be the norm, but there is no question it is increasing everyone's
stress levels.

Given the continued rise of the machines, I predict there
will be an equally strong counterbalance to this ever-increasing
stress and connectivity: a burning desire to unhook from our
electronic and media-saturated lives. The more ubiquitous
computers and robots become, the more luxurious it will be to
disconnect. Watch for an increase in digital detox as the new
luxury, perhaps as features of day spas or high-end vacations.
And I predict a new industry of experts who teach the digital native millennials exactly how to pull the plug—digital detox coach
may become a new career path.

Breathe

I tend to get annoyed when I'm completely freaking out about
something and someone says, "Just breathe." What's most annoying
is that it usually works. A few calm, deep breaths in and out can, at
the very least, slow your heartbeat and give you a moment to collect
your racing thoughts. When the toddlers at my daughter's preschool
get worked up, the teachers show them how to take deep breaths
by saying, "Smell the flowers in, then blow the birthday candles
out." When I think of those instructions during stressful moments, I
breathe . . . and also smile.

Take Breaks

If breathing exercises are not your cup of organic, fair trade, de-
caffeinated tea, then figure out what does help you destress. It might
involve listening to music, calling a friend, playing Tetris, getting a
chair massage, going to kickboxing class, or just staring out the win-

dow. No matter what, it's wise to take several breaks throughout the day for at least a few minutes, even on your busiest days, just to give your mind and body a chance to recharge.

**BY THE NUMBERS:
ARE WOMEN MORE STRESSED THAN MEN?**

For what it's worth, recent research suggests that professional women need stress management advice more than their male colleagues. A 2011 Captivate Office Pulse survey found that men are 25 percent more likely to take breaks throughout the day for personal activities, 7 percent more likely to take a walk, 5 percent more likely to go out to lunch, and 35 percent more likely to take breaks "just to relax."

The Myth of Multitasking

"Humans don't really multitask," concluded a groundbreaking 2009 Stanford University study.

You've got to be kidding, right? I'm multitasking while I'm writing this sentence: sipping an iced coffee, texting back and forth with my husband, and thinking about what time I need to leave for my afternoon meeting. And I'm guessing you're probably multitasking while reading this, too.

Well, apparently we're not. According to the Stanford study, literal multitasking (defined as doing two actions simultaneously) is not possible. What is really happening is that our brains are switching incredibly quickly between the tasks we think we're doing at the same time. As a result, it takes a lot longer to get any single one of those tasks done when your brain has to keep shifting its attention. So if you really want to complete an e-mail, a design, a proposal, or the first draft of that international peace treaty, then it's wise to close your door, turn off and put away all distractions, and focus completely on the task at hand.

THERE'S AN APP FOR THAT: FREEDOM

If you don't have the willpower to focus on one single task without checking Instagram, last night's box scores, or the Dow, you can pay for the privilege. For about $10, an app called Freedom—available for Mac, PC, and Android—will shut down your access to the Web for a time period you specify (Macfreedom.com). Writers like Zadie Smith and Dave Eggers swear by it.

"But wait," you say, "I absolutely need the Internet to *do* my work!" Not to fear: there's an app for that, too. If you only want to turn off the potential distraction of social media sites, check out the aptly named apps Anti-Social (Anti-social.cc) or SelfControl (Selfcontrolapp.com).

Or, as time usage expert Laura Vanderkam suggests, "Consciously use social media as a reward. If you can focus for thirty minutes [or any specific period of time] on a difficult problem you're trying to solve, or a difficult memo you're trying to write, you can reward yourself with ten minutes on Facebook. That's actually far more efficient than sneaking glances here and there and then losing time on every transition."

Interestingly, when I asked the various millennials I interviewed for this book what they thought the greatest strength of their generation of leaders would be, many identified multitasking. But when I dug a little deeper, their definition of multitasking was not the one I provided above: doing two (or more) actions simultaneously. It seemed to be more about being able to absorb and process a lot of diverse information at a much faster pace than previous generations ever had to do. Perhaps a better word for this is synthesizing rather than multitasking.

Most millennials grew up with multiple screens (from video games to cell phones to computers) and were overscheduled with activities (from T-ball to origami to bassoon), so maybe that's where your generation's synthesis strength comes from. Many young people also possess a healthy FOMO (fear of missing out) factor and are more afraid of losing an opportunity than losing focus on a task. This is neither bad nor good; it's just different from previous generations of leaders. I do encourage you to be aware, however, that your older colleagues may require more time and focus on projects, which to you might look like slacking. Instead, try to accept it as a different style of working. And if older workers question why you have four computer monitors on your desk, explain that you process information in a different way. Hopefully you can both learn from and live with each other's practices.

How to Delegate Without Being a Dictator

One of the many perks (and, alas, potential challenges) of being a leader is that you are not going it alone. Even if you're now a sole proprietor or the founder of an online movement with no team, you can still benefit from our next topic: delegation.

It has taken me a very long time to become even moderately proficient at delegation. As a card-carrying member of the perfectionist club, I have always found it really hard to trust other people with my work, whether it's responding to information requests from potential clients, negotiating speaking fees, or even booking business travel. For instance, I used to become overly worried about things like whether my virtual assistant signed her e-mails with *Best*, *Cheers*, or *Kind regards*. (Cary, if you are reading this: please accept my sincere apologies.)

What I learned—slowly and sometimes painfully—is that the more I focused on the small stuff, the less I focused on the big stuff that really mattered (remember Stephen Covey's rocks). While I still believe that "little" things like using proper grammar, responding to messages promptly, and confirming all reservations are essential to maintaining the brand of my business, I've learned to worry less about exactly how these tasks are accomplished.

Here is a collection of some of the best advice I've gathered about the art and science of delegation:

Create an "Only I" List

This tip is from millennial business owner Jess Lively, whom you met in the last chapter. She uses this strategy herself and recommends it to her clients: Write down on a piece of paper what you personally have to do for your business, your organization, or your team to succeed. Delegate everything that is not on that list. This will clarify your daily duties as the boss and also will help you avoid the common mistake of throwing all different kinds of work at your staff members whenever you feel overwhelmed. The more time you put into planning what you yourself need to do and what others need to accomplish, the more smoothly everyone's work will flow.

Spend More Time Upfront

As you're first learning to delegate, it will take far more time to teach someone how to do a task than it would take to just do it yourself. Don't get frustrated. Answer every question, go over every detail, and clarify every expectation you have. The more time you spend teaching and setting expectations, the better the results will be in the long run. When she was running her jewelry business, Lively actually worked with her staff members to create a manager book that documented every key task and how to do it. New staffers or interns could then refer to the book when they had questions so they wouldn't have to ask Lively to explain every assignment.

You also want to instill in your team members that when they do approach you with challenges they can't solve alone, they should come to you with suggested solutions. For example, if you assigned a junior staff member to reach out to several news outlets to pitch a story featuring your new client and she was unable to place the story, encourage her not to return to you saying, "Unfortunately no one would do a story on our client. What should we do?" Instead, you would teach her to come back and say, "Unfortunately I reached out to ten local media outlets and no one would do a story on our client. As alternate options, we could (1) pitch media in a slightly larger geographic radius, (2) pitch independent bloggers who cover the client's subject matter, or (3) consider changing the pitch to focus on a different area of the client's business. Let me know how you'd like me to proceed or what other strategy you'd like me to pursue."

Set Clear Deadlines and Regular Check-ins

Most leaders know that it's important to set a clear deadline when you delegate a task, but it's also important to set ongoing check-ins as well, particularly for longer projects. Tammy Tibbetts of She's the First sets specific check-in dates when she assigns tasks to her staff and volunteers (and to me as her board chair!) and marks them as to-do items in her calendar. On those dates, she sends a quick e-mail or text that says, "It's July 8 and we agreed I would check in to make sure you have everything you need . . ." These short check-ins will save enormous amounts of time you might have spent if a project falls behind schedule without your knowledge or if a team member never admits he is struggling with a task you've delegated. As mentioned earlier, this is a particular must when you are managing virtual employees.

Teach Delegatees to Close the Loop

I once worked with an assistant who drove me nuts because I never knew what she was and wasn't getting done. After a while I felt like I was sending e-mails into a black hole. When I sat down to talk to her about this issue she said, "Oh, when you don't hear from me you can just assume I've gotten the task done."

That, I told her, was not going to work for me. How would I know the difference between not hearing from her because a task was done and not hearing from her because she never received the assignment in the first place? Or because she was out of the office? Or for whatever reason it fell through the cracks? As a leader, I needed to know that everything was on track. And as I learned, if you don't clearly explain what you need to know, your employees may not choose to tell you. (Some employees feel that reporting in on completed tasks is "bothering" the boss.) While every leader has a different desire for information, it is essential to communicate to your direct reports when and how you'd like them to "close the loop" on completed work. Millennial leader James Duffy, the employee representative in the food service industry, likes to touch base with his reports at least once a day. "I just want to know that you and I have made contact," he tells his team members. "On a day-to-day basis, I want us to have seen each other. Maybe I had a question you needed to get back to me on. Maybe I had a suggestion you needed to look into. Even if the answer is no, I want to close that chapter in my mind."

Approach Delegation as Empowerment

Some leaders, particularly new ones, worry that delegating will feel like dumping work on people. Katharine Golub was especially sensitive to this perception because, as class president at Bucknell, she was a leader of her classmates. But she quickly realized how much people thrive when they have a sense of ownership. "Delegating is really important," she told me. "When you are working with a group, it helps people stay engaged if they feel accountable for something. When our group was selling baseball caps to students, I split up the tasks to make sure that everyone was contributing. For example, some students booked the table for selling the caps, while others were responsible for the design. You as the leader are in control of the overall project, but let everyone have an important role in making the project complete. When the project is done, they will have a sense of satisfaction."

MORE, PLEASE: HOW DO I DELEGATE WITHOUT BEING A MICROMANAGER?

Some leaders, myself included, have a really hard time letting go. People like us need to be especially careful not to become micromanagers. You're not really delegating if you're constantly looking over people's shoulders as they complete the work you've assigned.

As Carol Frohlinger of Negotiating Women points out, however, managing people closely is not always a bad thing; there is some nuance here. Yet again, you have to know your audience. She explains, "You really have to consider each situation. There are some people who want a lot of direction, want to check in with you very often. In that case, you might micromanage because they ask for it. With them, part of your job as a good manager will be helping them to wean themselves away from your constant guidance over an appropriate period of time. Support them to accomplish the results you are seeking, but give them the confidence they need to make decisions on their own as well."

With less dependent people, the best way to avoid being a micromanager is to set those regular check-in dates described above, so that you both have the same expectations about how often you as the manager will be involved in the person's work. Don't let a fear of micromanaging allow you to become too lax. Carol shared the story of a client of hers who was managing a group of interns. She gave them an assignment and future deadline, but never followed up. The client was shocked and dismayed at the end of the time period that the interns had not delivered what they had committed to. Frohlinger reminded the client that you always have to check in with people, especially interns or new employees. That's not micromanagement; that's just management.

Work/Life What?

During my stint at WorkingWoman.com, the hottest topic on our site was work/life balance. Every other article seemed to cover some aspect of "having it all," which at the time was defined for women as having a significant other, kids, and a fulfilling career. Because talent had the upper hand in the booming 1990s, large employers were bending over backward to offer maternity leave, paternity leave, backup childcare, lactation rooms, and annual Take Your Daughters and Sons to Work Days to attract and retain the best people.

At the time I was in my midtwenties, and, to be honest, I felt left out. All of the work/life balance perks seemed only to apply to people with kids, and I wasn't even dating someone. Plus, the deep dark secret we heard from employees of many companies was that most people didn't really take advantage of these benefits until they were senior enough in their organizations that they wouldn't fear repercussions for it. (That was particularly true of paternity leave, by the way.)

Times have changed. Work/life balance is now being referred to as "work/life integration"—or, frankly, just "life"—because we've come to realize that the issue is not about equally balancing one's personal and professional lives, but integrating them into a complete whole. This twenty-first-century change is attributable to two major factors:

- Demographics: The increasing numbers of women in leadership positions and the increase in millennials entering the workforce have changed the work/life conversation. Millennials are the children of America's first large generation of working mothers (boomer women who spearheaded the 1970s women's movement) and, therefore, grew up knowing firsthand how hard it can be to manage a job and a family. They want a better deal. I've had college students as early as freshman year attend my workshops and ask how they can build a career that allows them to have both personal and professional happiness.
- Technology: The ubiquity of technologies that allow people to conduct personal or professional business anytime and anywhere has made it almost impossible to separate one's life into neat little buckets of "work" and "home." If technology provides us with more options for flexible work, shouldn't we take advantage?

In the past, when work/life separation was the norm (in theory at least), employees considered it a perk to work from home or make a personal call at work. Most of the time, the two realms remained separate. Nowadays, almost everyone works from home at least occasionally and expects some level of flexibility. Millennials in particular have fully embraced the constantly connected work/life style. Most young professionals I know have no problem responding to a work e-mail at 10 p.m. on a Friday night, but they also won't hesitate to peruse Etsy at 10 a.m. on a Tuesday morning.

This is a good thing in many ways (particularly for those who deeply benefit from working at home and flexible schedules, such as the physically challenged), but it can lead to difficulties setting scalable and fair HR policies. For example, millennial leaders like you will be the ones to address future workplace issues such as:

- Will there be a concept of "regular work hours" in the future?
- If so, should hourly wage employees be paid overtime for responding to e-mails after hours? (Some companies now automatically shut off employees' e-mail accounts during non-working hours to avoid paying overtime.)
- Will it be legal to reprimand or fire an employee for something she shared on a personal, privacy-protected social media site?
- Will you allow employees to "bring your own device" (BYOD) to work, and if so, how will you protect sensitive data?

TREND WATCH: WORK/LIFE 3.0

When The Hartford first asked me to write trends forecasts, examples of which you've been reading throughout this book, we decided the very first topic in the very first report needed to address the way that millennials were changing the work/life discussion. We determined that over the next few years, the conversation will shift again, from 1.0 (work/life balance) to 2.0 (work/life integration) to the 3.0 iteration: wellness at work.

"Wellness at work," a concept fully embraced in Silicon Valley, is the idea of employers' supporting employees in all aspects of their lives, such as quitting smoking, eating healthily, exercising regularly, handling home maintenance, and investing. As more employees bring their work into their personal time and space, for better or worse, employers are addressing more personal issues at the office.

Now let's bring the work/life topic back to you as an individual. Even if you would happily describe yourself as a "casual workaholic" and you're very comfortable integrating "work" and "home," there inevitably will be times when personal events conflict with professional events. As the boss, your handling of such moments will be closely observed. Here are some coping strategies:

Don't Apologize for How You Spend Your Time

An admirable attribute I've observed in many successful leaders is that they don't feel the need to explain their schedules and their boundaries. Too many people give too much detail about where and how they spend their hours, which can harm their professional credibility. It is absolutely your right to schedule "me time" in your calendar so you can catch up on work, or think, or even take a nap. (I hereby acknowledge that occasionally—usually around 4 p.m. on a gray, rainy day—I take a nap. This is one of the reasons I love having a home office.)

Jeff Weiner, CEO of LinkedIn, publicly shared that he blocks off a few hours a day in his calendar for strategic thinking time. He calls these empty blocks in his day "buffers" and says they are "the single most effective productivity tool" he uses. I love that Weiner is forthcoming about his scheduled breaks, but you don't have to be. A perk of being a leader, especially if you're the top boss, is that you don't have to explain to anyone why you're closing your door, out of the office, leaving early, or declining a meeting. You can explain if you'd like (and the rising importance of transparency in today's leaders suggests you don't want to be too secretive), but only when you feel it's truly important.

Beyond not feeling the need to explain, never apologize for the choices you're making—as long as you're not being irresponsible, of course. For instance, if you decline a 5:30 p.m. meeting invitation from a board member because you want to be on time for your best friend's birthday party that night, you can simply say that you are unavailable or that you have a previous commitment. There is no need to say, "I'm so sorry I can't make that meeting time—it's my best friend's birthday and I really need to go home and take a shower first!"

Buy Every Tool Available

I don't like advising you to spend a lot of money, but I believe it's always worth the expense to acquire any tool that will help you better manage all the various elements of your life as a leader. Don't cheap out and then become stressed because you don't have a fast enough computer or access to the Internet when you need it. If you work for someone else you can ask your employer to foot the bill by making a case that you need the best equipment to do the best job. If you are self-employed or run your own business, most of these items can be claimed as business expenses on your taxes. No matter how you acquire these time- and energy-saving items, I recommend shelling out for:

- A lightning fast and totally reliable smartphone, tablet, and/or laptop, with an extra battery for each and the biggest data plan you can afford.
- Paying for the "priority" level of customer service that will guarantee you can get any device fixed quickly if anything goes wrong.
- A wireless or solar-powered phone charger so your phone never dies (the Mophie Juice Pack is my favorite).
- Your own MiFi card or other method for creating a personal hotspot anywhere you need to connect.
- Paying for a day pass to an airline lounge during a long layover or flight delay so you are guaranteed a desk, a power outlet, and Wi-Fi (and, not for nothing, a free cocktail).
- Taking a cab or car service instead of driving to a far-away meeting or event so you can work while you ride.
- Buying the extra legroom and Wi-Fi on airplanes so you can get real work done while you fly. (I was once so stressed and in need

of work time, and—oh, yeah, pregnant—that I paid an exorbitant amount of money to upgrade to first class on a cross-country flight. It was worth every penny.)

Once you have all the tools you need, use them every chance you get to support you when you need to work remotely or can't be in two places at once. I've sent professional e-mails from coffee shops, bars, diners, supermarkets, dressing rooms, waiting rooms, hair-dryer chairs, pedicure chairs, bathrooms, bathtubs, and my own bed. No one was the wiser. (Hint: I deleted that "Sent from my iPhone" signature line that might have blown my cover.)

Outsource What You Can

If you can delegate work tasks, there's no reason you can't delegate personal tasks as well. If it will save you time for more important personal or professional priorities, why not hire a virtual assistant or intern to take care of tasks such as grocery shopping, scheduling haircuts and doctor's appointments, running errands, hanging your new curtains, or even doing your holiday shopping?

THERE'S AN APP FOR THAT: TASKRABBIT

On TaskRabbit (TaskRabbit.com), you simply describe a task you need to have done (such as taking some big items to Goodwill or repairing your printer), set a price you're willing to pay for someone to do it, and then pay only when the work is done. TaskRabbit will even select the person who will complete the job if you'd like—all TaskRabbits are background-checked—and your payment is securely transferred through their site.

Wake Up Earlier

This trick is simple, yet hard. Obvious, yet ingenious. If you don't have enough time in your day to do everything you really want to do, then make more time in your day. Set your alarm for an hour earlier. (Ideally this means going to bed an hour earlier, too.) Whenever I'm particularly busy I implement this strategy to have some extra time in the morning to write a blog post, read the news, exercise, or indulge in a novel I can't put down. The rest of my day is always better when I wake up early.

"That is ultimately the amazing thing about mornings," says Laura Vanderkam, the author of an e-book called *What the Most Successful People Do Before Breakfast*. "They always feel like a new chance to do things right. A win scored then creates a cascade of success. The hopeful hours before most people eat breakfast are too precious to be blown on semiconscious activities. You can do a lot with those hours. Whenever I'm tempted to say I don't have time for something, I remind myself that if I wanted to get up early, I could. These hours are available to all of us if we choose to use them."

Get Better at Saying No

Why is it that saying yes—even when it means changing our entire schedule, canceling other plans, or doing something totally unpleasant—feels so much easier than just saying no? If saying no makes you nervous, then you'll love this story from EY's Dan Black: "A number of years ago I was asked to lead our recruiting efforts in Canada. I would have to leave New York every Monday and fly home every Thursday night. It was a huge opportunity, and even though it was before I had kids, it felt like too much time away from my wife and my friends. I said no. It turned out the next opportunity was to lead recruiting in the United States! Of course you can't always say no—you have to understand that balance—but if something is important to you, you need to stay true to it and trust that there will be more opportunities down the road. A good lesson for a young leader to learn is that saying no doesn't mean no not ever; it can mean no not now. Keeping this in mind gives you the power and level of comfort to sometimes say no."

For me, saying yes was a lifelong habit and was causing major stress as I built my business. I finally realized I needed to increase my no quotient a few years ago when my business coach asked me to bring my calendar to one of our sessions. Together we looked at the number of meetings, phone calls, networking events, personal events, deadlines, and errands I tried to fit into every week.

"Um, any guesses why you're stressed?" she asked with a smile.

It suddenly seemed so obvious. My calendar was packed. Overflowing. Like so many people, I was trying to do way too much. I was saying yes to absolutely every invitation and project. In the process, I was saying no to my own sanity and spreading myself so thin that I couldn't truly focus on any one project or goal.

This exercise happened to take place in the fall, so my coach assigned me the challenge of saying no more often in the hopes of clearing more space in my calendar. I decided to declare the eleventh month of the year the month of NO-vember and decline every nonessential activity or obligation that came my way during those thirty days. My default answer to every invitation or nonrequired assignment became "no," "not now," or "let me get back to you." (Of course this didn't include existing project deadlines and client requests.)

Here's what I experienced that November—and now every November since—and the perks you will enjoy if you get better at saying no:

First, I became significantly clearer on what I really wanted to do. Because I challenged myself to say no more often, when I felt myself desperately wanting to say yes to an opportunity, I realized what I really wanted—which projects got me most excited, which networking events felt most valuable, which activities really moved my career forward, which friends I most wanted to spend time with. If you find yourself undecided about where to take your career or personal life, try saying no more often and you'll find that the right opportunities make themselves clear and become what my coach called "absolute yesses."

Second, I accomplished more of my big goals. (Think back to Stephen Covey's rocks again.) By clearing my calendar, I had time to get things done and start on projects that had been on my to-do list forever. I ended each day with a true sense of accomplishment. I know this is a "duh"—when you have more time, you can accomplish more—but we often forget that if you want to get things done, you have to make time to do things.

Third, I learned that people would rather hear an honest no than a dishonest yes. In the past, when I really wanted to say no, I would often say yes first, in hopes that this would soften the later blow of canceling at the last minute. Wrong! I've learned that an honest, upfront answer is the best way to go. As my coach told me, "It's like ripping off a Band-Aid. It's better to say no quickly and definitively." I finally began to understand that it is kinder to other people when you say no honestly. It helps them move on and find someone who will give a genuine yes.

Fourth, I had more energy. When you work too hard and run from meeting to meeting to phone call to phone call to drinks to dinner to bed, you have no time to stop, reflect, and refuel. I really do love the buzz and energy of being busy, but the truth is that when I'm really overscheduled, I don't feel buzzed and energetic; I feel tired.

And here is my final and most surprising revelation about saying no more often: no one noticed! I thought all of my friends, family, and professional colleagues would react negatively to my nos. I thought I'd lose multiple opportunities. I thought I'd get angry e-mails or phone calls from people who felt ignored or rejected. Instead, almost every time I said no to something, the response was, "Okay." This was a complete revelation. I thought I had to say yes all the time to be successful. What I learned in my first annual month of NO-vember was that it is absolutely okay to say "no," "not now" or "let me think about it" any month of the year. For two little letters, *no* has made an amazing impact on my life and work. I highly recommend it.

Now that you've got a better handle on your time, we'll move into the final section of this book and the topic of professional networking. Networking is crucial for new leaders and is a fun and fruitful way to spend the many hours you've just freed up in your schedule.

PART III

Last

CHAPTER 7

Connect

Finding Your Champions, Networking Up, and Always Taking the Meeting

L iam E. McGee, now chairman and president of The Hartford, started his career as a junior salesperson at Wells Fargo, essentially "dialing for dollars." Describing himself as a shy person, he was so scared before his first in-person sales call that he got back in his car and drove away before walking in the front door! Slowly he began to overcome his fear—he knew he wouldn't keep his job if he didn't—and worked his way up the ranks. One day, on his way to a meeting with his mentor, he overheard the mentor say to a colleague, "I think that McGee kid can be on the twelfth floor someday," referring to where the top executives sat.

"That changed my life," McGee told me. "It confirmed to me that my goals were possible."

He went on to mention "five very important mentors who were very tough on me and gave me sometimes-too-candid feedback. They saw something in me and I trusted them."

How do you, like McGee, find true supporters and attract the interest of key decision makers who will help to fast-track your leadership ascent? And how do you build an authentic and valuable professional network overall (even if you hate networking)? That's what this chapter is all about.

Find Your Champions: The Five People You Need on Your Personal Advisory Board

First, let's set about finding your version of McGee's five very important mentors. I'm going to suggest that you approach this group as more of a rotating advisory board, with some ongoing relationships and some at-large supporters who play different roles at different times. Five is not a magic number by any means, but it's a good estimate of the number of people and the diversity of perspectives you'll want to have on your leadership speed dial at any given time.

Let's meet them:

A Traditional Mentor

The traditional concept of mentoring involves an older, more experienced person taking a younger, less experienced person under his or her wing. The two people generally work in the same organization or profession and meet or talk regularly. It's usually an official arrangement, where the mentor has agreed to be available and provide advice on a consistent basis. This may feel a little old fashioned in today's more ad hoc world, but there is still tremendous value in building a relationship with someone who has years of wisdom and wants to share that with you in a focused, formal way.

As a new leader, you'll want to find a mentor with extensive leadership experience—and the desire to share it. You may be taking on a leadership role at a much younger age than many baby boomers would have assumed a similar position, so you'll likely have a fair amount of catching up to do. A mentor can't do your job for you, but he or she can help you think through decisions, better understand complex people management issues, and anticipate leadership challenges you may face. The best mentors are forthcoming with advice, open to tough questions, honest with their feedback, and genuinely supportive of your success.

Don't discount that final characteristic—being genuinely supportive of your success. I once met with a woman I thought was a mentor and asked for her advice on negotiating a potential book project. When I told her the amount of money I was planning to ask for—which I had researched extensively through industry associations and conversations with other authors—she said, "Oh, no. You need to ask for less. You're way too young to get that kind of money." Needless to say, I moved on to other, more supportive advisors.

A Co-Mentor

I first wrote about co-mentoring in 2007 in *Getting from College to Career*, and the concept has become even more popular today. Co-mentoring, sometimes known as reverse mentoring, is more of a two-way street than traditional mentoring. In this case, the co-mentor, who, again, is someone older and more experienced, will seek advice from the younger person as well—perhaps about technology, social media, Gen Y shopping habits, or any other area of expertise the younger person possesses. Essentially, co-mentoring acknowledges the fact that young people have their own wisdom that is valuable for older colleagues. One of the cool things about the co-mentorship situation is that it gives you a great perspective on the questions and concerns that older generations might have about you and your peers and, in turn, provides you with a better perspective on how to manage and engage with your older colleagues.

HOW *NOT* TO SAY IT:
"WILL YOU BE MY MENTOR?"

When it comes to finding a traditional mentor or a co-mentor, do not start asking people, "Hey—will you be my mentor?" These are relationships that have to build organically over time. Because people are so busy these days, asking, "Will you be my mentor?" can sound too time-consuming for the type of successful, busy person you'll want to engage. Instead, ask the person to advise you on a specific project or issue as a first step. If you demonstrate through this interaction that you respect the person's time and that you took his or her advice to heart, it's likely that person will agree to advise you again in the future. The mentoring relationship will grow naturally from there. I've referred to several people in this book as my mentors, but I don't recall ever asking them to serve in that role.

That said, if you are shy or new to your organization or you're having trouble finding mentors for any reason, formal mentorship programs do exist and can be valuable. Check with your company, any industry groups you belong to, or your university or grad school alumni association to find a good match. If you find after a meeting or two that the mentor you received is not a helpful fit, don't hesitate to move on.

A Sponsor

While mentors will advise and support you, they will not directly provide you with a promotion or other professional opportunity. For that, you'll need a sponsor. The concept of sponsorship has been gaining traction in recent years, particularly among women in corporate America. Kate White describes the concept this way: "A sponsor is often more senior in an organization than a mentor and, rather than simply offering feedback, he (or she) uses his influence with senior executives to advocate for the sponsoree. A sponsor opens doors and works to get a candidate promoted." Adds White, "Women, unfortunately, tend to be overmentored and undersponsored."

A sponsor can be your boss, your boss's boss, or another senior person. And White points out one very important distinction between how you interact with a sponsor versus a mentor: "Do *not* turn to a sponsor for advice the way you might a mentor. You don't want her to have even a glimmer about any work dilemmas you're facing or doubts you may be struggling with. You want her to see only your strength because her role is to *sell* you."

A Peer

The next advisory board member to cultivate is someone who is a lot like you: this might be someone who manages a similar-size department to yours, or someone who owns a similar business to yours, or someone who is running for office in another county. I'm not talking about befriending a direct competitor who may not be trustworthy, but someone who will really understand the day-to-day experiences and challenges you're facing. Sometimes there is no one more valuable to turn to for ideas, recommendations, or just a sympathetic chat on a rough day.

If you don't have a professional network of peers, then industry associations, networking events, and conferences can be good places to meet them. Early in my career I went to every networking event I could, and while every event wasn't a winner, I can trace many of my current friends and professional supporters to those outings. The thing about professional associations and networking events is that people go to them because they want to meet people. Most attendees are friendly, generous, and eager to know you.

Mom and/or Dad

Another form of millennial shaming is the media's constant poking of fun at millennials for being too close to, and too dependent on, their parents. (Although I had to laugh at this headline from *The Onion*: "Study Finds Millennial Generation Stays on Phone with Parents throughout Entire Day.") Maybe it's because I'm now a mom myself, but I think it's a good thing when parents are involved with their kids' lives and want to be lifelong supporters. That is, as long as your parents stay in the background of your career in the role of coach and cheerleader and don't step over any lines by, say, calling your boss to negotiate your salary (seriously, HR professionals tell me all the time about parents doing this sort of thing). So go ahead and ask your parents for professional advice, support, and retweets, especially if you're fortunate to have a parent who works or has worked in a similar field to yours.

BY THE NUMBERS:

TAKING YOUR PARENTS TO WORK

According to a 2013 LinkedIn survey, 35 percent of parents confessed that they're not completely familiar with what their children do for a living. LinkedIn, Google, Deutsche Bank, and other companies have taken steps toward decreasing this gap by instituting "Take Your Parents to Work" days. I assume we'll see much more of this practice in the future. And why not? The more your parents know about the work that you do, the more they can support, advise, and encourage you.

Networking in the Twenty-First Century, Part 1: Eleven Ways to Reach Out

When I was in college, a very successful family friend told me that the most important thing I could do for my career was to keep building my contacts. I've followed that simple but profound advice ever since. In those days, of course, networking consisted of either a phone call, a face-to-face meeting, or, as you'll see below, an old-fashioned snail mail letter. As a leader today you have countless additional methods—LinkedIn, Twitter, Facebook, Skype, FaceTime, Google+ Hangouts, etc.—to leverage in your relationship building. The most successful twenty-first-century networkers use all of the tools— online and offline—available. My friend Diane K. Danielson calls this a "clicks and mix" networking approach.

No matter how or where your connections arise, what's important is building and maintaining a network of diverse, authentic relationships with people you genuinely like or respect—including people who seemingly have no connection to your current role or future career plans. You never know which people will turn out to be the ones who refer clients, job candidates, and opportunities to you, who support you in tough times, and who will ultimately make your career the most meaningful and enjoyable.

This is especially important today, when it's rare for anyone, even top executives, to remain at one company, or even in one industry, for an entire career. I know a networking expert who once pitched a corporate training program to an executive at one of the largest financial institutions in the country. "We don't need a professional networking workshop," the executive told my friend. "We're one of the top firms in the country. Our employees only need to know each other."

That firm was Lehman Brothers.

> ### TREND WATCH: RETRO ROLODEXING
>
> One vision of the future workplace is that it may end up functioning more like Hollywood: rather than committing to employment at one company (or movie studio), people will be more like free agents, working their networks to form multiyear alliances to work on a specific project or idea. (Think of the long-term affiliation among the producers, crew, and actors who created the three Lord of the Rings movies, for example.) If this proves to be the case, then your relationships will be by far your greatest asset as a future leader.

By the way, I know that a lot of people don't like the term *networking,* so you can call the activities recommended in this section whatever you'd like. What's important is that you commit to initiating, building, and maintaining professional relationships throughout your leadership journey. Ultimately it is people who will hire you, promote you, invest in you, buy from you, and introduce you to other great people. Here are my top eleven strategies for building relationships that matter.

1. Leave. Your. Desk.

It is way too easy these days to spend your entire life in front of a screen. You'll increase your relationship-building success exponentially if you actually go places. As often as possible, get thee to a conference, wine-tasting, trade show, workshop, fund-raiser, luncheon, golf outing, spin class, or wherever else you might strike up an interesting conversation with an interesting person.

In particular, start to learn where other leaders in your industry or community hang out. Go to the restaurants, bars, and coffee shops where more senior people are. Challenge yourself to join committees, nonprofit boards of directors, or professional organizations where you will be among the least accomplished people in the room. National organizations include the Young Presidents' Organization (YPO.org), Entrepreneurs' Organization (EONetwork.org), the Young Entrepreneur Council (YEC; TheYEC.org), and Summit Series (Summit.co). I know that large gatherings of high-level executives and entrepreneurs can be intimidating, but stretching your networking comfort zone is crucial at this stage of your career and will expand your horizons exponentially.

As you become more comfortable attending events, work your way up to being a panelist or featured speaker at such gatherings. There are few better ways to become known in your field than to be the one everyone else is watching on stage. How do you get asked to speak? What I've learned is that the more you speak, the more you are invited to speak. So get out there! As you know, I got my start by taking the podium at local Rotary clubs. Beyond that, as I was building my career I pretty much agreed to speak at any event or on any panel that invited me, including high school career days, Junior Achievement clubs, alumni panels for prospective applicants to my university, and even a Girl Scouts troop (where I spoke about how to write a business plan for that year's cookie sales). I also spread the word to my colleagues at WorkingWoman.com that I'd be happy to take on any speaking opportunity that someone else didn't want to do. (And, public speaking being such a common fear, it turned out there were a whole lot of speaking gigs that other people didn't want to do.) Most of these events involved sitting on a panel and answering questions about my work, which is something any young leader is capable of doing. So go do it!

2. Pick. Up. The. Phone.

Leaving your office and attending events helps you form relationships; the phone ensures you don't mess them up. As we've discussed, there will inevitably be times where you and a colleague, a client, or a friend have some sort of misunderstanding (or worse). When this happens, remember to take your fingers off the keyboard and pick up the phone. You'll work things out more quickly and won't risk the other person's misinterpreting your words or tone. Even if there is no misunderstanding at all, occasionally talking to someone, rather than always e-mailing or texting, can make a big difference to deepening a relationship.

3. Build Relationships Before You Need Them

Just like personal relationships, you can't snap your fingers and conjure up a group of supportive, loyal professional colleagues when you need them. You have to continuously build this foundation so that people will be there for you when you want to reach out. This is true at every level of your career, but particularly when you're in a leadership role. Congressman Aaron Schock told me, "I spent much of my first year in Congress getting to know my colleagues who were part of my freshman class and the more seasoned members of Congress who understood how the House works. This effort to connect with my colleagues helps when I need support for a bill I am introducing, so I know which members might be interested in joining me, and it's not the first time they have heard from me. Making the personal connection is a huge part of persuading people to support the goals you have in front of you."

4. Give First

The social media expert Gary Vaynerchuk starts his days by posting the question "What can I do for you?" to his hundreds of thousands of social media followers. His approach, true to Gary Vee's persona, is pretty extreme (and he does add the caveat, "keep it reasonable please"), but the concept is spot-on. I fully advocate the habit of giving to people as much as possible. Even little "gives" make a big difference: advice, compliments, referrals, ideas, happy birthday messages, "likes," and anything else that person needs. Reid Hoffman, cofounder of LinkedIn, calls this doing "small goods" for other people, and he says it's one of his favorite uses of the professional networking site. In most cases, people only ask for things occasionally and the goodwill you'll build up will likely be returned tenfold if you need anything from those people in the future.

One of the tips I often share with young professionals is always to ask anyone you meet with, "Is there anything I can do for you?" A college student who had attended one of my campus speeches once e-mailed a few weeks after the talk to tell me that she had used this advice during an informational interview with an alum of her university who was a CEO. She told me, "I remembered what you said about giving first, but I thought, 'What would I have to give to a CEO? Clearly I need her advice and connections more than she would need anything from me. But I followed your advice at the end of the meeting and said, "You have been so helpful and I am so grateful. I know I'm just a student, but is there anything I can do to help you?"

The CEO's eyes lit up and she replied to the student, "Really? Yes! I just got the new iPhone and I can't figure out how to find anything." The student said, "I can help you!" and she spent another thirty minutes giving the CEO a tutorial on how to use her new device. This was a small give, but in that moment it was what the CEO needed and it genuinely helped her. She will likely never forget that student and her generosity. I wouldn't be surprised if that iPhone incident marks the beginning of a significant co-mentoring relationship.

5. Ask, Too

I admire the student who offered to help, and I also admire the CEO who admitted she needed help using her new phone. It's part of good relationship building to ask for assistance when you need it. I've met a lot of young leaders who worry about appearing needy or overstepping their bounds, particularly when asking someone to make an introduction to another person in their network. I promise you this is definitely not inappropriate; it's how the world works, and it truly makes people feel good to help others (as long as the ask is appropriate). The key to making an appropriate ask is to be specific about the assistance you need and genuinely gracious in your request.

Angela Lee is both a Columbia Business School professor and founder of 37 Angels, an angel-investing network dedicated to empowering female investors. She often receives requests from her MBA students for introductions to the people in her extensive investor network. I asked Lee how she feels about such requests and what her advice is for other young leaders trying to network in a similar way. She said, "It doesn't bother me when I sense they are truly passionate about what they're going after, and that they have done their research on me and know they are asking for my core competency. It's about knowing your audience and having done your research and making that person feel like an individual and not a big Rolodex. Investors don't like it when entrepreneurs look at you as a big bag of money."

I agree with Lee. If someone reaches out to me and engages in a friendly, mutually beneficial conversation about our businesses, I'm usually happy to help if that person later requests an introduction to someone in my professional network. On the other hand, when a total stranger e-mails out of the blue and wants to tap into my network, I feel like that human Rolodex Lee described and I almost always say no.

HOW TO SAY IT: ASKING FOR HELP

When it comes to asking for anything from a professional contact—advice, information, an introduction to one of that person's contacts—you first want to make sure that the ask is proportional to your relationship with the person. If you know the contact only a little bit, then make it a little ask (e.g., an introduction to the person's Web designer). If you are close friends with the person and have worked with him for years, then it's more appropriate to make a big ask (e.g., to serve on the board of your nonprofit). No matter what your relationship, review the person's LinkedIn profile or website before reaching out so you can understand what is important to that person—such as a current project or longtime interest. (For example, when I invite people to attend events for She's the First, I look to see if they've shown an interest in education issues in the past.) Be concise in your request, but provide enough information so the person can make an informed decision about helping. And no matter what, you always want to give someone an out if they aren't comfortable fulfilling the request. Here is an example of what I would consider to be a medium-size ask:

Hi Valerie,
It was great to see you last month at the fund-raiser. I hope you've been well and congrats on your recent promotion! I'm writing to ask for a favor: I noticed on LinkedIn that you are connected to George Lamont, who is a big supporter of the arts in Dallas. I'd like to invite George to be the keynote speaker at our next conference and I'm wondering if you would be willing to introduce me to him? Of course I will understand if that's not possible.

Thanks so much for considering my request and, as always, please let me know if there is anything I can do to support you.

Best regards,
Vivian

6. Always* Take the Meeting

This tip comes from *People*'s Zoë Ruderman and is most relelvant when you are searching for a new position or promotion. "Go in for [job] interviews even if you don't think you're interested," she says. "Don't do a whole round and waste people's time if you know you'd never take it, but suss out the situation first. They could realize you're better suited for a higher role (that happened to a friend and she ended up getting the job!). And of course, if after the one interview, you let them know that it sounds like it's not a good fit, they could call you back in a few months with a job that is a good fit."

As you know, I advise saying no to requests that are not "absolute yesses" (see the box), but I do agree with Ruderman's advice for situations involving an intriguing opportunity such as a potential new job, even if you're happy in your current position. If you're not necessarily interested in the opportunity the person is offering but you feel the person may be a good connection anyway, then there's no reason not to go for it.

---

*MORE, PLEASE:
WHEN *NOT* TO TAKE THE MEETING

As we discussed in the last chapter, one of the ways to stay sane as a modern leader is to be protective of your time. The more successful and high profile in your organization or industry you become, the more meeting requests you'll receive. Some of these will be more than worthwhile. Others won't. A great way to tell the difference is to do what I call playing boomerang. The higher you rise in your career, the more people will want to connect with you, pick your brain (yuck), or otherwise take up your time. Some of these connections will be mutually beneficial, but many will simply be time-sucks. You can determine the difference by boomeranging the person's message back to him or her and asking for more clarity. Personally, I use Gmail canned responses (or a simple document from which you cut and paste works just as well) to save template responses to these types of inquiries. My responses look something like this:

> Thank you for your interest in [meeting/connecting/working together]. Can you send some more information or a brief proposal outlining [your idea/the reason you'd like to connect] and some additional information about [you/your organization]?

> The serious people will respond thoughtfully and thoroughly, and if their proposal doesn't match with your goals, you'll have a more specific reason to say no. The rest will simply fade away.

7. Diversify

If you only connected with people just like you, you wouldn't accomplish much (and you'd have a pretty boring life). In addition to networking with people more accomplished or established than you are, also challenge yourself to build relationships with people from other industries, countries, ethnicities, generations, regions, and political views. This may require stepping even further out of your comfort zone, and that's a good thing. Attend lectures or Google+ hangouts on topics you know nothing about (Barnes & Noble author events are great for this), sign up for a volunteer project in a neighborhood where you don't know anyone, or simply walk over and chat with a colleague from a different department. By the way, this includes administrative assistants, custodians, baristas, temps, and taxi drivers. Leaders learn from everybody they meet.

8. Network Up

Next, let's talk about meeting more high-level people. I encourage you to determine the key players in your field, your organization, or your department and proactively invite them to have a phone chat or join you for a cup of coffee (or, better yet, breakfast—it shows you are a go-getter who is up early). I know it might seem pretty random to just send an e-mail and ask someone to meet, but it's far more common than you think among leaders. All you have to do is introduce yourself and your role and explain why you want to connect with this person (and it never hurts to put an emphasis on what's in it for them). For example, "I've just taken on the role of IT manager and would love to learn more about how my team can support your group."

I can't encourage you enough to reach out to people you admire, especially as a new leader. Most established professionals—myself included—are well aware that today's new manager is tomorrow's CEO. We've all been in your shoes and most people are willing to pay it forward and connect with you in the early years of your career. This is how I met Kate White, the former editor in chief of *Cosmopolitan*, whom I've quoted several times in this book. When I first graduated from college, I read White's career advice book, *Why Good Girls Don't Get Ahead . . . But Gutsy Girls Do*. I absolutely loved the book, and it is one of the reasons I wanted to write career advice books myself. At the time, I was just a recent college grad looking for a job before going to grad school in Australia, so I was way too intimidated to ask White out for coffee (at the time she was editor of a different magazine). Instead, I wrote her a fan letter. This was in the early days of e-mail, so I actually printed out the letter and mailed it. I was amazed and thrilled when she wrote back a few weeks later and shared some advice with me about my career.

Fast-forward to about seventeen years (!) later. My wonderful editor at HarperCollins, Colleen Lawrie, sends me an e-mail asking if she can connect me to another one of her authors, who has just written a new book. That author? You guessed it: Kate White. We had a conversation by phone (during which I reminded her about our letter exchange), I had the opportunity to speak on a radio show she hosted, and, as you know, she graciously agreed to be interviewed for this book. You never know what might happen if you reach out to the people you truly admire at every stage of your career.

9. Take Notes

"Take notes" sounds like a beginner tip, but Ben Casnocha, a young entrepreneur and author, tells a story that will convince you it's an expert strategy. A friend of his attended an event where Facebook CEO Mark Zuckerberg was giving a speech to a large audience of young entrepreneurs in Silicon Valley. Zuckerberg was sharing his perspective on the state of the Internet industry. Every seat was taken, and the young audience members were hooked on Zuckerberg's every word. Among the young crowd sat two older gentlemen, John Doerr and Ron Conway, who are both renowned investors in Silicon Valley. As Casnocha describes, "They stood out not just because their gray hair shimmered in the sea of youth around them, but because they were the only people in the audience taking notes. Isn't it funny that arguably the two most successful people in the room after Zuckerberg were also the only two people taking notes?"

Taking notes is wise for a variety of reasons: it helps you retain information better, it shows other people that you value their thoughts and ideas, and it will serve as a resource in the future not only to remember the ideas you found valuable enough to write down, but also to give you reasons to follow up with people based on what you know is important to them. One of the things I remember most about the first time I met Ben Casnocha for a coffee and chat in New York is that he took notes. Needles to say, I now do the same.

THERE'S AN APP FOR THAT: EVERNOTE

I have years of journals and notebooks in boxes in the basement of my childhood home. In all honesty, I'll probably never go back and look at them. Thankfully, now we have Evernote (Evernote. com). This app allows you to store notes, Web pages, photos, e-mails, and a wide variety of other files and then syncs them across all of your devices so your notes are with you at all times. You can even record and save audio files. I use Evernote to keep track of everything—meeting notes, call notes, frequent flier account numbers, shopping lists, memorable e-mails, book ideas, and more. Everything is completely searchable, so unlike those boxes full of notebooks, I now go back and refer to my various notes all the time.

10. Follow Up Faster

As a general rule, whenever you meet with someone for the first time, ask for someone's business card or contact info at a conference, or promise to provide somebody with follow-up information after a call or meeting, do it within twenty-four hours. This sounds like a simple thing, but I promise you will blow people away if you act this quickly. The world moves so fast these days that if you don't follow up within twenty-four hours, people have basically moved on. Immediate follow-up is the best way to say, "I value you and our relationship is important to me." As Angela Lee commented to me, most people don't follow through at all. "For every four business cards I give out [at a networking event], I get one follow-up." Be the one. And do it fast.

11. *Know That* Thank You *Is a Form of Networking*

Similar to the above advice, you absolutely, positively must thank anyone who helps you in any way. I've found that few leaders do this. Even though your fellow leaders and other professionals are busy, they will always appreciate a polite and timely thank-you note— preferably via e-mail, within twenty-four hours of the conversation or interaction.

I once received an "Urgent!" request from a young professional the night before she was scheduled to go on an important job interview. She sent me the e-mail around ten p.m., saying that she was "desperate" for help. I happened to open the e-mail and had time, so I responded with some very specific advice and wished her luck. I never heard from her again.

Frankly, I was annoyed. She had e-mailed me late at night and begged for my help, and then didn't even write back to say thank you? A few weeks later I was still bothered by this, so I did something I rarely do: I e-mailed her back and told her that I had been disappointed not to hear from her after I had taken time to respond to her urgent e-mail. Well, this time she wrote back immediately, saying that she had been so grateful for the advice and the reason she hadn't written to thank me was that she didn't want to bother me again.

Trust me on this: it is never, ever bothering someone to gratefully thank them for their time, advice, help, or anything else. At the very, very highest levels of government, Hollywood, corporate America, international relations, and beyond, people still send and appreciate thank yous. In fact, one of the things you often notice about the offices of these super-successful people is that they are often decorated with dozens of framed thank-you notes.

MORE, PLEASE:
NETWORKING ADVICE FOR SHY LEADERS

Does some of the advice in this section feel challenging for you? Perhaps it's because you are shy. If this is the case, you are in not only large company (around 45 to 55 percent of Americans are introverts), you are in very good company. Self-declared introverts past and present include leaders such as Abraham Lincoln, Eleanor Roosevelt, Bill Gates, Larry Page, Steven Spielberg, Warren Buffett, Katharine Graham, and Charles Schwab.

Introverts don't just make fine leaders, they can also, surprisingly enough, make stellar professional networkers. Here's why:

They Ask for Personal Referrals
There's a myth that networking is all about cold-calling people and walking up to strangers at cocktail parties. Often the best connections are made through mutual acquaintances who make personal introductions. Shy people tend to feel most comfortable networking with the people they know, and then asking those people for referrals to others. That's a good strategy for anyone.

They Are Polite
Etiquette has become a bit of a lost art these days, and that's a shame. A woman I know once attended an event with Martha Stewart. She waited patiently as people hovered around the Domestic One, wielding business cards and loud voices. Eventually my friend made eye contact and said, "Excuse me, Ms. Stewart. May I introduce myself?" "Absolutely, I would love to meet you," was the reply. "Thank you for being so polite."

They Listen More Than They Talk
Shy people tend to ask questions and listen intently to the answers, talking only when they have something meaningful to add. When it comes to networking, you learn a lot about other

people by listening to them talk—information that will help you build a long-term, genuine, mutually beneficial relationship.

They Reach Out Online

Many shy people feel more comfortable networking online, where they can think about what they want to say and take time in their responses to other people's outreach. While a strong leader shouldn't spend all of his or her time connecting online, social networks are a great place to begin and maintain relationships that can then be carried over into the physical world.

Networking in the Twenty-first Century, Part 2: Six Online Tips

Now let's look at the *clicks* side of the clicks and mix networking approach. While you may be an expert user of social media for personal purposes, I find that many young leaders still need some guidance on the professional use of social media. Here are some suggestions:

Do Your Homework

Before reaching out to or meeting with anyone, even someone you've met before, always google the person and thoroughly review his or her LinkedIn, recent tweets, and other social media profiles. This is particularly important with new contacts. It's one thing to go into a meeting and say, "What exactly does your company or department do?" But it's so much more impressive to walk in and say, "I was reading all about your recent ad campaign. I saw what your competitors did and how you responded on your Twitter feed. I really admire how you handled it . . ." Now you sound like a respectful colleague who is serious about building a relationship. That's who people want to know, network with, and, ultimately, do business with: people who do their homework.

Follow Organizations

The above tip applies for organizations you'd like to connect with as well. Just like individuals, organizations are now tweeting, posting to Pinterest, Tumbling, updating their Facebook pages, and creating YouTube channels. If there's a company you are interested in in any way—as a future employer, customer, competitor, or funder—and they want to share information with you, then I want you to be there to listen. Follow them and subscribe to them. You don't ever have to write back or say a word (and most of the time whoever is posting on behalf of that organization will never reach out to you unless you make the first move), but good networkers gather all the information they can. I believe this is particularly important to do with clients and potential clients. It is a sign of respect to follow the companies you do business with.

Give People and Organizations Reasons to Reach Out to You: Post Status Updates

LinkedIn, Twitter, and other sites offer you the opportunity to share brief status updates with your connections or followers. This is a golden opportunity to heighten people's awareness of you and to spark their interest in your leadership brand. I think of my status updates like brief conversations I would have at networking events: "I just read a really interesting article you might enjoy" or "I'm attending our industry conference next week. Ping me if you're going too." You never know what nugget might catch someone's attention and initiate a conversation or opportunity.

I also recommend including "touch points" in your online profiles, which are little tidbits of information that might catch the eye of someone with a similar interest or just a bit of curiosity. Mention that you play squash, that you are an avid musical theater fan, or that you've traveled to over 100 countries. On my website I mention that my Starbucks order is a tall skim latte, which has sparked some fun conversations (and welcome invitations to treat me to one). It's the same reason people often include an "interests" section on their résumés: you never know when a networking contact is an avid skier, saxophone player, or latte drinker, too.

Customize Everything

Many social networks provide you with a generic outreach message, such as "I'd like to add you to my professional network on LinkedIn." My advice is to never ever, ever, ever send this message the way it is. Why not? Because part of being good at networking and being successful as a leader is to have authentic, one-to-one relationships. So erase the generic sentence and write your own words. Keep such personal notes short, but show that you are human. Here's an example:

> Hi, Jane,
> I hope all is well. I'm not sure if you remember me, but I was a summer intern at National Bank a few years ago and worked in your department. I'm now the VP of finance at a health care start-up and would love to reconnect and learn more about your consulting business.
>
> All the best,
> Rob

HOW TO SAY IT: BEING CONCISE

Whether you're reaching out to people on LinkedIn or elsewhere on the Web, a big mistake people make is writing too long of an outreach message. Remember that this is neither a cover letter nor your life story. You must be straightforward about who you are and what you are asking this person. And you must always show respect for the person's time. It's also a great idea to throw in a "small good," such as a compliment or perhaps a mention that you've bought the person's book (hint, hint!).

Here is an example of a concise outreach message if you admire the person but don't have anything or anyone in common.

Subject line: Inspired by your TED talk

Jonah,

I recently viewed your TED talk online and I was particularly inspired by your story of success as a digital journalist. I am in the process of launching a news Web site and I was wondering if you could offer any advice from a successful journalist's perspective. I know you are very busy, so any guidance or suggestions would be deeply appreciated. Thank you for inspiring me and for considering my request.

Best regards,

Max

Here is an example if you do have something in common, such as having attended the same university or working for the same company at some point:

Subject line: Career advice for a fellow Bruin?

Hunter,

I'm a fellow UCLA alum and came across your profile on LinkedIn. I graduated in 2003, also with a degree in history, and I have been working as a PR director for the past few years. I'm now job hunting and hoping to make the transition from the agency side into a communications leadership role at a nonprofit or university. I really admire your career and was wondering if you might be willing to offer some advice or perhaps chat by phone? I would really appreciate your time and would be happy to do anything I can to help you.

Thank you and Go Bruins!

Kira

Remember that the goal of networking outreach online is to establish rapport and perhaps receive some general information and advice that can lead to more communication in the future.

Try Alternate Methods of Outreach

Sometimes you can write the world's most perfectly crafted outreach e-mail and you still don't receive a response. Perhaps it's because your e-mail arrived on a day when the recipient's in-box was overflowing, or perhaps you reached out on Facebook and the person never checks her messages there. (Or, once in a while the person you want to connect with is, for whatever reason, "just not that into you.") Because there are so many social networks and communication methods out there, I believe it's worth trying a few different approaches if necessary. Try your best, through observation, to determine where the person tends to be most active, or just try a few different networks. And even with people you know and communicate with often, sometimes it's a nice idea to switch things up a bit and send a quick tweet instead of an e-mail.

Just Because You Can Doesn't Mean You Should

Finally, remember that one of the benefits and dangers of social media is that it's easier than ever to research other people, particularly those with a relatively public persona. If you come across very personal information about someone (e.g., that she is going through a divorce or that he struggles with depression), I hope it goes without saying that you should not use that information in your professional outreach or conversations. I wouldn't even mention that you know someone is married or has children or just went on vacation if the person doesn't bring it up himself or herself. When you do step over the line, it can backfire completely. For example, I once received an e-mail from a woman who said that she had applied for a job on my husband's sales team but hadn't received a response. So she googled him, found our wedding announcement from several years earlier, then googled me, found my Web site and e-mail address, and forwarded her résumé to me and asked me to pass it along to my husband.

While a tiny piece of me admired her creativity, the rest of me felt annoyed and a bit invaded.

Since I give people career advice for a living, sometimes I'll reply to a request I consider out-of-bounds and politely let the person know that his or her tactic backfired. In this case I didn't, but if I had, I would have advised this woman that just because you can find information on the Internet doesn't mean you should use it professionally. If my husband and I talked frequently about each other professionally or linked to each other's Web sites, our relationship would be fair game for someone to use in a job search. In this case, the woman google-stalked me through our personal wedding announcement, which in my opinion is not appropriate. Plus, if my husband wasn't interested in her résumé, why would I take her side instead of his?

Mentor Others Early and Often

Finally, as a leader in any realm, you have the unique opportunity to give back to people younger or less experienced than you are. Do it. We've talked a lot in this chapter about how much you can gain by asking other people for help, assistance, connections, and support. Be sure to give back to those for whom you are the higher-up or VIP as well. You'll not only help the other person, but you'll also see how enjoyable it is to be the one providing the mentorship, which will give you extra confidence when you reach out to your aspirational contacts.

Take it from someone who loved being a mentor so much in college that I figured out how to turn it into my livelihood: mentoring people just starting out in their careers is one of the most enjoyable things you can do as a leader in any profession. The final question in my online leadership survey was the typical, "Is there anything else you'd like to share?" My favorite answer came from Daisy Colina, executive director for hair color for Aveda Canada. She wrote simply and eloquently, "There is nothing more rewarding than seeing people grow."

VOICES OF MILLENNIAL LEADERS

When I was a lot younger, I thought that being a good leader meant gaining more recognition for myself. As I've gotten older, I now realize I find the greatest self-worth in watching others succeed because of my leadership skills. I like knowing that my team depends on me, but that they also know I depend on them and am appreciative of their work.

—Denise M. Gardner, extension enologist, Penn State University

As we head into the home stretch, it's time to plan ahead for the next steps in your leadership journey. How do you make decisions about when to make a big move in your career? When is the right moment to launch a new venture or change course completely? And the most important question of all: what will it take for you and your fellow millennial leaders to make a major impact on the world?

CHAPTER 8

Grow

Getting Better, Falling with Style, and Truly Changing the World

As I mentioned early on, my goal in this book has been to share everything I possibly could about being a young leader today. As we approach the end of these pages, I sincerely hope you are not feeling overwhelmed.

So let's return to where we began: you. I've found that when leaders, particularly new ones, become overwhelmed by their responsibilities (or simply overworked), they tend to lose sight of their own career and personal development. For previous generations of leaders this was probably okay; you could simply do your job and tread water for a while before preparing for your next big career step. But that's not an option anymore. In our fast-changing times, you need to continually focus on your own development as well. The good news is that the FOMO-y, YOLO-y millennials—who crave regular change and challenge—are perfectly suited for this kind of world.

But by regular change and challenge I don't necessarily mean changing jobs or career paths every few years (although we'll talk about when you should consider making such moves), or that you need to be constantly charging ahead at a million miles an hour. I think of career movement today as being more like software releases:

some are big and bold (and require a total reboot), and others are just slight bug fixes or fine-tuning. My goal is for you to continually thrive in these ever-evolving times while still maintaining your sanity and sense of purpose.

Oh, and did I mention that you'll also change the world?

Nine Ways to Get Better All the Time

Leadership is most definitely a marathon and not a sprint. So what is the right training plan to keep you going over the long haul of months, years, and decades? The mix is different for everyone, so here are a variety of expert strategies for evolving over time. Some of these suggestions may not apply to your particular realm or career stage, so focus on the ones that feel most applicable to you and return to this section whenever you need an energy boost.

1. Trust Your Training

There is a reason this book included a lengthy overview of leadership history. Yes, a whole lot is changing and will continue to change over the course of your leadership journey, but certainly not everything. The vast majority of the lessons and guidance in this book will remain true whether you are leading a conference call in 2015 or a meetup on Mars in 2035. No matter what stage of your career you're in or what future generations you're working with, you will still encounter challenging people and still need to manage your time effectively. So trust the foundation of your leadership training and the experience you build every day. This is what members of the military do in combat situations. This is what aid workers do after natural disasters. This is what you should do as the world changes around you: never forget the basics.

2. Make Yourself Feel Old

At the same time, of course, you'll have to work hard to stay current. You'll be amazed at how fast the next generation sneaks up and you're the one complaining about kids today. (Trust me; it happens to the best of us.) So just as I recommended that you serve as a reverse mentor to an older colleague, it's also smart to find a reverse mentor of your own. Build a relationship (or, better yet, several) with some smart, interesting people in your field who are younger and hipper than you are. You can talk to them about things like how they shop, how they vote, what global issues they worry about, what tech devices they're craving, what music they're downloading—or, preferably, all of the above. I do my best to keep up/feel old by having several younger mentors (thank you, Tammy, Christen, and Kevin!), spending a lot of time on college campuses, and regularly reading youth-focused media sources such as YPulse, PolicyMic, and Her Campus.

3. Stay Humble

There are times it will pay to be brash as a leader. There are infinitely more times it will pay to be modest. Particularly if you're introverted by nature, do not feel the need to grow your head along with your career. In fact, you might be doing yourself a disservice if you do so. Susan Cain, in her book *Quiet*, points out that many of the highest-performing companies have had chief executives who "were known not for their flash or charisma but for extreme humility coupled with intense professional will." The quintessential example is Darwin Smith, who served as CEO of Kimberly-Clark for twenty years and is widely considered one of the greatest corporate leaders of all time. In *Good to Great*, Jim Collins describes Smith as "an individual who blends extreme personal humility with intense professional will," and reports that Smith once said of his career, "I never stopped trying to become qualified for the job." Never stop trying to become qualified for every leadership role you hold.

4. Decide to Be Great

Jim Collins's entire book strove to answer the question, What makes a company—and a leader—become not just good but great? I posed the same question during my interviews with leaders. People tended to respond by talking about the importance of hard work, which really is the price of admission to great leadership. When I pressed for my interviewees to tell me more, to really explain what launches someone to the very elite levels of his or her field, this is what many of them revealed to me: at a certain point as you are rising in your success, you need to *decide* to be the best. In other words, you can't just wait and hope that you rise to the top. You intentionally choose to go for it.

Can you really just decide to be a big success? I believe that if you make a definitive, no-turning-back-now choice to be the best and you couple that with hard, diligent work—and you do both of those things day in, day out, year in, year out—then, yes, there is no reason you can't achieve your biggest, boldest dreams.

5. Commit!

Notice that in the last tip I mentioned making a definitive, no-turning-back-now choice to be the best. Leadership is not a job for commitment-phobes. I've talked a few times in this book about the FOMO (fear of missing out) factor and how many millennials avoid making decisions that would close off any of their options. While it's great to have options and be open to new opportunities, there comes a point where you have to start making some choices. If you want to be a great leader, you have to let that FOMO go. It will hold you back and frustrate the people around you. (In fact, one of my corporate clients insisted that I include in my training to her company's millennial leaders that it was not appropriate to reply with maybe to meeting invites from managers or clients. Trust me that this habit has a tendency to drive people of other generations crazy. So next time you feel the urge to reply maybe or that may work to an invitation, please force yourself to decide yes or no, or wait a short time until you can reply with a definitive answer.)

Here's another reason to get better at commitment: research has shown that keeping one's options open is ultimately a recipe for less happiness and success. As psychologist Dr. Heidi Grant Halvorson has said, "[R]eversible, keep-your-options-open decisions reliably lead to *lower* levels of satisfaction than irreversible ones. In other words, we are significantly less happy with our choices when we can back out of them." Why? Because, according to Halvorson, when we make a definitive choice, our "psychological immune system kicks in"—i.e., our minds focus on feeling good about the decision we made and we stop thinking about the what-ifs. On the other hand, if you keep your options open, you continue trying to decide if you made the correct choice or not. That immune response never happens and you feel less happy. Plus, as Halvorson reports, "When you're still deciding what you *should* do, you don't have the cognitive resources to devote yourself fully to what you're *actually* doing" and your performance suffers.

Take it from someone who has wasted way too much time and energy second-guessing decisions large and small—my college major (American studies, but would English have been more prestigious?), my business entity (LLC, but would an S corp have had more tax advantages?), and even the winter coat I just bought (a gorgeous navy blue, but would black have been more practical?). While it's certainly important to make careful, thoughtful decisions, there is absolutely no value in constantly questioning those decisions after the fact. You'll just drive yourself crazy and take your focus away from more important things. Commit! Commit! Commit! (We can work on this one together.)

6. Hatch Some Big Ideas

When your mind is free of second-guessing past decisions and wondering about roads not taken, you'll have a lot more time and brain space to come up with the huge, innovative ideas that can truly catapult your career. This is particularly true in artistic fields. "In my industry," says Zoë Ruderman, the style editor of *People*, "it's all about pitching big, creative ideas. Executives don't tend to hear about the editor who comes in on time every day and always hands in her story on time and with no typos, but they do hear about the editor who pitched a sellable, interactive new tool for awards season, or found a new way to partner with Twitter. It's not to say coming in on time and writing clean copy doesn't matter, but that gets you noticed by your own manager (a good thing, too), just not her manager and her manager's manager." You may not have a big, bold idea every day, but I know you have a few zingers you've been mulling over in your mind. If you want to grow in your career and your leadership, take time to craft those ideas into a pitch and share them with your team or higher-ups ASAP. And keep pitching those big ideas now and forever.

VOICES OF MILLENNIAL LEADERS

We all start out wet behind the ears. It's the risk taking that shapes us into true leaders.

—Krystal Kohler, campaign associate, the Arts Partnership

---

7. Seek Professional Help

Don't be afraid to engage paid supporters as well. I've mentioned a few times the various coaches I've hired to help me with both personal and professional goals, and I've also worked with a wonderful therapist to address various fears, insecurities, and challenges. I sometimes joke that it takes a village to be me, and it's kind of true. We engage experts to help manage our health, our cars, our money, and even our hair, so why not engage experts to help manage our emotional and professional issues when necessary? Professional coaches, in particular, can help you handle difficult work relationships, trouble with your own performance, and other issues you'd be reluctant to discuss with an internal colleague or HR rep. Sometimes you just need one or two sessions with a coach, or you may develop an ongoing relationship. To find a good coach, ask for a referral from someone you trust or from a professional association you belong to.

8. Make Your Own Rules

All of the previous tips in this section make the assumption that you already know what your next career or leadership step is or what action would be required to get there. But, speaking as an entrepreneur, I realize that sometimes you have absolutely no idea what your next step will be because you're the very first person to forge your particular career path. The way I've navigated this situation is to research as much as I can about people who've created similar businesses or careers to what I envision for myself, and then I've invented the rest. While my business plan has been a bit more detailed than "make it up as I go along," I do place a lot of emphasis on creating my own destiny. In fact, the quote I have hanging over my desk reads, "You don't want to be better than the competition. You want to be considered the only one that does what you do."

I think that I am simply part of a larger trend toward customization in all areas of our lives, including our careers. This trend was born from necessity: because the world is changing so fast, there are no longer many prescribed career paths to follow. Even doctors, lawyers, and professors are finding ways to buck ages-old systems and forge new and unique career destinies. I encourage you to do the same: don't be afraid to take a detour, make a lateral move, start a business on the side, or break out of what appear to be the prescribed rules of career development.

TREND WATCH: CUSTOMIZATION NATION

The trend of customization is going to grow only stronger in the future. The more customization we experience—from the personalized fit of our jeans, to the unique mix of benefits we receive from our employer, to the infinite combinations of online and IRL courses that comprise a university degree—the more we will want. Be prepared to lead and work with employees who want customized job tiles, customized job descriptions, customized performance incentives, customized schedules, and customized compensation plans. Clients and customers will want customized service along with customized payment schedules as well. Technology will likely aid us in handling all of this personalization, but you'll be smart to embrace this trend early and prepare for a one-size-fits-one work environment of the future.

---

9. Change Jobs

Finally, no matter how happy you are in your current role or how much you are creating your own customized path, thoughts of whether or not to change jobs will cross your mind at some point during your career. Should you start your own firm with some friends? Take a sabbatical to write a book? Jump to the competition? Pursue that mega job that will push you to your limits? How do you know when it's time to make a major move? Below are some guidelines.

MORE, PLEASE: WHEN TO MAKE A MAJOR MOVE

Here are some questions to ask yourself when evaluating a major job move:

Is It Truly an Amazing Opportunity?

You may be content where you are, with coworkers you like, an important title, and work that's meaningful. And then the phone rings and you receive an offer that's beyond anything you had ever imagined (or perhaps it's exactly the dream opportunity you have been imagining your whole life). Career-catapulting opportunities don't come around often, and if you take a pass, you might always wonder "What if?" Some opportunities have the potential to change your entire career—and life—trajectory. For example, once you have the title of CEO on your résumé or have launched a start-up that is acquired or goes public, you'll be playing in the big leagues from that point forward.

Are You Following a Trusted Mentor or Sponsor?

It's flattering when your mentor asks you to come with her to her next gig, especially if it's high profile. But before you leap, ask yourself whether you're going because it's the right move for *you* or because you feel like you can't say no to this particular person. You won't succeed if you're following someone else's dream, and your mentor, while disappointed, will ultimately respect you for staying true to yourself.

Are You Chasing a Dream?

Have you always imagined yourself building a business from the ground up? Or does your childhood vision of writing songs and singing them to sold-out crowds keep rattling around in your brain? Or have you been planning for years to turn a side gig into a full-time job? As long as you feel confident that you have a financial and personal plan for making your dream path a viable reality, then I would never stand in your way if the time feels right to leap toward your destiny.

Will You Be Making the World a Better Place?

Is your new opportunity one in which you'll have an impact on a cause you care deeply about? Members of previous generations often pursued nonprofit or cause-related work as second careers after retiring from something else. Millennials don't want to wait, and this is one of the characteristics I most admire about your generation. If this is the type of move you want to make, then it can be a wise one.

Will You Leave Your Current Organization Better Than You Found It?

For leaders, I think this final question is quite important. You have to consider how your personal career decisions will affect the organization in which you are now serving as a leader and the people you now manage. While you can't make choices based solely on these factors, you can strive to make choices that will not actively hurt your current team and projects. Even if you leave to take a job with your organization's biggest competitor, as many people do, you can still wrap up your current role in a professional, positive way and do your best to leave each employee and project with a strong plan and your genuine best wishes.

In general, when mulling a career change, there are no guarantees that you are making the right decision. But as you'll see in the next section, every choice you make, even perceived career mistakes, will ultimately help you develop and grow.

How to Fall with Style

My toddler daughter's favorite movie at the moment is *Toy Story*. She especially loves the scene in which the brand-new astronaut toy Buzz Lightyear tries to prove to the skeptical, old-fashioned cowboy Woody that he is not a toy but a real astronaut who can fly. He proceeds to jump off a bedpost and, through a series of lucky accidents (like getting caught on a rotating ceiling fan), he appears to fly gracefully around the room. Buzz lands proudly, raises his arms in triumph, and all of the other toys applaud.

A frustrated and irritated Woody says: "That wasn't flying! That was falling with style!"

The toys ignore Woody and proceed to worship Buzz Lightyear all the same. This is how I recommend handling the inevitable mistakes you will make in your career. You're going to make mistakes and fail sometimes. So do your best to fall with style.

Here are some strategies for falling with style, whether you've spearheaded a failed project, missed a crucial deadline, overseen disappointing sales results, lost an election, received a pink slip from your job, or experienced any other mistake, failure, disaster, debacle, or embarrassment, public or private:

Own It

In the early years of building my speaking business, I worked as an independent consultant for a corporate training company. The company offered clients a wide variety of training program topics—cold-calling, presentation skills, negotiation, etc.—but I was one of the few consultants who felt comfortable teaching the courses on business writing and grammar (thank you again, English teacher dad). I soon learned that one of the biggest mistakes that professionals make in their writing is overuse of the passive voice—e.g., "This book is being read by you" vs. "You are reading this book." The reason to avoid passive voice, particularly in business writing, is that it places emphasis on the action taken rather than the person taking that action. And in many instances, you can use the passive voice to avoid mentioning the action-taker at all.

What does passive voice have to do with making mistakes? The prime example we shared to explain why business leaders should avoid passive voice was this: "Mistakes were made."

The phrase, popular with politicians, is a way that the speaker admits that something went wrong but totally avoids taking (or, for that matter, assigning) any blame. Using an evasive phrase such as *mistakes were made* would be, in my opinion, the opposite of falling with style. Leaders take responsibility not just for wins, but also for losses. While you don't want to apologize every day for every tiny error (like, for instance, using the passive voice in an e-mail), I do believe that leaders can and should apologize for important mistakes and still retain credibility. In fact, most people say they respect leaders more when they acknowledge their mistakes and take responsibility when appropriate.

HOW TO SAY IT: ADMITTING MISTAKES

So what's a better admission of wrongdoing than "mistakes were made"? Here are some general guidelines for making good apologies:

Keep It Short
A concise apology or admission of a mistake remains professional. A long, rambling sob story starts to sound inauthentic and threatens your credibility. Make your amends and move on.

Be Specific About What You Did Wrong
"I'm sorry that I did not alert you sooner that we would miss this quarter's fund-raising goals by 30 percent" is more effec-

tive and professional than "I totally failed in the fund-raising this quarter."

Explain What You Will Do Differently Next Time

Before you make your apology or admit your error, give some thought to how you will do things differently in the future. For example, "I've already added three additional fund-raising calls to my daily schedule to make sure we avoid missing next quarter's goal. I'll update you weekly on our progress so there are no more surprises." When you share your plan as part of your apology, you'll show people that you are already learning from the mistake.

Lick Your Wounds. Privately.

I've just shared some suggestions for how to act and speak when you mess up as a leader, and I'll share more below. But before moving on I want to mention the fact that it's okay to be upset about a failure or mistake. It's okay to feel angry at yourself or others, to wish it hadn't happened, to bang your fists on the desk, to journal about it, to cry. I have done all of those things and more. But here is the key: I've done them in private. I don't see any advantage to freaking out publicly, and particularly not in front of the people you lead. You can express your concern in a professional way after you've pulled yourself together, but overt displays of anger or emotion can frighten the people you lead and cause additional problems. I know there are many bosses who throw public tantrums (I had a boss during a college internship who—I kid you not—was so angry about some issue that she picked up a computer printer and threw it on the floor. A printer!). But those leaders are rarely respected or admired.

When it comes to career failures, such as getting fired, receiving a demotion, or having a business go bankrupt, keep in mind that most people aren't paying such close attention to your career that they would give significant thought to such happenings. When they do become aware, people generally react the way you do. If you bemoan the news and write long, depressing blog posts about a failure, then people will feel sorry for you. If you share the news and say, "Onward!" then people will get on board with your next project. I'm not saying this to lessen the personal pain of such failures, but to remind you that what feels like a total crisis to you is often just mildly interesting news to your general network.

Don't Make the Same Mistake Twice

When I've done something I've regretted—such as sharing a not-well-thought-out idea in a client meeting or undercharging for a time-consuming project or even taking a job that turned out to be a bad decision—I let myself wallow for a while and then I do my best to rectify the mistake and figure out how to avoid that same pain again. (Sometimes I'm more successful than other times, but I'm only human.) And I remember another gem of advice from my mom. She likes to call a mistake, screwup, or disappointment an AFLE: another freakin' learning experience. That never fails to make me smile and remember that life is long and will be filled with many more mistakes to come. We can't avoid them, but we can get better at handling them.

Remember That Leadership Is Hard

As a leader, you'll have the opportunity to experience more AFLEs than most people. Never forget that by taking on a leadership role you have assumed a certain amount of risk. It's that famous *Spider-Man* line, "With great power comes great responsibility." Leadership will expose you to criticism, challenges, and annoyances large and small. And the more successful you become, the more impediments you are likely to face. (My friend Janet, a small-business advisor, assures clients panicked by a lawsuit that "you're not truly successful until someone tries to sue you.")

It helps in tough situations to remain focused on why you wanted to be a leader in the first place. As Congresswoman Tulsi Gabbard told me, "As long as you are motivated by a desire to make a positive impact, you cannot fail and will overcome the naysayers and the inevitable obstacles. You won't win every single battle, and there will be challenges. But every battle and every challenge is actually an opportunity—an opportunity to learn, to expand, to change course, to build character, and ultimately, to be a better servant leader."

Bounce Back Quickly

I've already shared the advice to make an apology short and sweet. The same advice applies on a macro level: do your best to get back to your regular, day-to-day work as quickly as possible after a setback. Think of a quarterback moving on to the next play after throwing a dropped pass. Think of a movie star moving on to the next role after a box office bomb. Think of a politician who loses a very public election and runs again the next time. JetBlue Airways chairman Joel Peterson has said that "Most Likely to Bounce Back after a Fall" would be a much better yearbook category than "Most Likely to Succeed," and I wholeheartedly agree. (And I suppose this is the one chance I'll get to boast that I was voted "Best Dressed" in my eighth-grade yearbook, which almost made up for the burning shame I felt in sixth grade when I showed up for school wearing the exact same paisley blouse as my science teacher, Mrs. Rosenkrantz.)

Share Your Lessons With Others

Finally—and I've done my best throughout this book to implement this tip myself—make your mistakes more valuable by helping other people to avoid them. One of my favorite writers, the late Nora Ephron, famously said that if you slip on a banana peel, you're the butt of the joke, but if you tell the story of slipping on a banana peel, then you're the hero of the story. It's true; I always find that the more I share my painful, embarrassing life lessons with others, the less painful and embarrassing they become. And even better, when you tell the story of slipping on that banana peel, you serve as a valuable lesson to others to beware of the banana peels lurking in their own paths.

The Future of Millennial Leadership: What Will It Take to Change the World?

As I've addressed throughout this book, the leadership success of the millennial generation is no small issue. You are poised to take over and determine the direction of the companies, governments, universities, armies, hospitals, families, and communities that make up the world we all share. The choices you make will truly change the world.

A VIEW FROM THE TOP

I am so bullish on this generation. They have so much to bring to the table. I meet tens of thousands of students and I am continually impressed by their excitement and commitment, and the skill sets they have that I can't even imagine. They are diverse, culturally aware, connected, and networked in ways my generation never knew how to be. These kinds of skills make them uniquely prepared to be successful in the coming decade or two.

—Dan Black, director of recruiting, EY Americas

BY THE NUMBERS: THE SMARTEST GENERATION?

Despite the fact that one critic penned a book calling millennials the "dumbest generation" (how's that for millennial shaming?), there is no doubt in my mind that millennials are smart enough to change the world. There is even research to prove this. Professor Jim Flynn of New Zealand's University of Otago, who has tracked IQ scores across generations, says that scores have been steadily rising in the United States since 1947 and that, on average, millennials hold a six-point IQ advantage over people born twenty years earlier. Flynn has identified these gains mostly in vocabulary and logical reasoning and says that these increases "potentially, could help them make better judgments about the world."

I say this not to scare you but to empower you. And because I know that you are up to the challenge. I see evidence in my work every day that despite economic crises, political gridlock, environmental disasters, and social challenges, countless millennials remain optimistic and undaunted. No, not every millennial is succeeding today and not every millennial will (or wants to) change the world. But as a generation, you have the diversity, talent, and skills to do so. And young leaders like the ones I've profiled throughout this book are working hard every day to change their small parts of the globe and address the issues that affect us all.

However, just because millennials have the potential to be another "greatest generation" doesn't mean there are any guarantees. As Jimmy Lepore Hagan of Nanette Lepore cautions his fellow millennials, "Thinking about ourselves uncritically is really problematic. There is a danger in overstating how great we are going to be as a generation. We are still in the early throes of implementing and

doing our work. [Positive predictions about the millennial genera-
tion] should be taken with a grain of salt and not a spoonful of sugar."

So here is your grain of salt: just like becoming a great leader,
changing the world takes an incredible amount of hard, ongoing
work. Over the years to come, you'll need to continually be, listen,
manage, prioritize, connect, and grow in order to reach your—and
your generation's—highest potential. I hope that the information in
this book will be a helpful resource along your journey.

And here, because I can't resist, is your spoonful of sugar: I believe
to the core of my being that the millennial generation can and will
make the world a better place, and in ways that we probably can't
even fathom yet. Your creativity, authenticity, and kindness inspire
me every day, and I know you are only at the beginning of your potential. I wish you the very best, and I can't wait to see where your
leadership takes us all.

RESOURCES

Looking for more inspiration, education, and networking? Here are some leadership organizations to check out for further information and opportunities. Descriptions are adapted from each organization's own Web site. Note that listing here does not necessarily imply official endorsement by the author or publisher of this book.

AMERICAN MANAGEMENT ASSOCIATION

Amanet.org
@amanet

The American Management Association works to advance the skills of individuals, teams, organizations, and government agencies through a comprehensive range of offerings such as business seminars, webcasts and podcasts, conferences, books, white papers, and articles. Its approach is to improve professional performance by combining experiential learning with opportunities for ongoing professional growth at every step of a person's career journey.

BRAZEN CAREERIST

Brazencareerist.com
@brazencareerist

Brazen Careerist is a community for young leaders and hosts a blog, *Brazen Life*, that offers career advice from authors and experts (blog. brazencareerist.com). The team at Brazen also hosts virtual networking events for employers and universities, connecting top talent around the world. Check out the "Best of Brazen" blog post series for the site's best tips on leadership topics such as freelancing, networking, and succeeding at work.

CENTER FOR CREATIVE LEADERSHIP
CCL.org
@ccldotorg

The Center for Creative Leadership offers an exclusive focus on leadership education and research as well as expertise in solving the leadership challenges of both individuals and organizations. Their programs focus on developing strong interpersonal skills grounded in personal reflection and self-awareness, and they have a special offering for women in leadership.

DALE CARNEGIE TRAINING
Dalecarnegie.com
@dalecarnegietraining

Dale Carnegie Training offers courses for individuals on leadership and communication throughout the United States and in eighty additional countries. The trainings emphasize practical principles and processes that help people understand how they add value to business.

ENTREPRENEURS' ORGANIZATION
EOnetwork.org
@entrepreneurorg

Entrepreneurs' Organization is a global business network with 131 chapters in forty countries. It enables small and large business owners to learn from one another, leading to greater business success and an enriched personal life. They offer resources in the form of events, leadership-development programs, an online entrepreneur forum, and business owner education opportunities.

FORTÉ FOUNDATION
Fortefoundation.org
@fortefoundation

Forté Foundation is a nonprofit consortium of companies and business schools working together to launch women into fulfilling careers through access to business education, opportunities, and community. The organization has reached more than fifty thousand women and offers programming at the undergraduate and graduate level.

INTERNATIONAL LEADERSHIP ASSOCIATION
ILA-net.org
@the_ila

The International Leadership Association is a global network for those who practice, study, and teach leadership, and it promotes a deeper understanding of leadership knowledge and practices for individuals and communities worldwide. Members have access to a leadership webinar series, a virtual community, and an annual conference.

JAYCEES
JCI.cc
@usjaycees

The United States Junior Chamber, known commonly as the Jaycees, is a membership-based nonprofit organization with two hundred thousand members in one hundred countries around the world. The Jaycees' philosophy is "to improve the world to create lasting positive change in the world." There are local Jaycees groups in five thousand communities globally, and the national organization also organizes conferences and leadership development opportunities for members.

JOB ACCOMMODATION NETWORK
Askjan.org
@JANatJAN

The Job Accommodation Network provides free consulting services for individuals with physical or intellectual limitations that affect employment. Services include one-on-one consultation about job accommodation ideas, requesting and negotiating accommodations, and rights under the Americans with Disabilities Act (ADA) and related laws.

LEVO LEAGUE
Levo.com
@levoleague

Levo League is a community of professional women seeking advice, inspiration, and the tools needed to achieve personal and professional success. The organization provides mentorship and guidance to young women in their careers by offering content, community, and weekly Office Hours, which are thirty-minute group video chats with career experts and successful businesswomen. There are also several local chapters of Levo League around the country.

MANAGEMENT LEADERSHIP FOR TOMORROW
ML4T.org
@mltorg

Management Leadership for Tomorrow is a career development organization that equips high-potential African Americans, Hispanics, and Native Americans with skills, coaching, and "door-opening" relationships to help them become corporate, nonprofit, and entrepreneurial leaders. It offers programs at the undergraduate, MBA, and executive levels.

MILLENNIAL ACTION PROJECT
Millennialaction.org
@MActionProject

The Millennial Action Project's goal is to advance millennial values, ideas, and leaders to foster post-partisan policymaking and political collaboration. Its vision is to make creative cooperation—rather than ideological conflict—the dominant mode of American political decision making. It offers a fellowship program for young leaders along with other opportunities to become involved in its agenda.

THE MUSE
Themuse.com
@dailymuse

The Muse is a Web site for people in all stages of their careers, from entry level to the C-suite, offering information about top companies and a blog with expert career advice. Visitors to the Web site can explore the company cultures of a wide variety of potential employers and read advice on management, entrepreneurship, and productivity.

MY TOMORROW
thehartford.com/tomorrow
@TheHartford, #mytomorrow

This interactive Web site helps young professionals understand and choose employee benefits, including suggestions about life and disability insurance. The site offers videos, a "real world roadmap" to assist with financial planning, and regular workplace trends forecasts (as featured throughout this book) to guide millennials through their careers.

NATIONAL URBAN LEAGUE YOUNG PROFESSIONALS
NULYP.net
@nulyp

National Urban League Young Professionals is a volunteer organization for young professionals ages twenty-one to forty to empower their communities and change lives. Its mission is to support the Urban League movement through volunteerism, philanthropy, and membership development.

NEGOTIATING WOMEN
Negotiatingwomen.com

Negotiating Women is an organization committed to helping women in business to maximize opportunities and recognize that success in business means more than delivering great results. The organization offers live negotiation training and consulting to organizations and works with corporations, nonprofits, women's associations, governmental offices, and individuals.

PERSONAL BRANDING BLOG
Personalbrandingblog.com
@DanSchawbel

The *Personal Branding Blog* is led by millennial workplace expert Dan Schawbel and provides helpful articles, podcasts, expert interviews, and research reports on the topic of personal branding and career success. Its sister site, StudentBranding.com, caters to the collegiate audience.

ROTARY INTERNATIONAL
Rotary.org
@rotary

Rotary International is an organization of 1.2 million community leaders comprising differing occupations, cultures, and countries that seek to make their communities better. Their Rotaract program brings together people ages eighteen to thirty to organize and participate in service activities, develop leadership and professional skills, and have fun.

SANDBOX
Sandbox.is
@sandbox_network

Sandbox is a global community of more than eight hundred young leaders in twenty-five cities worldwide. Its members are entrepreneurs, designers, opera singers, investment bankers, academics, and more, all driven by a desire to change the world for the better. Sandbox connects members online and through more than 150 yearly events.

TOASTMASTERS INTERNATIONAL
Toastmasters.org
@toastmasters

Toastmasters International is a nonprofit educational organization that teaches public speaking and leadership skills through a worldwide network of meeting locations. Since 1924, Toastmasters International has helped people of all backgrounds become more confident in front of an audience.

U.S. BUSINESS LEADERSHIP NETWORK
USBLN.org
@usbln

The U.S. Business Leadership Network is a national nonprofit that helps businesses succeed by leveraging disability inclusion in the workplace and marketplace. This organization also serves as the voice of network affiliates across the United States, representing more than five thousand businesses. It hosts an annual conference every year and provides mentorship opportunities to students and recent graduates with disabilities, helping them succeed in the workplace.

USVeteransMagazine.com
@usveteransmag

U.S. Veterans Magazine's goal is to provide employment and business opportunities for veterans, transitioning service members, and veteran business owners. Their Web site provides career opportunities, a blog, and listings of events and conferences for its constituents. The organization also connects veterans with universities for further education, promotes opportunities within the federal government, and has several corporate partners.

THE YOUNG ENTREPRENEUR COUNCIL
TheYEC.org
@theyec

The Young Entrepreneur Council is an invitation-only membership organization comprised of hundreds of successful young entrepreneurs. Its goal is to provide entrepreneurs with access to everything they need to succeed today and in the future, including a virtual mentorship program called #StartupLab. Its members represent every market sector and industry.

YOUNG NONPROFIT PROFESSIONALS NETWORK
YNPN.org
@ynpn

Young Nonprofit Professionals Network is an organization that seeks to develop emerging leaders who will advance the social sector. Young professionals can become involved locally in one of their chapters across the country or attend the national conference that the group hosts for members each year.

YOUNG PRESIDENTS' ORGANIZATION
YPO.org
@ypo

YPO connects successful young chief executives in a global network, uniting approximately twenty thousand business leaders in more than 120 countries. The organization emphasizes the value of a peer network and trusted mentors, the importance of ongoing education, and the need for a safe haven where issues can be aired in an environment of confidentiality.

ABOUT THE AUTHOR

Lindsey Pollak is a keynote speaker, corporate consultant, and internationally recognized expert on millennial workplace issues. She is an official ambassador for LinkedIn and the author of *Getting from College to Career: Your Essential Guide to Succeeding in the Real World*. She also serves as the spokesperson for The Hartford's "My Tomorrow" campaign, a national educational effort targeted to millennials, and as chair of *Cosmopolitan* magazine's Millennial Advisory Board. *Forbes* selected her career advice blog as one of the Top 100 Websites for Your Career. A graduate of Yale University, she lives in New York City with her husband and daughter.